CASEBOOK
ON
SALE OF GOODS

CASEBOOK

ON

SALE OF GOODS

By

E. R. HARDY IVAMY, LL.B., Ph.D., LL.D.

Of the Middle Temple, Barrister,
Professor of Law in the University of London

FOURTH EDITION

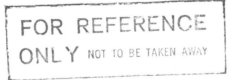
LONDON

LLOYD'S OF LONDON PRESS LTD.

1980

First published 1965
Second Edition 1969
Third Edition 1973
Fourth Edition 1980

E. R. HARDY IVAMY

1980

X

ISBN 0-904093-83-2

Printed in Great Britain by

Holmes & Sons (Printers) Limited, Andover, Hampshire

PREFACE

The need for this new edition has been brought about by the enactment of the Sale of Goods Act 1979, which came into force on 1st January, 1980.

The book is now divided into seven Parts.

Part I ("The Sale of Goods Act 1979") has involved considerable up-dating of the numbering of the sections of the Sale of Goods Act 1893. Since the Act of 1979 is a consolidating Act the cases on the Act of 1893 are still law where the wording of the statutes is the same, and accordingly have been retained in this edition.

Part II ("The Sale of Goods Act 1893") contains a case interpreting s. 26, which is the only section in the Act of 1893 which still remains.

Part III ("The Factors Act 1889") includes a selection of the cases on this Act, which is unaffected by the Sale of Goods Act 1979.

Part IV ("The Hire-Purchase Act 1964") deals with the sale of motor vehicles which are the subject of hire-purchase agreements and includes *Barker* v. *Bell* (*Ness, Third Party*), [1971] 2 All E.R. 867, C.A., and *Stevenson* v. *Beverley Bentinck Ltd.*, [1976] 2 All E.R. 606, C.A.

To Part V ("International Sales") has been added *M. Golodetz & Co. Inc.* v. *Czarnikow-Rionda Co. Inc.* [1980] 1 All E.R. 501, C.A. ("clean" bill of lading).

In Part VI ("Bankers' Commercial Credits") *Discount Records Ltd.* v. *Barclays Bank Ltd.* [1975] 1 All E.R. 1071 is set out.

Edward Owen Engineering Ltd. v. *Barclays Bank International Ltd.* [1978] 1 All E.R. 976, C.A. forms Part VII ("Performance Guarantees").

I am grateful to Butterworth & Co. (Publishers) Ltd. (the publishers of the "All England Law Reports"), to "Lloyd's Law Reports" and "The Times" for giving me permission to use extracts of the judgments from the law reports concerned.

I should like to thank Mr P. F. Vivian, of the Legal Publishing Department of Lloyd's of London Press Ltd., for seeing the book through the press.

University College London, **E. R. HARDY IVAMY**
June 1980.

TABLE OF CONTENTS

PART VI—BANKERS' COMMERCIAL CREDITS

PART VII—PERFORMANCE GUARANTEES

INDEX

TABLE OF CASES

Page numbers printed in heavy type indicate where an extract from the case is set out

TABLE OF STATUTES

THE SALE OF GOODS ACT 1979

A. CONDITIONS AND WARRANTIES

(1) STIPULATIONS AS TO TIME

Thames Sack and Bag Co. Ltd. *v.* Knowles & Co. Ltd.

(1918), 119 L.T. 287

By s. 10(1): "*Unless a different intention appears from the terms of the contract, stipulations as to time of payment are not of the essence of a contract of sale*".

The sellers sold a quantity of hessian bags to the buyers. The contract of sale stated "all conditions as per United Kingdom Jute Goods Association's spot contract form, terms net cash against delivery order on or before 19th September, delivery prompt". On 19th September the sellers had not been paid the price, so they repudiated the contract.

Held, by the King's Bench Division, that if the only matter in which the buyers failed was to pay in time, the sellers were not justified in repudiating the contract, for, on the facts, the time of payment was not of the essence of the contract. But the sellers were entitled to repudiate the contract because the buyers had not removed the goods by the required date.

SANKEY, J. (at page 289)

The conclusion I draw from that is that if the only matter in which the defendants failed was to pay in time, then the sellers were not justified in repudiating. One has to look to see the nature of the contract in order to see whether mere failure to pay was enough. It was a contract in respect of bags described at a certain price per 100 "ex wharf London". The delivery was to be prompt and there was a slip attached under which the sellers were to pay insurance until delivery. Was that a contract of such a character that if the buyers did not comply by 19th September, the sellers were entitled to say the matter was at an end? I think the whole object of this contract was to make a bargain which should be completed by the buyers at least by 19th September, and the object of the contract was that by that date the matter was to be entirely finished, and therefore any party who neglected to perform was guilty of a breach of a term going to the root of the contract: "All conditions as per the 'spot' contract form". That points to goods being available and ready for immediate delivery and removal on a certain date from a certain place. Therefore the failure of the buyers to carry out the terms of payment and to remove was a failure justifying the sellers in saying they were no longer bound.

McDougall *v.* Aeromarine of Emsworth Ltd.

[1958] 3 All E.R. 431

By s. 10(2): "*Whether any . . . stipulation as to time [other than one as to the time of payment] is or is not of the essence of the contract depends on the terms of the contract". Thus, the time for delivery of the goods may be of the essence of the contract.*

A firm of yacht builders agreed to supply a pleasure yacht according to a certain specification. Delivery was to be on 1st May, 1957, but cl. 3 in the contract stated that "owing to the effect of delays and shortages such delivery date cannot be guaranteed". The yacht was not delivered on that date, and on 19th September, 1957, the buyer repudiated the contract since delivery had still not been made, and 4/5ths of the yachting season was over by the beginning of September.

Held, by the Queen's Bench Division, that he was entitled to do so, for the time of delivery was a condition of the contract, and the sellers had not delivered within a reasonable time after 1st May, which, in the circumstances, had expired by the beginning of September.

DIPLOCK, J. (at page 438)

It thus becomes relevant to decide what is the period for delivery permitted by the contract. Clause 3 states a specific date for delivery, namely, 1st May, 1957, but expressly states that such delivery cannot be guaranteed. A clause in this form, in my view, places on the seller the duty to deliver within a reasonable time of the specified date. What is a reasonable time from the specified date is a question of fact depending on all the circumstances of the case as they exist up to the time when delivery is or ought to be made. In my opinion, in the circumstances of the present case, which relates to the sale of a pleasure yacht built in accordance with the buyer's special requirements for use by him in the 1957 yachting season, and where delays in completion after 3rd June, 1957, were due solely to the prior bad workmanship or the prior incorporation of defective materials by the [builders], a reasonable time had certainly expired by the beginning of September, 1957, that is three months after 3rd June, and at a time when four-fifths of the 1957 yachting season had passed. Whether this stipulation as to time of delivery is a condition or a warranty depends, under s. 10 of the Sale of Goods Act . . . , on the terms of the contract. In my view, the obligation to deliver within a reasonable time of 1st May, 1957, is a condition. It was conceded by counsel for the [builders] that this was so and a general rule in mercantile transactions, but he contended that it did not apply to the sale of a vessel for use by the purchaser solely for his own pleasure, not for commercial use or for re-sale. I am not impressed by this argument. Where a purchaser buys a yacht for use for his own pleasure from the beginning of a particular yachting season, I think that it must, as a matter of common sense, be of the essence of the contract that he should receive delivery in time to make substantial use of it during that season. It may be that he expects to use it also in subsequent seasons, but he cannot foretell whether he will be able to do so, and in any event it will have deteriorated in some degree by the time the next season comes round. Where, as was contemplated in this case, the yacht incorporates modifications to suit the buyer's personal taste, its value on sale by him is likely to be less than the price which he paid. Furthermore, it does not seem to me that he can be adequately compensated in damages for any breach of the stipulation, since, although it was suggested in *Mediana (Owners)* v. *Comet (Owners), The Mediana*[1] that real and not merely nominal damages may be given for the loss of a chattel which has amenity but not a commercial value, there is little assistance to be gained from the cases on the question how such damages are to be assessed, and indeed it is impossible adequately to equate loss of some amenity or pleasure to pounds, shillings and pence. For these reasons, I am of opinion that it was a condition of the contract and not a mere warranty that the seller should deliver the yacht within a reasonable time of 1st May, 1957, which time had, as I have held, expired by the beginning of September, 1957.

Charles Rickards Ltd. *v.* Oppenheim

[1950] 1 All E.R. 420

Where the buyer has waived a stipulation making the time of delivery of the essence of the contract, he can again make it of the essence of the contract by giving reasonable notice of his intention to do so.

Charles Rickards Ltd., a firm of coachbuilders, agreed to supply Oppenheim with a special body for a Rolls Royce within seven months. The contract stated that time was of the essence of the contract. The body was not delivered at the correct time, and Oppenheim waived the original condition as to the time of delivery. But later he gave the coachbuilders four weeks' notice that, if they did not deliver the body within that period, he would repudiate the contract. The body was not delivered until after the four weeks had expired, so Oppenheim refused to pay the price.

Held, by the Court of Appeal (without deciding whether the contract was for the sale of goods or for work and labour), that Oppenheim was justified in refusing to pay. He was entitled to give a reasonable notice making time once more of the essence of the contract, and this he had done.

DENNING, L.J. (at page 422)

It is clear on the findings of the Judge that there was an initial stipulation making time of the essence of the contract between the plaintiffs and the defendant, namely, that it was to be completed "in six, or, at the most, seven months". Counsel for the plaintiffs did not seek to disturb that finding—indeed, he could not successfully have done so—but he said that that stipulation was waived. His argument was that, the

---

[1] [1900] A.C. 113.

stipulated time having been waived, the time became at large, and that thereupon the plaintiffs' only obligation was to deliver within a reasonable time. He said that, in accordance with well-known authorities, "a reasonable time" meant a reasonable time in the circumstances as they actually existed, i.e., that the plaintiffs would not exceed a reasonable time if they were prevented from delivering by causes outside their control, such as strikes or the impossibility of getting parts, and so forth, and that, on the evidence in this case, it could not be said that a reasonable time was in that sense exceeded. He cited the well-known words of Lord WATSON in *Hick* v. *Raymond and Reid*[2] to support the view that in this case, on the evidence, a reasonable time had not been exceeded. If this had been originally a contract without any stipulation in regard to time, and, therefore, with only the implication of reasonable time, it may be that the plaintiffs could have said that they had fulfilled the contract, but, in my opinion, the case is very different when there was an initial contract, making time of the essence, of "six or, at the most, seven months". I agree that that initial time was waived by reason of the requests for delivery which the defendant made after March, 1948, and that, if delivery had been tendered in compliance with those requests, the defendant could not have refused to accept. Supposing, for instance, delivery had been tendered in April, May, or June, 1948, the defendant would have had no answer. It would be true that the plaintiffs could not aver and prove that they were ready and willing to deliver in accordance with the original contract. They would have had, in effect, to rely on the waiver almost as a cause of action . . . If the defendant, as he did, led the plaintiffs to believe that he would not insist on the stipulation as to time, and that, if they carried out the work, he would accept it, and they did it, he could not afterwards set up the stipulation in regard to time against them. Whether it be called waiver or forbearance on his part, or an agreed variation or substituted performance, does not matter. It is a kind of estoppel. By his conduct he made a promise not to insist on his strict legal rights. That promise was intended to be binding, intended to be acted on, and was, in fact, acted on. He cannot afterwards go back on it. . . .

Therefore, if the matter stopped there, the plaintiffs could have said that, notwithstanding that more than seven months had elapsed, the defendant was bound to accept, but the matter does not stop there, because delivery was not given in compliance with the requests of the defendant. Time and time again the defendant pressed for delivery, time and time again he was assured that he would have early delivery, but he never got satisfaction, and eventually at the end of June he gave notice saying that, unless the car was delivered by 25th July, he would not accept it. The question thus arises whether he was entitled to give such a notice, making time of the essence, and that is the question which counsel for the plaintiffs has argued before us. He agrees that, if this is a contract

---

[2] [1893] A.C. 22, at pp. 32, 33.

for the sale of goods, the defendant could give such a notice. He accepted the statement of McCardie, J., in *Hartley* v. *Hymans*,[3] as accurately stating the law in regard to the sale of goods, but he said that that statement did not apply to contracts for work and labour. He said that no notice making time of the essence could be given in regard to contracts for work and labour. The Judge thought that the contract was one for the sale of goods, but, in my view, it is unnecessary to determine whether it was a contract for the sale of goods or a contract for work and labour, because whichever it was, the defendant was entitled to give a notice bringing the matter to a head. It would be most unreasonable if, having been lenient and having waived the initial expressed time, he should thereby have prevented himself from ever thereafter insisting on reasonably quick delivery. In my judgment, he was entitled to give a reasonable notice making time of the essence of the matter. Adequate protection to the suppliers is given by the requirement that the notice should be reasonable.

The next question, therefore, is: Was this a reasonable notice? Counsel for the plaintiffs argued that it was not. He said that a reasonable notice must give sufficient time for the work then outstanding to be completed, and that, on the evidence in this case, four weeks was not a reasonable time because it would, and did, in fact, require three and a half months to complete it. In my opinion, however, the words of Lord Parker of Waddington in *Stickney* v. *Keeble*[4] apply to such a case as the present, just as much as they do to a contract for the sale of land. Lord Parker said:[5]

> "In considering whether the time so limited is a reasonable time the Court will consider all the circumstances of the case. No doubt what remains to be done at the date of the notice is of importance, but it is by no means the only relevant fact. The fact that the purchaser has continually been pressing for completion, or has before given similar notices which he has waived, or that it is specially important to him to obtain early completion, are equally relevant facts . . .".

To that statement I would add, in the present case, the fact that the original contract made time of the essence. In this case, not only did the defendant press continually for delivery, not only was he given promises of speedy delivery, but, on the very day before he gave the notice, he was told by the sub-contractors' manager, who was in charge of the work, that it would be ready within two weeks. He then gave a four weeks' notice. The Judge found that it was reasonable notice and, in my judgment, there is no ground on which this Court could in any way differ from that finding. The reasonableness of the notice must, of course, be judged at the time at which it is given. It cannot be held to be a bad notice because, after it is given, the suppliers find themselves in unanticipated difficulties in making delivery.

---

3 [1920] 3 K.B. 475, at p. 495.
4 [1915] A.C. 386.
5 *Ibid.*, at p. 419.

(2) Implied Condition as to Title

Niblett Ltd. *v.* Confectioners' Materials Co. Ltd.[6]

[1921] All E.R. Rep. 459

By s. 12(1): *"In a contract of sale . . . there is an implied condition on the part of the seller that in the case of a sale, he has a right to sell the goods, and in the case of an agreement to sell, he will have a right to sell the goods at the time when the property is to pass". A seller has no right to sell the goods where he can be restrained by injunction from so doing at the instance of a third party.*

The sellers sold a quantity of tins of condensed milk c.i.f. London. The buyers discovered that they could not sell them without removing the labels on them which were marked "Nissly Brand", for the Nestlé Co. could have obtained an injunction against them if they had sold the tins with the labels still on them, because the term "Nissly Brand" infringed the Nestlé trade mark. The buyers sued the sellers for damages for breach of s. 12(1) on the ground that they had no right to sell the goods.

Held, by the Court of Appeal, that the action succeeded.

SCRUTTON, L.J. (at page 462)

This was an English contract in writing whereby the buyers bought 3,000 cases of sweetened full cream condensed 1919 season's milk of a quality equal to federal standard. The milk came from the United States. The price was 42s. a case c.i.f. London nett cash against documents. The documents which were tendered under this contract had reference to certain cases which had on them labels with the words "Nissly Brand". The Nestlé and Anglo-Swiss Condensed Milk Co. thought that the word "Nissly" was an infringement of their registered trade mark, and that they could stop the sale of these goods. They attacked the sellers, and the sellers, not wishing to contest the matter, admitted that the cases were an infringement of the Nestlé Co.'s trade mark, and undertook not to sell condensed milk under the title of "Nissly". Neither were the buyers prepared to fight the Nestlé Co.; and after an unsuccessful attempt to export these cases, they were driven to remove the labels and sell the goods as condensed milk unlabelled. . . .

The second point arose on s. 12(1) . . . which provides that there is an implied condition on the part of the seller that in the case of an agreement to sell he will have a right to sell the goods at the time when the property is to pass. The property was to pass when the documents were tendered for the cases containing the goods. The sellers impliedly warranted that they had then a right to sell them. In fact, they could have been restrained by injunction from selling them, because they were infringing the

---

6 Another aspect of this case is treated under "Implied Warranty as to Quiet Possession". See p. 9, *post.*

rights of third persons. If a vendor can be stopped by process of law from selling, he has not the right to sell. Therefore, the purchasers so far have made out a cause of action for breach of s. 12(1).

Rowland *v*. Divall

[1923] All E.R. Rep. 270

Where the seller is in breach of s. 12(1), *because he has no right to sell the goods, the buyer is entitled to recover the full purchase price which he has paid, even though he has used the goods.*[7]

A buyer of a car used it for about three months, and then found that it was stolen property, and had to return it to its true owner.

Held, by the Court of Appeal, that even though he had used it for this period, he could recover the price, for there had been a total failure of consideration.

ATKIN, L.J. (at page 274)

It seems to me that in this case there has been a total failure of consideration, that is to say, that the buyer has not got that which he paid his price for. He paid the money in order that he might have the property, and he has not got it. It is true that the seller handed over to him the *de facto* possession, but the seller had not the right to possession and could not give to the buyer the right to possession, so that the buyer, during the time he had this car in his possession, had no right to possession, and was at all times liable to the true owner of the car in damages for the conversion of the car. There is no doubt that what he had the right to get was the property in the car because that is provided for by s. 12(1) . . ., which expressly provides that in every contract of sale there is an implied condition on the part of the seller that he has the right to sell the goods. . . . A seller cannot sell the goods which are not his property. I think that the right view is to say that there was a term of the contract implied, namely that the condition could be treated as a ground for rejecting the goods, and for repudiation under the contract. I think that would be the true implied term. One difficulty in actually reading the Sale of Goods Act seems to be that in this case there must be a right to reject, and not merely a right to reject, but a right to sue for the price upon failure of consideration for the sale, and also that there is no obligation on the part of the buyer to return the goods, for *ex hypothesi*, the seller has no good title to receive the goods back. On the facts of this case . . . the trouble arises because the goods have been taken from the buyer because some third person has the right to take them from

---

7 In April 1966 the Law Reform Committee in their 12th Report (Transfer of Title to Chattels) (Cmnd. 2958) recommended in par. 36 that in an action under s. 12(1) "the buyer should be entitled to recover no more than his actual loss, giving credit for any benefit he may have had from the goods while they were in his possession".

him. In these circumstances can it make any difference that the buyer has received and has used the goods before he has found out that there was a breach of the condition? To my mind, it makes no difference at all. The buyer accepted them upon the representation by the seller that he had the right to deal with the goods, but, inasmuch as the seller had no right and could convey to the buyer no right to use the goods at all, the seller cannot say: "You have got a benefit under the contract which you have not become entitled to, and that must be taken into account". It seems to me that in these circumstances the buyer has not received any part of that which he is entitled to receive. He has not received the goods, he has not received the right to possession of the goods, and in those circumstances there has been a complete failure of consideration.

Scrutton, L.J. (at page 273)

When one once gets a condition, and that condition is broken, the contract can be rescinded, and with the rescission of the contract, one can demand the return of the purchase money. Treating it as a condition, unless the purchaser with knowledge of the facts has held on to the bargain so as to waive the condition, and will himself be relying on his claim for breach of warranty in damages, there appears to be no difficulty whatever in recovering the purchase money. . . . It certainly seems to me that in a case of rescission for the breach of a condition that the seller has a right to sell the goods, it cannot be that the purchaser is deprived of his right to get back his purchase money because he cannot restore the goods which, from the nature of the transaction, are not the goods of the seller at all, and which the seller has, therefore, no right to in any circumstances. . . . The [buyer] is entitled to recover the whole of the purchase money, as and for the total failure of the consideration, inasmuch as the seller did not give that which he contracted to give, namely, the legal ownership of the car and the legal right to possession of it.

(3) IMPLIED WARRANTY AS TO QUIET POSSESSION

Niblett Ltd. *v.* Confectioners' Materials Co. Ltd.[8]

[1921] All E.R. Rep. 459

By s. 12(2): "In a contract of sale . . . there is . . . an implied warranty that . . . (b) the buyer will enjoy quiet possession of the goods . . .".

The sellers sold a quantity of condensed milk c.i.f. London. The buyers discovered that the labels on the tins infringed the Nestlé trade mark so that the only possible way of obtaining possession of them and dealing with them was to strip off the labels and sell them without labels. This they did, and suffered a loss in doing so, and claimed against the sellers for damages for breach of the warranty implied under s. 12(2) that "the buyer shall have and enjoy quiet possession of the goods".

Held, by ATKIN, L.J. (in the Court of Appeal), that the action succeeded.

ATKIN, L.J. (at page 465)

I think there was also a breach of the implied warranty in s. 12, that the buyer shall have and enjoy quiet possession of the goods. It may be that possession would not be disturbed if the only cause of complaint was that the buyer could not dispose of the goods, and that the warranty is confined to disturbance of possession of the goods delivered under the contract of sale. The warranty so interpreted was broken. The buyers were never allowed to have a quiet possession. They had to strip off the labels before they could take possession of the goods.

(4) IMPLIED CONDITION AS TO COMPLIANCE WITH DESCRIPTION

Arcos Ltd. *v.* E. A. Ronaasen & Son

[1933] All E.R. Rep. 646

By s. 13(1): "Where there is a contract for the sale of goods by description, there is an implied condition that the goods shall correspond with the description". Whether they do so correspond is a matter of fact in each case.

The sellers agreed to supply a quantity of staves of timber c.i.f. River Thames. They were to be $\frac{1}{2}$ inch thick. When they arrived at London, about 85% of them were found to be between $\frac{1}{2}$ inch and $\frac{9}{16}$ inch thick, while about 9% were between $\frac{9}{16}$ inch and $\frac{5}{8}$ inch thick.

Held, by the House of Lords, that the buyers were entitled to reject the goods, because there had been a breach of the implied condition of description under s. 13(1).

---

[8] Another aspect of this case is treated under "Implied Condition as to Title". See p. 6, *ante*. For another illustration of the warranty, see *Mason* v. *Burningham*, [1949] 2 All E.R. 134; p. 103, *post*.

LORD ATKIN (at page 650)

The simple question is whether the goods when shipped complied with the implied condition . . . that they should correspond with the description. . . . It was contended that in all commercial contracts the question was whether there was a "substantial" compliance with the contract; there always must be some margin, and it is for the tribunal of fact to determine whether the margin is exceeded or not. I cannot agree. If the written contract specifies conditions of weight, measurement and the like, those conditions must be complied with. A ton does not mean about a ton, or a yard about a yard. Still less, when you descend to minute measurements, does half an inch mean about half inch. If the seller wants a margin, he must, and in my experience does, stipulate for it. Of course, by recognised trade usage, particular figures may be given a different meaning, as in a baker's dozen, or there may be even incorporated a definite margin more or less, but there is no evidence or finding of such a usage in the present case. No doubt, there may be microscopic deviations which businessmen, and, therefore, lawyers will ignore. And in this respect it is necessary to remember that description and quantity are not necessarily the same, and that the legal rights in respect of them are regulated by different sections of the Code,[9] description by s. 13, quantity by s. 30.[10] It will be found that most of the cases that admit any deviation from the contract are cases where there has been an excess or deficiency in quantity which the Court has considered negligible. But apart from this consideration, the right view is that the conditions of the contract must be strictly performed. If a condition is not performed, the buyer has a right to reject. I do not myself think that there is any difference between businessmen and lawyers on this matter. No doubt in business men often find it unnecessary or inexpedient to insist on their strict legal rights. In a normal market, if they get something substantially like the specified goods, they may take them with or without grumbling and claim for an allowance. But in a falling market I find that buyers are often as eager to insist on their legal rights as Courts of law are ready to maintain them. No doubt at all times sellers are prepared to take a liberal view as to the rigidity of their own obligations and possibly buyers, who in turn are sellers, may also dislike too much precision. But buyers are not, as far as my experience goes, inclined to think that the rights defined in the Code are in excess of business needs. . . .

---

[9] I.e. the Sale of Goods Act.
[10] As to the delivery of the wrong quantity, see pp. 73 to 78, *post*.

Re Moore & Co. Ltd. and Landauer & Co.

[1921] All E.R. Rep. 466

The method of packing of the goods may form part of their description, and if it is not complied with by the seller, he is in breach of s. 13(1).

The sellers agreed to sell a quantity of tinned pears, which were to be packed in cases containing 30 tins each. When the goods were delivered, it was found that about half of the cases contained 24 tins only in each of them. The buyers refused to accept them.

Held, by the Court of Appeal, that the goods had been sold by description and the method of packing was part of the description. The sellers were therefore in breach of s. 13(1), and the buyers were entitled to refuse to accept the goods. Further, the method of packing would be particularly important if the buyer had sold the goods under the same description to a sub-purchaser.

SCRUTTON, L.J. (at page 469)

In this case sellers sold to buyers about "3,100 cases of Australian canned fruits consisting of about" and then follow five items, of which the first is 2,500 dozen $30/2\frac{1}{2}$ nominal tins Vickar pears at 27s. 6d. per dozen. We are informed that $30/2\frac{1}{2}$ means 30 tins in a case, each tin being of a nominal weight of $2\frac{1}{2}$ lb. When the goods arrived, the sellers tendered 698 cases, 30 tons to the case, and 781 cases 24 tins to the case, making in all a tender of 1,479 cases. The buyers, who rejected without giving a reason, at the arbitration gave as one of their reasons that they were not bound to accept such part of the tender as was 30 tins in a case. In view of the provisions of s. 30 of the Sale of Goods Act, I should have thought that the buyers were clearly right. One may adopt as one's own the language in which McCARDIE, J., dealt with a point of this sort in *Manbre Saccharine Co. Ltd.* v. *Corn Products Co.*[11] where the contract was for the sale of starch in 180 lb. bags, price so much per hundredweight, and the seller tendered 220 lb. bags and 140 lb. bags. McCARDIE, J., said:[12]

"In my opinion it is clear that such words were an essential part of the contract requirements. They constitute a portion of the description of the goods. The size of the bags may be important to a purchaser in view of sub-contracts or otherwise. A man may prefer to receive starch either in small or large or medium bags. If the size of the bags was immaterial, I fail to see why it should have been so clearly specified in the contract. A vendor must supply goods in accordance with the contract description, and he is not entitled to say that another description of goods will suffice for the purposes of the purchases. The tender by the defendants of starch in bags other than 180 lb. bags was a failure to comply with their contract".

---

[11] [1919] 1 K.B. 198.
[12] *Ibid.*, at p. 207.

In this case for some reason the sellers and buyers have put into their contract: "About 3,100 cases, with 30 tins to the case". They have put that in as a description, and that is what the seller must tender to the buyer. The arbitrator finds that 24 tins to the case are as valuable commercially as 30 tins to the case. That may be so. Yet a man who has bought under contract 30 tins to the case may have sold under the same description, and may be put into considerable difficulty by having goods tendered to him which do not comply with the description under which he bought, or under which he had re-sold. On that point I think the arbitrator was clearly wrong, and that ROWLATT, J.,[13] was clearly right.

(5) IMPLIED CONDITION AS TO FITNESS

Griffiths *v.* Peter Conway Ltd.

[1939] 1 All E.R. 685

Where the buyer suffers from an abnormality, e.g. a special sensitivity of the skin, he must make this known if he wishes to be able to rely on the implied condition under s. 14(3) that the goods shall be reasonably fit for the purpose.

A buyer of a Harris tweed coat suffered from dermatitis as a result of wearing it. Her skin was abnormally sensitive, but she did not make this fact known to the seller. There was no ingredient used in the manufacture of the coat which would have been harmful to the skin of a normal person. She claimed damages for breach by the seller of s. 14(3), on the ground that the coat was not "fit for the purpose", i.e., of wearing it.

Held, by the Court of Appeal, that the action failed. The coat had only to be reasonably fit for the purpose of being worn by a normal person. To enable her to sue for breach of s. 14(3) she should have made known to the seller the sensitivity of her skin, and this she had not done.

SIR WILFRID GREENE, M.R. (at page 691)

No normal skin would have been affected by this cloth. There was nothing in it which would affect a normal skin, but the plaintiff unfortunately had an idiosyncrasy, and that was the real reason why she contracted this disease.

On the basis of that finding, which is not challenged, [counsel] says: "Take the language of the section, and the present case falls within it". He says that the buyer, Mrs Griffiths, expressly made known to the [seller] the particular purpose for which the coat was required—that is to say, for the purpose of being worn by her, Mrs Griffiths, when it was made. Once that state of affairs is shown to exist, [counsel] says that the language of the section relentlessly and without any escape imposes upon the seller the obligation which the section imports.

---

13 In the Court below: [1921] K.B. 73.

It seems to me that there is one quite sufficient answer to that argument. Before the condition as to reasonable fitness is implied, it is necessary that the buyer should make known, expressly or by implication, first of all, the particular purpose for which the goods are required. The particular purpose for which the goods were required was the purpose of being worn by a woman suffering from an abnormality. It seems to me that, if a person suffering from such an abnormality requires an article of clothing for his or her use, and desires to obtain the benefit of the implied condition, he or she does not make known to the seller the particular purpose merely by saying: "The article of clothing is for my own wear". The essential matter for the seller to know in such cases with regard to the purposes for which the article is required consists in the particular abnormality or idiosyncrasy from which the buyer suffers. It is only when he has that knowledge that he is in a position to exercise his skill or judgment, because how can he decide and exercise skill or judgment in relation to the suitability of the goods that he is selling for the use of the particular individual who is buying from him unless he knows the essential characteristics of that individual? The fact that those essential characteristics are not known, as in the present case they were not known, to the buyer does not seem to me to affect the question. When I speak of "essential characteristics", I am not, of course, referring to any variations which take place and exist within the class of normal people. No two normal people are precisely alike, and, in the matter of sensitiveness of skin, among people who would be described as normal, their sensitiveness must vary in degree.

This does not mean that there is a line which it is the function of the Court, or of a medical witness, to draw with precision, so as to define all cases where normality ceases and abnormality begins. The impossibility of drawing such a line by reference to some scientific formula or something of that kind does not mean that, for the present purpose, the difference between normality and abnormality is a thing that must be disregarded, or cannot be ascertained. It is a question that no Judge and no jury would have any real difficulty in deciding on the evidence in any particular case. In this particular case, the [trial] Judge[14] has found the existence of abnormality, and, that being so, it seems to me impossible to say that the seller here had the particular purpose pointed out to him so as to show that the buyer relied on his skill or judgment. After all, the object of that is to enable the seller to make up his mind whether or not he will accept the burden of the implied condition, and the effect of the argument addressed to us would be to impose that implied condition upon the seller without his having the opportunity of knowing the vital matter which would affect his mind.

---

14 BRANSON, J.

Geddling *v*. Marsh

[1920] All E.R. Rep. 631

The implied condition under s. 14(3) *that the goods shall be reasonably fit for the purpose applies not only to the goods sold but to the goods* supplied *under a contract of sale*.

Mineral water in bottles was sold by a manufacturer to a retailer. The bottles themselves were not the subject matter of the sale, but had to be returned to the manufacturer when their contents had been drunk. One of the bottles exploded as a result of a defect in it, and injured the buyer.

Held, by the King's Bench Division, that the sellers were liable to her for breach of the implied condition under s. 14(3) that the goods should be reasonably fit for the purpose, for, although the bottle itself had not been sold, it had been "supplied" under a contract of sale.

BRAY, J. (at page 633)

The case for the [buyer] is that it is immaterial whether in fact the property in the bottle passed or not, because, in either case, whether there was a sale or a bailment, the case comes within the provisions of s. 14. . . . There is only one contract here. The [buyer] applied to the [seller] to supply her with mineral waters, that must mean mineral waters in bottles because mineral waters cannot be supplied except in bottles. Therefore she was seeking to have mineral water supplied to her in bottles. That undoubtedly is a contract of sale, and I assume that there may be a condition of that contract that the bottles are not to be bought, but hired; but the question which the [trial Court] had to consider was whether there bottles were supplied under a contract of sale. This was a contract of sale, and none the less a contract of sale because there was a particular provision with regard to the bottles. In my opinion, therefore, these bottles were supplied under a contract of sale, and it follows that there was an implied condition that the bottles should be reasonably fit for the purpose for which they were supplied; they were not in fact reasonably fit. The contention on the [seller's] behalf is that the implied warranty as to the fitness of the goods supplied applied only to the goods actually bought. It seems to me that the common-sense meaning of [sub-s. (3)] of s. 14 is that the warranty extends to goods not only actually bought, but to goods supplied under a contract of sale. In my opinion, the bottles were supplied under a contract of sale, and that, therefore, the warranty applies.

(6) IMPLIED CONDITION AS TO MERCHANTABLE QUALITY

Jackson v. Rotax Motor and Cycle Co.[15]

(1910), 103 L.T. 411

By s. 14(2): "Where the seller sells goods in the course of a business, there is an implied condition that the goods supplied under the contract are of merchantable quality". Goods are not of merchantable quality even though they can be made so at a very slight cost.

The sellers, who were manufacturers of motor horns, sold 609 horns under a contract of sale by description. 364 were defective for various reasons. Some were dented, but could have been made of merchantable quality at a very slight cost. The buyers rejected them on the ground that the sellers were in breach of s. 14(2).

Held, by the Court of Appeal, that they were entitled to do so, for the goods when delivered were not of merchantable quality.

COZENS-HARDY, M.R. (at page 413)

The official referee has found not merely that the horns were damaged in transit, but that, owing to defective packing, many of the horns as delivered were not in a merchantable state in the sense that they could without more have been disposed of reasonably and properly by the buyers as dealers in horns to people who wanted then and there a horn for a motor-car, but he found also that they could be made merchantable at a trifling cost. I will read a passage from his judgment. [The Master of the Rolls read the passage set out above, and proceeded:] What does this amount to? The plaintiff is suing for the contract price of the goods, and the defendants are held bound to take the goods, part of which were, as the official referee finds, unmerchantable, with an allowance of £35. The case then went to the Divisional Court, and that Court put what, so far as I am aware, is an entirely new meaning on the word "merchantable"—that goods are "merchantable" if they only want some trifling thing done to make them immediately saleable; that they are to be considered as merchantable, although not immediately saleable, and although a further expenditure of money is required by the purchaser to make them saleable. I am not aware of any authority for that view. It seems to me to be inconsistent with the language of the Sale of Goods Act . . ., to which our attention has been called.

---

15 This case has been retained in this edition because it would seem that it is still good law. The Sale of Goods Act 1979, s. 14(6) merely states:—"Goods of any kind are of merchantable quality . . . if they are as fit for the purpose or purposes for which goods of that kind are commonly bought as it is reasonable to expect having regard to any description applied to them, the price (if relevant) and all the other relevant circumstances . . .".

Sumner, Permain & Co. *v.* Webb & Co.[16]

[1921] All E.R. Rep. 680

The term "merchantable quality" in s. 14(2) does not mean that the goods are legally saleable in the particular place at which the buyer intends to re-sell them.

The manufacturers of "Webb's Indian Tonic Water" sold a quantity of it f.o.b. London to buyers, who carried on business in the Argentine. The sellers knew that it was to be sent there on shipment. An Argentine law prohibited the sale of drink containing salicylic acid. The tonic water contained this chemical, so the buyers brought an action against the sellers on the ground that the goods were not of merchantable quality, since they could not be sold in the Argentine.

Held, by the Court of Appeal, that the action failed. The term "merchantable quality" did not mean that the goods were legally saleable.

BANKES, L.J. (at page 683)

Then we come to sub-s. (2) of s. 14. I emphasise the fact that the section does not speak of goods being either "saleable" or "merchantable", but of being of "merchant-able quality", and the introduction of the word "quality", in my opinion, qualifies and restricts the meaning which must be put upon "merchantable". But the statute goes further than that because it speaks of "quality of goods" in the definition section, which is s. [61], as including their state or condition. I do not propose to attempt any definition which will comprise every case, but all I need say about this sub-section is that, in my opinion, it is not really possible to include under that language the contention of the present buyers that the state of the law of the country in which the goods are to be re-sold is a matter which comes under that language at all. Quality or state or condition seem to me to refer to something essentially different in their nature. . . .

There is no complaint here, either with regard to the quality of the goods, their state, or their condition—they were all perfectly good; and there was no objection which could be taken to them except that by the law of the Argentine the goods which contained one of the ingredients of these goods could not be dealt with in that country. BAILHACHE, J.,[17] has dealt with that point shortly as follows:

"The quality of the goods was perfectly all right in most countries—nothing the matter with them. Can it be said that because they were prohibited from being sold in the Argentine therefore they were of unmerchantable quality? I agree one must have regard to the place in which the goods are to be sold, and I have come to the conclusion that these goods were of unmerchantable quality in the Argentine".

---

[16] This case has been retained in this edition because it would seem that it is still good law, although the Sale of Goods Act 1979, s. 14(6) defines "merchantable quality". The sub-section is set out in footnote 15, p. 15 *ante*. The new definition would appear not to be exhaustive, and not to cover the facts which arose in this case.
[17] In the Court below.

He does not elaborate the reasons upon which he comes to that conclusion, but on the ground which I have endeavoured to state I am not able myself to come to the conclusion that, upon the grounds stated, the case falls within the sub-section at all.

SCRUTTON, L.J. (at page 686)

I have looked a little further into the matter, and I can now finally express my opinion that "merchantable quality" does not cover legal title to goods or the legal right to sell. In my view, "merchantable quality" means that the goods comply with the description in the contract, so that to a purchaser buying goods of that description the goods would be good tender. It does not mean that there shall be, in fact, buyers of the article. For instance, take the case that I put during the argument. If you sell vestings of a particular fancy pattern for sale in China, you do not warrant that the Chinese buyer will like that pattern and will buy it, when it goes out there. If the goods are vestings, fancy pattern, they are merchantable though nobody likes the fancy pattern when it has got there. Similarly, I do not think "merchantable quality" means that there can legally be buyers of that article. If the goods are of the contract description, the possibility of legally making a sale of them does not, in my view, come within "merchantable quality" or the word "saleable".

ATKIN, L.J. (at page 688)

The other way in which it was put is that there was a breach of the implied condition in s. 14(2) of the Sale of Goods Act that the goods shall be of merchantable quality. I agree with what has been said by the two other members of the Court that that cannot in itself refer merely to the fact that the goods are unsaleable because there is a law of the place in which they are sought to be sold prohibiting that sale. One has to remember, when one is dealing with this subject, that one is clear of all questions with regard to whether the goods are fit for a particular purpose. This is a general obligation applying to all sales, and it appears to me merely to mean that there shall be a warranty that the article delivered is the article described in the contract, not so differing from the normal quality, including state or condition, required by the contract, as to make it unsaleable. In this particular case, the article that was described was the article contracted for, and it was delivered in its normal state or condition, which would ordinarily be required in performance of a contract for the delivery of these goods f.o.b., and it appears to me impossible to suggest that in this warranty the seller warrants that the goods shall be sold in the particular place to which they are delivered to the buyer—in other words, warrants that there shall be no legislation or that there is no existing legislation prohibiting their sale. A case was put in argument, which, I think, illustrates fairly clearly what the contention of the buyers in this case amounts to—that where a buyer, resident in America when there was a complete legislative prohibition against the sale of alcohol, ordered from another country goods containing alcohol to be imported into America, the seller must be taken to have warranted that the goods should be capable of being sold in America. I think the proposition need only be stated to show that it is impossible that the Act of Parliament can have contained a warranty which would have an effect such as that, and, to my mind, the warranty extends no further than I have stated.

(7) Sale by Sample

E. & S. Ruben Ltd. *v.* Faire Bros. & Co. Ltd.

[1949] 1 All E.R. 215

By s. 15(2)(a): "In the case of a contract for sale by sample there is an implied condition that the bulk shall correspond with the sample in quality". This condition is broken even though only a simple process is required to make the bulk correspond with the sample.

The sellers agreed to supply the buyers with a quantity of "Linatex" [a type of vulcanised rubber] in 41 ft. rolls, 5 ft. wide, in accordance with a small sample. The sample was flat and soft, but the rubber delivered was crinkly and folded, though these defects could have been put right if it were warmed.

Held, by the King's Bench Division, that the goods had been sold by description, and that the sellers were in breach of s. 15(2)(a), for they were not in accordance with the sample though only a simple process was required to make them correspond with it.

Hilbery, J. (at page 218)

Having found, as I have, that the contract was for the goods which were offered by the [sellers], namely, Linatex in 41 ft. rolls, 5 ft. wide, at 1s. 9d. a lb. as per the small sample, I am satisfied that the goods were in rolls, inasmuch as they were rolled up in lengths, but they were not according to the measurements that were specified when the goods were described, and there is no doubt that the measurements given in this case were words of description. The goods were not in accordance with the description, but it is said that they were in accordance with the sample, although they were crinkly and folded in some cases, while the sample was flat and soft. The hardness of some of the pieces seems to me to be a matter which is incidental to the article, it being a rubber sheet article. A difference in temperature will cause it to go hard or relatively hard, and I am not satisfied that anyone in the trade who was dealing with a piece of this sheet rubber material would not expect there to be some variation in the nature of the hardness or pliability between sheets as they were when delivered to him rolled up and the sample, because the mere handling of the small sample piece, carrying it in, perhaps, warm conditions, will make it soft or extra soft, or pliable, but the folding of the material is a matter of considerable importance because, if the material is to be used by shoe manufacturers, as this article was, the flatness of the sheet is essential if it is to be put in a cutting machine and not into a clipping machine, because in a cutting machine, the sheet has to be lifted and brought up against the knives which are fixed, and the material has to be flat to make the cuts correct. It was unfortunate that so small a sample was used, because it was a perfectly flat sample, and the goods delivered were not flat.

In regard to the fact that the goods showed signs of folding, and were, in some respects, crinkly, it is said that that could have been corrected by warming them and pressing out the crinkles when the rubber was warm. It is not in compliance with a contractual obligation if an article is delivered which is not in accordance with the sample, but which can, by some simple process—no matter how simple the process is—be turned into an article which will be in accordance with the sample on which the contract was made. In the circumstances, I think that the goods were not in accordance with the description, nor were they according to the sample.

Polenghi Brothers *v.* Dried Milk Co. Ltd.

(1904), 92 L.T. 64

By s. 15(2)(b): "In the case of a contract for sale by sample there is an implied condition that the buyer shall have a reasonable opportunity of comparing the bulk with the sample".

The sellers sold a quantity of dried milk powder to the buyers. The contract of sale was a sale by sample and stated, "The prices to be paid . . . 6d. per lb. c.i.f. London . . . Payment to be made in cash in London on the arrival of the powders against shipping or railway documents". The buyers refused to pay for any delivery on production of the shipping documents, and contended that they had a right under s. 15(2)(b) to a reasonable opportunity of comparing the bulk with the sample.

Held, by the King's Bench Division, that they were entitled to have such an opportunity.

KENNEDY, J. (at page 66)

The point is a narrow one—whether on the construction of the contract the buyer is entitled, in respect of the goods contracted for, to insist on the provisions of s. 15, sub-s. 2(b), of the Sale of Goods Act, and to have an opportunity of comparing the bulk with the sample before paying the price. The goods in question were manufactured abroad, and were sent, partly by sea and partly by rail, to London. The goods having arrived, the difficulty arises between the parties by the refusal of the buyers to pay the price until they have found out whether the goods correspond with the sample. The goods were arrived goods at the railway company's warehouse. They were goods in respect of which the sellers were in a position to tender to the buyers the shipping documents. The buyers refused payment until they had had an opportunity of satisfying themselves that the goods were equal to sample. What is the reasonable meaning of cl. 9 of the contract? Generally, s. 15 of the Sale of Goods Act applies, and gives the buyer a reasonable opportunity of inspecting the goods before payment. The contract contains these words: "Payment is to be made . . . in London on the arrival of the powders against shipping or railway documents". That is an express provision. With regard to payment, there are two stipulations, and two only. The seller must (1) show that the goods are arrived goods, and (2) produce the shipping documents. Payment on delivery is excluded by express stipulation, which provides for payment on arrival. The plain meaning of the contract is that on those two conditions being fulfilled payment is to be made. If the goods do not answer the description, the buyer has a right to reject, which right is not impaired by the express condition in the contract that "payment is to be made . . . in London on the arrival of the powders against shipping or railway documents".

Godley *v*. Perry (Burton & Sons (Bermondsey) Ltd., Third Party, Graham, Fourth Party)

[1960] 1 All E.R. 36

By s. 15(2)(c): "*In the case of a contract for sale by sample there is an implied condition that the goods shall be free from any defect, rendering them unmerchantable, which would not be apparent on reasonable examination of the sample*". *It is to be emphasised that the Act speaks not of* "*practicable*" *but of a* "*reasonable*" *examination.*

A retailer purchased from a wholesaler a quantity of toy catapults, the sale being by sample. One of them was sold to a small boy who injured his eye when it broke into pieces because of its faulty construction. The retailer was held liable for damages to the boy, and claimed an indemnity from the wholesaler. The defect in the catapult would not when the retailer pulled back the elastic of the catapult.

Held, by the Queen's Bench Division, that the wholesaler was liable for breach of s. 15(2)(c). The test made by pulling back the elastic was all that could reasonably be expected of a potential purchaser.

EDMUND DAVIES, J. (at page 40)

I hold that this was indeed a sale by sample, and that the implied condition accordingly existed. . . . That in breach of such condition, what I may call the accident catapult was so defective as to be unmerchantable is clear. Nevertheless, learned counsel . . . submitted that a reasonable examination of the sample would have revealed its defects, and that accordingly no such condition could be implied. The fragility of the toy was, he submitted, perfectly obvious, and however widely his clients might have departed from the proper standard of mercantile ethics in placing large supplies of such an object on the market, to be snapped up by juveniles, liability under s. 15(2)(c) could not be established as against them. Counsel . . . demonstrated that by squeezing together the two prongs of the catapult in the hand they could be fractured, and further suggested that by holding the toy down with one's foot and then pulling on the elastic, its safety could be tested and, as I understand it, its inherent fragility would thereby inevitably be discovered. True, the potential customer might have done any of these things. He might also, I suppose, have tried biting the catapult, or hitting it with a hammer, or applying a lighted match to ensure its non-inflammability, experiments which, with all respect, are but slightly more bizarre than those suggested by learned counsel. But, looking at the matter realistically, as one must, in my judgment none of these tests is called for by a process of "reasonable examination", as that phrase would be understood by the common-sense standards of everyday life. All these suggested tests were reasonably practicable, but the Act speaks not of a "practicable" but of a "reasonable" examination. In my judgment, to pull back the elastic as [the retailer] did . . . was all that could reasonably be expected of any potential customer, and such an examination wholly failed to make apparent to [him] or even to render [him] alive to the possibility of, such a defect as undoubtedly existed in the accident catapult.

B. TRANSFER OF PROPERTY AND RISK AS BETWEEN SELLER AND BUYER[18]

(1) SALE OF SPECIFIC GOODS

Re Anchor Line (Henderson Brothers) Ltd.

[1936] 2 All E.R. 941

By s. 17(1): *"Where there is a contract for the sale of specific or ascertained goods, the property in them is transferred to the buyer at such time as the parties to the contract intend it to be transferred".*

The Anchor Line Ltd. signed an agreement with the Ocean S.S. Co. Ltd. for the purchase of an electric crane at a deferred purchase price of £4,000. Annual payments in respect of "interest" and "depreciation" were to be made. The amount paid for "depreciation" was to be deducted from the purchase price on completion of the purchase. In the meantime the Anchor Line Ltd. was to "have entire charge of and responsibility for" the crane. Payments in respect of "interest" and "depreciation" were made regularly for some years by the Anchor Line Ltd., but it went into liquidation. One of the issues which arose was whether the property in the crane had passed to the Anchor Line Ltd.

Held, by the Court of Appeal, that it had not passed. The terms of the contract showed an intention (within the meaning of s. 17) that it was not to pass until the purchase was completed.

---

[18] For the transfer of property in the case of c.i.f. contracts, see p. 130, *post*; in f.o.b. contracts, p. 158, *post*; and ex-ship contracts, p. 164, *post*.

LORD WRIGHT, M.R. (at page 945)

If one looks at the Sale of Goods Act . . ., the material section, to my mind, is s. 17, which states the general rule, that the property passes when it is intended to pass:

"(1) Where there is a contract for the sale of specific or ascertained goods the property in them is transferred to the buyer at such time as the parties to the contract intend it to be transferred.

(2) For the purpose of ascertaining the intention of the parties regard shall be had to the terms of the contract, the conduct of the parties, and the circumstances of the case".

In s. 18 there are certain specific rules which are to apply. But, as I understand this case, s. 18 does not apply here, because, in my judgment, s. 18 can only apply, according to its terms, "unless a different intention appears". That refers back to s. 17, and, as I construe the contract, a different intention does appear. I find, in the contract read as a whole, a clear intention that the property shall not pass until the purchase is completed.

The transaction, as I understand it, was simply this. The crane, being on the berth occupied by the Anchor Line, was in their occupation. They wanted to use it in the course of their ordinary business. It was, I say, in their "occupation"; it was a chattel and not a fixture to the realty; but I use the word "occupation" for convenience, in the sense that they were possessing and using it. They wanted to possess and use it. They were not, however, prepared there and then to pay the price for the crane, namely, £4,000. They entered, therefore, into this agreement, which was to operate, according to its language, "in the meantime"—that is to say, to tide them over their immediate financial difficulties. They were not to pay the purchase price at the moment or in one sum, but it was to be paid by the arrangement which is specified: £350 per annum was to be paid for the first two years; £450 per annum for the second two years, and £400 per annum thereafter. Of those sums, I take it, £350 is the starting amount. The sum of £240, which was 6% of the purchase price of the crane, was to be regarded as depreciation. That I understand to mean this: the crane, being treated as the property of the Ocean Steamship Company, was year by year depreciating, and, according to business practice, they would write off, on the footing that it was their property, a sum for depreciation year by year, and that would have appeared in their books as a debit. But that amount year by year was to be paid over to them, and paid in that way by the Anchor Line. The amount of the purchase price was to be reduced proportionately, just as the crane in question was being reduced year by year in value. That explains, I think, the provision as to the payment of depreciation.

On the other hand, the payment appropriated to interest was on a different footing. The word "interest" might seem to indicate that there was a debt for the whole purchase price or for the balance each year of the purchase price, the payment of which was foreborne at interest. If that were its meaning, then it would be rather consistent with the view that the debt of £4,000 was due and outstanding from beginning to end. But I do not so regard it. I think the word "interest" is used here somewhat loosely as indicating a payment year by year in the nature of rent, or for use and occupation of the crane. As that was paid on that footing, it was not to go in reduction of the £4,000, because the Anchor Line were getting value in return—namely, the use of the crane in the meantime.

There is a further provision which to my mind is only consistent with the view that the property in the crane was still vested in the sellers: that is the clause "In the meantime you"—that is the Anchor Line—"will have entire charge of and responsibility for the crane in every respect". I think that indicates that the Anchor Line did not become owners of the crane but were merely bailees, and, as bailees, were responsible for its safety and its preservation to the bailors, who were the owners—namely, the Ocean Company.

Finally, I attach very great importance to the language "completion of the purchase", read with the remaining words. The first clause states the agreement as one for "a deferred purchase price of £4,000". Now, a deferred purchase price might be construed as meaning a price for a deferred purchase, or a price for a purchase which was to become complete at once, though the payment of the price was deferred. In that state of ambiguity I attach importance, as solving the ambiguity, to the words immediately following: "Until the completion of the purchase", and to the similar words: "balance actually to be paid by you on completion of the purchase, whenever that may take place". I agree that these words are not conclusive, but, read in the context in which they are, they support the view which I otherwise arrive at: that what we have here is a contract, the intention of which is that there should be an agreement to purchase, but that that agreement should not be completed or carried out until some time, "whenever that may take place"—the time, it is implied in the contract, when the balance of the purchase price is paid; and then, and then only, the property in the crane is to vest in the Anchor Line. That certainly agrees with the business probabilities. It is always dangerous to rely on business probabilities in construing any contract, because it does not necessarily follow that the parties have contemplated all that might happen. I prefer, therefore, to rest my judgment on the construction which I attach to the terms of the contract, which, to my mind, show an intention within the meaning of s. 17 as to the time at which the property is to be transferred.

Underwood Ltd. *v.* Burgh Castle Brick and Cement Syndicate

[1921] All E.R. Rep. 515

By s. 18, r. 1: "Unless a different intention appears . . . where there is an unconditional contract for the sale of specific goods in a deliverable state, the property in the goods passes to the buyer when the contract is made . . .". Whether the goods are "in a deliverable state" is a matter of fact.

The sellers sold to the buyers a horizontal condensing engine for £650 f.o.r. London. It weighed 30 tons and was bolted to a concrete emplacement. It took two days for it to be disconnected and two weeks for it to be dismantled and placed on the rail. While it was being loaded on a railway wagon, it was accidentally damaged. The buyers refused to accept the engine, so the sellers sued them for the price.

Held, by the Court of Appeal, that the property in the engine had not passed to the buyers and the action failed, because the goods were not in a "deliverable state".

BANKES, L.J. (at page 517)

The only question is whether the property in this engine had passed to the buyers before the damage to it was done. The contract of sale was in writing. The subject-matter of the sale was a horizontal condensing engine, which, at the date of the contract, was in place and securely fixed at the works of some firm at Millwall. The sellers agreed to sell it to the buyers at the price of £650 f.o.r. London. The engine weighed 30 tons. It was bolted to a concrete emplacement in which it had become embedded by its own weight, so that it had first to be unfastened, a work of two days, and then to be dismantled, a process which required a further two weeks' work and an expense of some £50, after which another sum of £50 might be required to place it on rail.

Did the property in this engine pass on the contract of sale? No general rule can be laid down which will answer the question when the property passes in every contract of sale. In many sales of specific articles to be delivered, the property passes on the making of the contract. A man may select and agree to buy a hat and the shopman may agree to deliver it at the buyer's house. There, notwithstanding the obligation to deliver the hat, the property passes at the time of the contract. But that is far from this case. Considering the risk and expense involved in dismantling and moving this engine, I have no hesitation in holding that the proper inference to be drawn is that the property was not to pass until the engine was safely placed on rail in London. In my view an elaborate discussion of the rules in s. 18 of the Sale of Goods Act . . . is unnecessary. They only apply where a different intention does not appear, and in this case a different intention does appear, assuming for the moment that this machine was in a deliverable state when it was fixed in its position at Millwall. . . . But was this engine in a deliverable state when in its position at Millwall? The sellers contended that where a specific article is complete in itself, for example a complete engine or a complete cart—that is to say, where nothing more has to be done to make it an engine or a cart—it is then in a deliverable state within the meaning of s. 18, r. 1, and, if the owner agrees to sell it, the property passes to the buyer when the contract is made, and it is immaterial whether the time of payment or the time of delivery, or both, be postponed. I do not accept that test. A "deliverable state" does not depend upon the mere completeness of the subject-matter in all its parts, but on the actual state of the goods at the date of the contract and the state in which they are to be delivered by the terms of the contract. Where the vendors have to expend as much trouble and as much money as the sellers had to expend before this engine could be placed on rail, I cannot think that the subject-matter can be said to be in a deliverable state.

SCRUTTON, L.J. (at page 518)

On some of the points raised I do not think it necessary to express a final opinion, because I have formed a clear opinion on one point. I assume that this was a sale of a chattel, and not of a mere right to sever. It was a sale of a specific engine f.o.r. London. At the time of the sale the specific engine was fixed by bolts and embedded by its own weight in concrete. It had first to be detached, which could not be done in less than two days. And then it required a further sum of, perhaps, £100, and two or three weeks' work before it could be put on rail. The sellers had to detach it and take it to pieces; both the expense and the new work were to be provided by them. It is a well-known rule, now embodied in s. 18, r. 2, of the Sale of Goods Act . . . that

> "where . . . the seller is bound to do something to the goods, for the purpose of putting them into a deliverable state, the property does not pass until such thing [is] done . . .".

The sellers contended that, if an engine, the subject-matter of a sale, is in its place as an engine, it is in a deliverable state, and that it is immaterial that it has to be taken to pieces by the vendor before it can be delivered. I do not agree. I find it impossible to apply the definition in s. [61] of the Sale of Goods Act of a "deliverable state" as "a state in which the buyer is bound to take delivery" of the goods, to this case where the buyers find an engine so firmly attached that it takes two days before it can be got loose, and in such a state that it cannot be put on rail, where they stipulated to have it, until a further two weeks' work has been done on it. I decide this case on the ground that the sellers were bound to do something for the purpose of putting this engine in a deliverable state, though I do not dissent from the view of BANKES, L.J., that, in all the circumstances, the property was not intended to pass until the engine was placed on rail.

Dennant *v.* Skinner

[1948] 2 All E.R. 29

By s. 57(2): *"A sale by auction is complete when the auctioneer announces its completion by the fall of the hammer . . .". Property in the goods passes at that moment to the buyer unless a different intention appears.*

Dennant, an auctioneer, knocked down at an auction a van to the highest bidder, who said his name was King, taking from him in return a cheque and a signed statement that the property was not to pass until the cheque was paid. King was allowed to remove the vehicle and sold it to another person who in turn sold it to Skinner. Dennant then sued Skinner for the return of the van.

Held, by the King's Bench Division, that the action failed. On the facts, there had been no mistake as to the identity of the contracting parties when the sale took place. The property in the van passed to King on the fall of the hammer under ss. 57 and 18, r. 1, and therefore Skinner obtained a good title to the vehicle.

HALLETT, J. (at page 34)

The second point on which the plaintiff relies is that the property in the circumstances of this case did not pass until the price was paid by the cheque being in order or cash substituted for it. A contract of sale is concluded in an auction sale on the fall of the hammer, and, indeed, the Sale of Goods Act . . . [s. 57(2)], so provides. Section 18 provides:

"Rule 1: Where there is an unconditional contract for the sale of specific goods, in a deliverable state, the property in the goods passes to the buyer when the contract is made, and it is immaterial whether the time of payment or the time of delivery or both be postponed".

Accordingly, on the fall of the hammer the property of this car passed to King unless that *prima facie* rule is excluded from applying because of a different intention appearing or because there was some condition in the contract which prevented the rule from applying. In my view, this was clearly an unconditional contract of sale, and I can see nothing whatever to make a different intention appear. The only evidence on which it was ever suggested to exist was the printed conditions, but I can see nothing in those conditions to negative an intention that the property should pass on the fall of the hammer. I think the conditions are entirely consistent with such an intention. If, however, the conditions are to be regarded as incorporated in the contract of sale, as to which I have some doubt, that makes no difference to the claim of the plaintiff. By the Sale of Goods Act . . ., s. 28: "Unless otherwise agreed, delivery of the goods and payment of the price are concurrent conditions", and, finally by s. 39(1)(a) and (c), an unpaid seller of goods has a lien on the goods or right to retain them for the price while he is in possession of them and he also has a right of re-sale as limited by the Act.

However, the passing of the property and the right to possession are two different things. Here, in my judgment, the property had passed on the fall of the hammer, but still the plaintiff had a right to retain possession of the goods until payment was made. If, when he was ready to deliver the goods, payment was not made, he could have sued for the price, or he could have exercised powers of re-sale, and he could have secured himself by way of lien on the goods for the price, but once he chose, for reasons good, bad, or indifferent, as a result of statements fraudulent or honest, to part with the possession of the vehicle by giving delivery of it, he then lost his seller's lien and he no longer had·a right to possession of the vehicle. He had a right until it was delivered, but as the right of retainer was not exercised, he had no right in the vehicle. The property in the vehicle had passed to King. In my view, therefore, the second contention for the plaintiff also fails. His right to the property had gone and his right to possession had gone.

Kursell *v.* Timber Operators & Contractors Ltd.

(1926), 135 L.T. 223

The term "specific goods" which is used in s. 18, r. 1, means "goods identified and agreed upon at the time a contract of sale is made".

On 10th September, 1920, the sellers agreed to sell to the buyers all the "merchantable timber" growing in a forest in Latvia on 20th August, 1920. "Merchantable timber" was defined as "all trunks and branches of trees but not seedlings and young trees of less than six inches in diameter at a height of four feet from the ground". The buyers took possession of the forest and began to cut the trees, but on 1st October the whole of the forest became State property as a result of a law passed by the Latvian Government, and all private rights in it were annulled. The sellers sued for the price of the timber, claiming that the property in it had passed to the buyers.

Held, by the Court of Appeal, that the property in the timber had not passed to the buyers, because under s. 18, r. 1, the sale did not constitute a sale of specific goods, for the sale was of "merchantable timber" as defined above, which could be only determined and identified from time to time as the trees grew.

SCRUTTON, L.J. (at page 225)

This appeal from the decision of ROWLATT, J., on a case stated by a legal arbitrator involves the effect on the purchase of a forest in Latvia of a Latvian law appropriating the forest and annulling all private rights in relation to it. The vendor sues for the price of the forest on the ground that the property in it has passed to the purchaser, and any subsequent loss of the subject-matter is for the purchaser's account. The purchaser replies that the property has not passed. . . . The arbitrator and ROWLATT, J., have decided in favour of the purchaser's contention.

The contract in question was made on 10th September, 1920, and provided for the sale of all merchantable timber growing in a specified forest on 20th August, 1920. Merchantable timber was defined as "all trunks and branches of trees, but not seedlings and young trees of less than six inches in diameter at a height of 4 ft. from the ground". The timber was to be cut not more than 12 in. from the ground. The measurement of the trunk was, therefore, uncertain till cutting. The purchaser had 15 years in which to cut the timber, and was to have the use of the vendors' sawmills, plant and huts, and the right to occupy every part of the forest. The price was £225,000 and the payments were to be made £15,000 on each of the first three quarter-days in the year, and for the fourth quarter a sum equal to £4 a standard of exportable timber cut in the forest during the year, less £45,000 (the three previous instalments). The amount was to be certified by the authorised agents of the vendors and purchaser, the measurements having been agreed by them. The purchaser, unless prevented by some act or enactment of the government of the country, or by *force majeure*, was to cut timber at the rate of 15,000 standards per annum, and if he was so prevented, the 15 years' period was to receive a corresponding extension. During the period of prevention the £15,000 instalments of price were to be reduced to £4 a standard of timber cut, carried away, and sold or exported during the quarter. So long, therefore, as there was complete prevention, no price would be payable.

The contract having been made on 10th September, on 16th September the Latvian Assembly passed an agrarian law, by which from 1st October, 1920, the forest became the property of the Latvian State and the contract was annulled and all property and rights of vendor and purchaser in the forest were confiscated. In other words, for the last 5½ years it has been illegal to perform the contract in the place where alone it can be performed; and the obstacle to performance is continuing. A small quantity of timber was cut between 2nd and 14th October, 1920, amount unknown; but as the purchasers have paid £30,000 to the vendors covering the first six months, it is not possible to argue that a default of payment of sums due has made the whole price payable.

What is the legal result of these facts? In the first place, has the property passed? It was said that this was a contract for the sale of specific goods in a deliverable state under s. 18, r. 1, of the Sale of Goods Act. Specific goods are defined as goods identified and agreed upon at the time a contract of sale is made. It appears to me these goods were neither identified nor agreed upon. Not every tree in the forest passed, but only those complying with a certain measurement not then made. How much of each tree passed depended on where it was cut, how far from the ground. Nor does the timber seem to be in a deliverable state until the buyer has severed it. He cannot under the definition be bound to take delivery of an undetermined part of a tree not yet identified.

I refer to and adopt Lord JOHNSTON's discussion of a similar question in the Scotch case of *Morison* v. *Lockhart*.[19]

For these reasons, in my opinion, the property had not passed under s. 18, r. 1, and, therefore, the timber was not at the risk of the purchaser.

LORD HANWORTH, M.R. (at page 225)

In my judgment the determination of what trees fulfil the definition of merchantable timber is to be determined from time to time, as and when it is proposed to fell them, and the words "growing on August 20, 1920", are inserted in order to lay down the condition that such trees must have been part of the forest growing at the date, and not part of those replanted later under cl. 10(3), some of which might reach the required measurements in the course of the lapse of 12 or 14 years from their planting by the vendors. This conclusion negatives the contention that the agreement of 10th September, 1920, made a sale of specific or ascertained goods. The definition of specific goods in s. [61] of the Sale of Goods Act . . . is: "Specific goods means goods identified and agreed upon at the time a contract of sale is made". It is clear that this definition will not fit trees of which it cannot be determined that they are merchantable and within the contract until the time for felling them has approached and when the time for their measurement has arrived—that may be any number of years up to nearly 15 after the contract was made.

It is not necessary, however, to base my judgment upon this point of interpretation of its terms alone. From a careful study of the agreement, and in particular the clauses which I have set out above, I have come to the conclusion that the agreement was not executed on the part of the vendors at its date. They still had to agree the timber to be cut, its measurement when cut, and its value, and the instalments due in respect of it. The question whether the property in the timber then passed depends first upon whether it is "specific or ascertained goods" within s. 17 . . ., and next if it be such, whether the parties intended the property in it to be transferred. Further, by sub-s. (2) "for the purpose of ascertaining the intention of the parties regard shall be had to the terms of the contract, the conduct of the parties and the circumstances of the case". The law as stated in the Code[20] is similar to the proposition as to the passing of the property in specific and ascertained goods laid down in his judgment in *Heilbutt* v. *Hickson* by BOVILL, C.J.,[21] where he adds:

"unless from other circumstances it can be collected that the intention was that the property should not at once vest in the purchaser. Such an intention is generally shown by the fact of some further act being first required to be done: such, for instance, in most

---

[19] 1912 S.C. 1017.
[20] I.e., the Sale of Goods Act 1893.
[21] (1872), L.R. 7 C.P. 438, at p. 449.

cases, as delivery—in some cases actual payment of the price—and in other cases weighing or measuring in order to ascertain the price, or marking, packing, coopering, filling up the casks or the like".

In my judgment the terms of the agreement point to such other circumstances, and negative the intention that the property should at once, on the execution of the agreement, vest in the purchaser. The case is very different from *Tarling* v. *Baxter*,[22] which was much pressed upon us, where a haystack standing in a field was sold and paid for by a bill of exchange and afterwards lost by fire. In that case, however, the same principle stated in *Heilbutt* v. *Hickson*[23] and in the Code is referred to:

> "In the case of a sale of goods, if nothing remains to be done on the part of the seller as between him and the buyer before the thing purchased is to be delivered, the property in the goods immediately passes to the buyer—but if any act remains to be done on the part of the seller, then the property does not pass until that act has been done . . .".[24]

Coming to the actual subject-matter of the sale in the present case, authority is not lacking that although for some purposes *fictione juris* the tree may be treated as divided from the freehold, yet in fact and in truth the vendor cannot take them before severance: "for it was said that timber trees cannot be felled with a goose quill" (see *Liford's* case[25], quoted in *Benjamin on Sale*, 6th Edn., p. 218[26]). This appears to be authority for PARKER, J.'s dictum in *James Jones & Sons Ltd.* v. *Tankerville*.[27]

> "A contract for the sale of specific timber growing on the vendor's property on the terms that such timber is cut and carried away by the purchaser certainly confers on the purchaser a licence to enter and cut the timber sold, and at any rate as soon as the purchaser has severed the timber the legal property in the several trees vests in him": (see also *Morison* v. *Lockhart*).[28]

The contention of the vendors appears to strain the agreement in their favour, and to leave out of sight many important terms which remained to be operative on their part during its continuance. It is, in my judgment, impossible to hold that the intention of the parties was that the property passed immediately at the date of the agreement.

---

[22] (1827), 6 B. & C., 360.
[23] *Supra.*
[24] See HOLROYD, J.: (1827), 6 B. & C., at p. 365.
[25] (1614), 11 Co. Rep. 46b, 50a.
[26] See now Benjamin's *Sale of Goods* (1st Edn. 1974), par. 92.
[27] [1909] 2 Ch. 440, at p. 442.
[28] *Supra.*

(2) SALE ON APPROVAL

Kirkham *v.* Attenborough

[1895-9] All E.R. Rep. 450

By s. 18, *r.* 4(a): "*Unless a different intention appears . . . when goods are delivered to the buyer on approval or 'on sale or return' or other similar terms the property in the goods passes to the buyer when he signifies his approval or acceptance to the seller or does any other act adopting the transaction*". *A pledge of the goods is an "act adopting the transaction".*

> Jewellery was delivered by Kirkham, a manufacturing jeweller, to Winter "on sale or return". Shortly afterwards, Winter pledged the goods with Attenborough, a pawnbroker. The price remained unpaid, so Kirkham brought an action to recover them from Attenborough.
>
> *Held*, by the Court of Appeal, that by pledging the goods Winter had "adopted the transaction" within the meaning of s. 18, r. 4(a). Consequently the property in the goods had passed to Winter, and therefore the claim to recover the goods from Attenborough failed. The only remedy was to claim the price from Winter.

LORD ESHER, M.R. (at page 451)

In this case there was a contract between the plaintiff and Winter, the terms of which were that the goods were delivered to Winter "on sale or return". That is a contract which is so common in business, that it has become well known to the Courts, and it has been interpreted. Where a particular kind of contract has become well known, and the Courts have determined what is its true construction, all the Courts adopt that construction in subsequent cases. The construction which has been put on this contract is, that, if those are the only terms, the contract does not pass the property in the goods at the moment when the contract is made, but at a subsequent time on the happening of certain events. The contract by which goods are delivered "on sale or return" means this: the purchaser may return the goods within a reasonable time, and the option of return belongs solely to the purchaser; the other party cannot even ask for the return of the goods, and his only right is to sue for the price if the goods are not returned. That being the meaning of the contract, we have to see how the party who has the option is to exercise that option.

The rules for determining that question are now put in a code, though they are somewhat unhappily expressed. What has the purchaser to do in order to show that he has accepted the goods, as sold and bought? The Sale of Goods Act . . ., s. 18, says that

> "Unless a different intention appears, the following are rules for ascertaining the intention of the parties as to the time at which the property in the goods is to pass to the buyer. . . .

Rule 4: When goods are delivered to the buyer on approval or 'on sale or return' or other similar terms the property [in the goods] passes to the buyer:—(a) When he signifies his approval or acceptance to the seller or does any other act adopting the transaction".

"Acceptance" means acceptance of that part of the contract which makes him the purchaser absolutely. Such acceptance gives the seller the right to be paid, and sue for the price; that is the only right of the seller, and he cannot ask for the return of the goods. The words "does any . . . act adopting the transaction" are difficult to construe. What "transaction" is the buyer to adopt? It cannot be the transaction by which the goods were delivered to him "on sale or return". That transaction had already been adopted. The words must, therefore, mean an adoption of the transaction so as to make the buyer the absolute purchaser of the goods. That will be some act which signifies that he intends to be the absolute purchaser. If he does some act which would be right only if he were the absolute purchaser, that signifies an acceptance or adoption within the statute.

It has been argued that the buyer must do something which is quite inconsistent with a power to return the goods. That proposition is too wide. The act must be an act which is inconsistent with his not being the absolute purchaser of the goods. If a man has become a buyer under a simple contract of "sale or return", and nothing has been said as to time of payment, the price must be paid within a reasonable time. That is a transaction on credit. In this case, an act was done by the man who was in possession of the goods under a contract of "sale or return"; he pawned the goods. He had not then the power of returning the goods, unless he repaid the amount advanced by the pawnee. That is inconsistent with his free power to return the goods. He ought not so to deal with the goods unless he means to treat himself as being the absolute purchaser. The evident conclusion is that he has treated himself as the absolute purchaser. On the terms of the section we must hold that, by doing such an act, the buyer became the absolute purchaser, and the property in the goods passed. The only right of the seller was to sue for the price.

Weiner *v.* Smith

[1904-7] All E.R. Rep. 773

Where goods are delivered to the buyer on approval, the property will not pass to him even though he has adopted the transaction if there is a different intention deducible from the contract or the conduct of the parties, for s. 18, r. 4(a) applies only "unless a different intention appears".

Weiner delivered jewellery to Huhn under the terms of a document stating:—"On approbation. On sale for cash only or return. . . . Goods had on approbation or on sale or return remain the property of [Weiner] until such goods are settled for or charged". Huhn delivered them to Longman, who represented that he had a customer for them. Longman, however, pledged them with Smith. Weiner was never paid the price, so he claimed the goods from Smith.

Held, by the Court of Appeal, that the action succeeded. The property in the goods had never passed to Huhn under s. 18, r. 4 for, although he had adopted the transaction by delivering the goods to Longman, there was "a different intention" (within the meaning of that section), since property was not to pass until the price had been paid or Weiner had agreed to give him credit.

LORD ALVERSTONE, C.J. (at page 775)

Then comes the point upon which BRAY, J.,[29] decided in favour of the plaintiff— that is, that the property in the goods never passed from Weiner to Huhn so as to give the latter a right to sell or dispose of the goods and give a good title to them to any other person. If this were an ordinary case of the delivery of goods "on sale or return", *Kirkham* v. *Attenborough*[30] would be a conclusive authority in favour of the defendants. In that case, which is binding upon us, it was held by the Court of Appeal that, where a person who has received goods "on sale or return", pledges them, he has done something inconsistent with their return, and thereby adopts the transaction and becomes the purchaser so that the property in the goods passes to him. Therefore, as I have said, if this were an ordinary contract for the delivery of goods "on sale or return", *Kirkham* v. *Attenborough*[31] is a distinct authority in favour of the defendants. Under such a contract the person to whom the goods are delivered has the privilege of getting the goods on credit for a time, with the right to purchase them or to return them; but, if he does any act which is inconsistent with their return, he becomes a purchaser, or, if he retains the goods for an unreasonable time without giving notice of rejection, the property passes to him. The learned Judge decided that the contract in the present case did not bring the case within the decision of *Kirkham* v. *Attenborough*.[32]

---

[29] In the Court below.
[30] [1895-9] All E.R. Rep. 450, p. 31, *ante.*
[31] *Supra.*
[32] *Supra.*

I may say here that I think that the Scottish case of *Bryce* v. *Ehrmann*[33] does not help us much, although there are in that case some expressions of opinion as to this kind of contract. The case on behalf of the defendants has been put shortly in this way. Huhn had power to try to find a purchaser for these goods, but not to deliver them to any other person for any other purpose; therefore, when he gave the goods to Longman, he did an act which was equivalent to the act which was held in *Kirkham* v. *Attenborough*[34] to pass the property in the goods, and, therefore, he exercised such rights under the contract that the property in the goods passed to him.

The question, therefore, depends upon whether the learned Judge took the right view of the contract contained in the document in this case. Section 18 of the Sale of Goods Act . . . provides:

> "Unless a different intention appears, the following are rules for ascertaining the intention of the parties as to the time at which the property in the goods is to pass to the buyer . . . Rule 4.—When goods are delivered to the buyer on approval or 'on sale or return' or other similar terms the property [in the goods] passes to the buyer—(a) When he signifies his approval or acceptance to the seller, or does any other act adopting the transaction . . .".

Does the intention to pass the property in goods at a different time sufficiently appear from the document in the present case? The document commences thus: "On approbation. On sale for cash only or return". If the document had stopped there, I think that some difficulty might have arisen. It might be said that the purchaser was given credit until approval, or the doing of some act adopting the transaction as in *Kirkham* v. *Attenborough*.[35] It seems to me to be an essential part of this bargain that credit should be given to the purchaser up to the time when the purchaser approves or does some such act; and I cannot see why the seller could not say to the purchaser that if he approves, or if he adopts the transaction, in that case he must pay cash at once. This document, however, goes further, and says that:

> "Goods had on approbation or on sale or return remain the property of Samuel Weiner until such goods are settled for or charged".

I think that, if there is no legal objection to those terms, there is a specific statement that the property is not to pass until Huhn says that he approves of the goods, and either offers cash for them or asks Weiner to debit him with the price and Weiner consents to do so.

---

[33] 1904, 7 F. (Ct. of Sess.) 5.
[34] *Supra.*
[35] *Supra.*

The result is, therefore, that by the terms of the contract the property does not pass until one of those events has happened—that is, until the goods have been paid for or credit given to the buyer. I think, therefore, that an intention is indicated that the property is not to pass until some other event than those specified in s. 18 has happened. The terms contained in the contract were not complied with, and the property in the goods did not pass. That being so, it is obvious that the decision in *Kirkham* v. *Attenborough*[35a] does not apply. The remaining words of the document—"The consignees are responsible for these goods until they are returned to my possession"—do not, in my opinion, in any way affect the question. I base my judgment upon the ground that the learned Judge took the true view that the property in the goods did not pass until one of the events specified in the contract happened.

Genn *v.* Winkel

[1911-13] All E.R. Rep. 910

A buyer of goods on "sale or return" is deemed to have "adopted the transaction" for the purpose of s. 18, r. 4(a) (thus passing the property in them to him) where he cannot return them to the seller because they have been lost while in the possession of a third party to whom he himself has delivered them on similar terms.

On 10th January, 1910, the plaintiff delivered some diamonds to the defendant on sale or return. On the same day the defendant delivered them to a third party on the same terms. On 16th January the third party handed them on the same terms to a fourth party who lost them.

Held, by the Court of Appeal, that since the defendant was unable to return the goods to the plaintiff, the transaction had been adopted, and he was responsible to him for their loss.

VAUGHAN WILLIAMS, L.J. (at page 911)

The defendant took up the position that he could not return them because he could not obtain them from the third person. The question, therefore, is whether the loss of the goods has resulted from an act of the defendant. In my opinion, it has, and I think it was entirely due to the defendant's act that he could not return the goods. That being so, the defendant comes clearly within the principles laid down by Lord ESHER, M.R., and LOPES, L.J., in *Kirkham* v. *Attenborough*.[36] I do not read those judgments as limiting the liability of persons who take goods on sale or return to cases where there was an intention on their part to adopt the transfer of the goods. It was quite sufficient here that the defendant knowingly transferred the goods to another agent, who then transferred them to a third person, and when the defendant was called upon to return

---

35a *Supra*
36 [1895-9] All E.R. Rep. 450, C.A.

them he became liable because he did not in fact return them. A reasonable time had elapsed; the defendant said he could not return the goods, and he explained it by saying simply that he was not in a position to return them. *Prima facie* the defendant is liable because he could not return the goods. He has given no explanation and no reasonable excuse for his inability to return the goods.

FLETCHER MOULTON, L.J. (at page 911)

I am of the same opinion. I think that this case might be decided very shortly against the defendant on the grounds that VAUGHAN WILLIAMS, L.J., has stated towards the end of his judgment. The goods were received on sale or return and the defendant has not returned them, and he has given no adequate excuse for not returning them. The facts have been gone into to some extent, and, therefore, I should not content myself with putting it so briefly as that, and I would indicate two ways in which the facts may be looked at, both of which lead to exactly the same conclusion, and in both of which I make the same hypothesis as to what was proved by the defendant under the head of "excuse".

The first line of defence is that the defendant was a mere bailee. He delivered the goods to a third person, who delivered them to a fourth party, who lost them without any fault on his (the defendant's) part, and, therefore, it is said he is not liable. I will assume, without deciding it, that the person to whom the goods were delivered on sale or return is a mere bailee. But if a bailee chooses to avail himself of the powers of the contract by which he is bailee to entrust the goods to other persons on contractual terms so that he parts with the possession of the goods and can only have a right to get possession again under the terms of the contract he has made with these other persons, he is responsible if he does not get them back. He could no longer plead that he merely held them as bailee and had not been guilty of negligence. He has made a contract by which the goods are delivered to third persons with whom his bailor has nothing to do and who may not have known his bailor, and he can no longer say, "I am not liable unless I personally have been negligent". If he cannot get them back under his contract with the third person so as to be able to hand them back to his bailor, he is liable. I think there is not the faintest evidence as to how the goods were lost, whether it was due to carelessness or not, but I do not think it is important. I think that the defendant can no longer defend himself merely on the ground of being a bailee after he has chosen to hand the goods on to other persons.

I will now take the second line of defence by which the defendant assumes that he has proved that he delivered the goods on sale or return to another agent who then delivered them to a fourth party on the same terms. That is an assumption very much in favour of the defendant, because there is no evidence that he delivered them to the third person on any terms which entitled him to demand them back at all; but I will assume in his favour that all these contracts were on sale or return. I am not prepared to decide that if a person receives goods on sale or return and immediately hands them on to someone else on the same terms, that is in law an act adopting the transaction. The contract of sale or return appears to me clearly to be a contract whereby the person to whom the goods are delivered acquires a right to hold them for a reasonable time, during which he can make up his mind to keep the goods, in which case it becomes a sale on credit, and he is liable to pay the price, or he can return the goods. Under those circumstances a person who receives goods on sale or return and at once passes them on to someone else under a like contract is entitled to demand them from that third person just as soon as the original owner of the goods has the right to demand them from him, and, therefore, I do not see that he has lessened or impeded his power of returning the goods when the owner of the goods has a right to demand them back, but I am clear that, if he allows a period to elapse before he hands them to a third person on sale or return, he has done an act which limits and impedes his power of returning the goods as soon as the owner of the goods demands them. For instance, if 14 days be a reasonable time in such a contract in this particular trade, and if he waits seven days before entrusting the goods to a third person on sale or return, that third person has a right to keep them as against him for 14 days, whereas the original owner of the goods has a right to the return of them within seven days from that date, and I think that that is clearly an act inconsistent with anything but his having adopted the transaction. Therefore, I think that in that case it would be taken that the purchase was made.

Here the defendant handed the goods to a third party at once and that was not necessarily an adoption of the transaction. The third party waited two days and handed them on, I will suppose, on the same terms to a fourth person. That was, in my opinion, an adoption by the third party of the purchase from the defendant, and, therefore, the defendant must be taken to have sold these goods to the third person on credit. Having thus sold the goods on credit, it is quite clear that that act was inconsistent with not adopting the transaction within the meaning of s. 18 of the Sale of Goods Act . . . Therefore, under those circumstances it seems to me that the defendant adopted the transaction and that the plaintiff is entitled to sue him for the value of the goods.

BUCKLEY, L.J. (at page 913)

If A. delivers goods to B. on sale or return and B. having received them immediately delivers them to C. on sale or return, the reasonable time in the one case must, I think, be co-extensive with that in the other case, and if that reasonable time elapses and C. brings back the goods to B. and B. takes them back to A., everybody is acting within his rights, and it appears to me that the property never passes. That is not the point for decision in this case, and those are not the facts here, but that is a first step towards explaining the reason why I arrive at my conclusion. If under like circumstances A. delivers goods to B. and B. delivers them to C., in each case on sale or return, and the reasonable time be, let us say, 14 days, and C. after four days sells the goods or elects to buy the goods, the result will be, I think, that the property will have passed, because C. will have done an act which renders it impossible for B. to return the goods to A.

This is the reason why that is so. The contract under which B. received the goods was a contract under which it was competent to him to offer to sell the goods. That is the very purpose for which he was to have them. If he sold them, he bound himself to buy them. In the first case which I took he does nothing more than offer to sell them. B. had offered to sell to C., but C. had never bought, and, therefore, B. had simply done something authorised by the power which A. had given him, and he was entitled to say: "Although I offered my goods under that power, nothing has resulted, and, therefore, I am entitled to return them to you". In the second case which I put he has also done something under the power which A. had given him. He has offered to sell them to C., and C. has bought them. The result would be that the transaction had resulted, not in a mere offer, but in a contract, and in that case, an act had been done adopting the transaction. If that is right, the moment at which the property passes is not the moment at which B. offers the goods to C. on sale or return, that moment being the same moment at which B. has received the goods, but it is the moment at which under that offer made by B. to C., C. does something, with the result that B.'s offer has resulted in a contract, and if it has resulted in a contract, then the property has passed.

Poole *v*. Smith's Car Sales (Balham) Ltd.

[1962] 2 All E.R. 482

By s. 18, *r.* 4(b): "*Unless a different intention appears . . . where goods are delivered to the buyer on approval or on 'sale or return' or other similar terms the property in the goods passes to the buyer . . . if he does not signify his approval or acceptance to the seller but retains the goods without giving notice of rejection, then . . . if no time has been fixed [for the return of the goods], on the expiration of a reasonable time". What is a reasonable time is a question of fact.*

In August, 1960, Poole, a car dealer, sold a secondhand Vauxhall to Smith's Car Sales (Balham) Ltd. on "sale or return". The car was not returned by October, 1960, so Poole wrote to them stating that if it was not returned by 10th November, the car would be deemed to have been sold to them. The car was not returned until the end of November.

Held, by the Court of Appeal, that the property had passed to the buyers under s. 18, r. 4(b), for a reasonable time had expired without the car being returned.

ORMEROD, L.J. (at page 486)

I can see nothing which warrants the conclusion that any different intention is to be discovered from the circumstances of the case.

So we are thrown back on r. 4. By that rule, if the parties have fixed a time for the property to pass, then the property will pass at that time. In this case there is no suggestion that any time had been fixed. Failing that, and it is a question of fact, the time for the property to pass is at the expiry of a reasonable time, and the question which arises is what is a reasonable time.

It has been argued with some cogency in this case that there was no evidence before the Court to show what was a reasonable time, and in the circumstances it is impossible to say that a reasonable time has expired. I cannot accept that. There is an appreciable amount of evidence. There is the evidence, for instance, of the plaintiff, who said that he was asking continually for the return of the car; that on 7th November he wrote a letter setting out his final terms relating to it, and the plaintiff is entitled to pray in aid the passage in the affidavit of Mr Smith himself when he was asking for leave to defend the summons under R.S.C. Order 14, because there he says in para. 3—and this affidavit was sworn in an early stage of the proceedings, on 4th May, 1961—

"In or about August, 1960, the said Colin Savage stated his brother had inquired whether my company would take two cars on a sale or return basis whilst his brother was on holiday and I agreed".

That would be some indication, I think, that the car was sent on a sale or return basis; but the important part is this:

"at the end of September, or early October, 1960, I gave instructions to the company's sales manager that as there was no prospect of the vehicle being sold, it should be returned to the brother of the said Colin Savage forthwith and the Wyvern car was accordingly removed from my company's premises by the said Colin Savage".

Accepting that for the moment, there is the sworn statement of Mr Smith that in early October at the latest the time, in his view, had gone by for selling the car as no purchaser was forthcoming.

That I would have thought to be cogent evidence on the question of what is a reasonable time, but there is a further matter which must be taken into account. The motor car in these days is a chattel in almost universal use, and in consequence, of course, dealers in motor cars, either new or secondhand, abound. It appears that certain habits have either been formed or have come to the surface as a result of the practice of using motor cars. It is a well known fact that people go on holidays in the months of July, August and September. It has become obvious, I think, in recent years that when people go on holidays, they like to take their cars with them. It may be that many people, when the holidays are over, like to sell those cars and therefore it is, I think, a well recognised fact that the sellers' market for secondhand motor cars in October and November is not so good as it is before the holiday season begins or is the summons under R.S.C. Order 14, because there he says in par. 3—and this still at its early stages. In any event, I see no reason why in these days a Court should not take judicial notice of the way the market in secondhand cars is carried and on come to a conclusion as to what is a reasonable time.

I am fully satisfied, both on the knowledge which has come to me in the ordinary course of life and through sitting in these Courts, and from the evidence before the Court in this case, that a reasonable time for the return of this car had expired, certainly in November, and if that reasonable time had expired, it is clear by reason of the operation of s. 18 of the Sale of Goods Act . . . that the property in the car had passed from the plaintiff to the defendants. If that be so, it is immaterial what happened afterwards or what was said afterwards by the parties or what action they chose to take.

Re Ferrier, ex parte Trustee v. Donald

(1944), 60 T.L.R. 295

For the property in goods, which are sold on approval, to pass to the buyer under s. 18, r. 4(b), the "retention" of them by him without giving notice of rejection must be voluntary. Retention of them by the sheriff in the course of execution on the buyer's goods is not sufficient to cause the property to pass.

On 12th, 13th, 14th November, 1941 Mrs Donald sold some antique furniture to Mrs Ferrier on approval for one week. On 15th November the sheriff levied execution on Mrs Ferrier's goods on behalf of two of her creditors. Among the goods was the antique furniture. On 24th April, 1942, Mrs Ferrier was adjudicated bankrupt, and her trustee in bankruptcy claimed that he had a good title to the furniture because the property in it had passed to Mrs Ferrier under s. 18, r. 4(b), because she had retained the goods after 20th November.

Held, by the Chancery Division, that the property in the goods had not passed, and they still belonged to Mrs Donald, for after 15th November they were "retained" by the sheriff, and not by Mrs Ferrier.

MORTON, J. (at page 296)

[Counsel] contended that as the goods were delivered on sale or return, and the time fixed for their return had expired on 20th November, and Mrs Ferrier had retained the goods without giving notice of rejection, the property in them passed to her on that date, and that there was nothing to show a different intention within the meaning of s. 18. Counsel also referred me to s. 26 of the Sale of Goods Act of 1893, which, so far as is material, provides: "A writ of *fieri facias* or other writ of execution against goods shall bind the property in the goods of the execution debtor as from the time when the writ is delivered to the sheriff to be executed".

I think that there is a very short and simple answer to that argument: I do not take the view that Mrs Ferrier retained the goods until 20th November within the meaning of s. 18, r. 4. She retained them until 15th November, when, according to the applicant's own evidence, the goods were seized under the execution. From that time on I think that the position was that the goods were retained by the sheriff; they were retained until, pursuant to the order of the Master, the sheriff withdrew from possession of them. The result is that, the goods having been sent on sale or return, the event which is referred to in r. 4 of s. 18 never happened, and the goods simply remained goods which had been sent on sale or return and which never became the property of Mrs Ferrier. These goods were handed back to Mrs Donald pursuant to the order of Master Horridge, and, in my view, she is entitled to retain them.

(3) Sale of Unascertained Goods

Laurie and Morewood *v.* Dudin & Sons

[1925] All E.R. Rep. 414

By s. 16: "Where there is a contract for the sale of unascertained goods no property in the goods is transferred to the buyer unless and until the goods are ascertained".

Alcock & Sons sold Wilkes & Sons Ltd. 200 out of 618 quarters of maize lying in their warehouse, and gave them a delivery order addressed to the defendants who were the owners of the warehouse. Wilkes & Sons Ltd. endorsed the delivery order "Please hold against our sub-order", and sent it to the defendants. Wilkes & Sons Ltd. then sold the 200 quarters to the plaintiffs and gave them a delivery order which was sent to the defendants. Wilkes & Sons Ltd. did not pay Alcock & Sons for the maize, so Alcock & Sons told the defendants to stop delivery. The defendants refused to deliver the maize to the plaintiffs. The plaintiffs claimed the maize from the defendants on the ground that the property in the maize had passed to them, and also claimed damages for detention.

Held, by the Court of Appeal, that the action failed, for the property had not passed since by s. 16 in the case of a contract for the sale of unascertained goods by description the property did not pass unless and until the goods were ascertained, and in the present case no "ascertainment" had taken place.

SCRUTTON, L.J. (at page 420)

There is no doubt that the goods were not ascertained here. They were 200 quarters, part of the quantity then lying in the defendants' warehouse, but those 200 quarters had never been ascertained. It seems to me that it is no good going into ancient authorities when one has got a statute. I have looked at the Lord President's judgment in the Scottish case of *Hayman & Son* v. *M'Lintock*.[37] There a trustee in bankruptcy was claiming property in a bankrupt's goods which the bankrupt had sold, as against a number of people who had various titles. It is not necessary to sort out all the various people who claimed the bankrupt's goods. Some of them claimed under bills of lading and some of them claimed under other documents, but some claimed under delivery warrants accepted by a warehouseman. It was not an action against the warehouseman, but it was an action against the bankrupt. . . . The Lord President said:[38]

> "That leaves 424 bags in the hands of the trustees representing the bankrupt, and upon these 424 bags arises a subsequent question with persons of the name of M'Connell and Reid and J. K. Stewart. The question arises out of this, that after the bankrupt had got the flour into the store he entered into a contract sale for certain of those bags in favour of these parties. There is no question as to the contract of sale of the flour lying in the store, but before anything was done in the way of separating the bags there came the bankruptcy. The trustee in the bankruptcy appeals simply to s. 16 of the Sale of Goods Act . . . , which specially provides that where there is a sale of unascertained goods the property shall not pass until the goods shall have been ascertained. Here nothing was done to ascertain the goods. These flour bags were not separately marked, and although doubtless if the buyer here had gone to the storekeeper and had got him to put aside the sacks, or mark them, or put them into another room, that would have passed the property, yet, as he did none of these things, the property, it seems to me, did not pass. It is not enough merely to get an acknowledgment in general terms that so many of those bags belonging to the bankrupt are held for him".

That seems to me to be merely repeating the language of the Sale of Goods Act . . . , and as far as the question of property is concerned, it appears to me that the plaintiffs had no claim because the goods were not their property since they had never been ascertained.

Carlos Federspiel & Co. S.A. *v.* Charles Twigg & Co. Ltd.

[1957] 1 Lloyd's Rep. 240

By s. 18, r. 5(1): "Unless a different intention appears . . . where there is a contract for the sale of unascertained or future goods by description and goods of that description and in a deliverable state are unconditionally appropriated to the contract either by the seller with the assent of the buyer, or by the buyer with the assent of the seller, the property in the goods then passes to the buyer . . .".

The sellers agreed to sell a number of cycles and tricycles "f.o.b. U.K. port". They made preparations for shipping them, and had the boxes, in which the goods were packed, marked with the port of destination. The goods, however, were never shipped, and the

---

37 1907, 44 Sc. L.R. 691.
38 *Ibid.*, at p. 698.

sellers went into liquidation. The buyers claimed the goods from the liquidator on the ground that the property had passed under s. 18, r. 5(1), since they had been "unconditionally appropriated" to the contract.

Held, by the Queen's Bench Division (Commercial Court), that the action failed. It was the intention of the parties that no property in the goods should pass until shipment. Although preparations for shipment had been made, this did not amount to an "unconditional appropriation" so as to pass the property.

PEARSON, J. (at page 255)

I think one can distinguish these principles. First, Rule 5 of s. 18 of the Act is one of the Rules for ascertaining the intention of the parties as to the time at which the property in the goods is to pass to the buyer unless a different intention appears. Therefore the element of common intention has always to be borne in mind. A mere setting apart or selection of the seller of the goods which he expects to use in performance of the contract is not enough. If that is all, he can change his mind and use those goods in performance of some other contract and use some other goods in performance of this contract. To constitute an appropriation of the goods to the contract, the parties must have had, or be reasonably supposed to have had, an intention to attach the contract irrevocably to those goods, so that those goods and no others are the subject of the sale and become the property of the buyer.

Secondly, it is by agreement of the parties that the appropriation, involving a change of ownership, is made, although in some cases the buyer's assent to an appropriation by the seller is conferred in advance by the contract itself or otherwise.

Thirdly, an appropriation by the seller, with the assent of the buyer, may be said always to involve an actual or constructive delivery. If the seller retains possession, he does so as bailee for the buyer. There is a passage in *Chalmers' Sale of Goods Act*, 12th Edn., at p. 75, where it is said:[39]

"In the second place, if the decisions be carefully examined, it will be found that in every case where the property has been held to pass, there has been an actual or constructive delivery of the goods to the buyer".

I think that is right, subject only to this possible qualification, that there may be after such constructive delivery an actual delivery still to be made by the seller under the contract. Of course, that is quite possible, because delivery is the transfer of possession, whereas appropriation transfers ownership. So there may be first an appropriation, constructive delivery, whereby the seller becomes bailee for the buyer,

---

[39] See now 17th Edn. (1975), at p. 153.

and then a subsequent actual delivery involving actual possession, and when I say that, I have in mind in particular the two cases cited, namely, *Aldridge* v. *Johnson*[40] and *Langton* v. *Higgins*.[41]

Fourthly, one has to remember s. 20 of the Sale of Goods Act, whereby the ownership and the risk are normally associated. Therefore as it appears that there is reason for thinking, on the construction of the relevant documents, that the goods were, at all material times, still at the seller's risk, that is *prima facie* an indication that the property had not passed to the buyer.

Fifthly, usually but not necessarily, the appropriating act is the last act to be performed by the seller. For instance, if delivery is to be taken by the buyer at the seller's premises and the seller has completed his part of the contract and has appropriated the goods when he has made the goods ready and has identified them and placed them in position to be taken by the buyer and has so informed the buyer, and if the buyer agrees to come and take them, that is the assent to the appropriation. But if there is a further act, an important and decisive act to be done by the seller, then there is *prima facie* evidence that probably the property does not pass until the final act is done.

Applying those principles to the present case I would say this. Firstly, the intention was that the ownership should pass on shipment (or possibly at some later date) because the emphasis is throughout on shipment as the decisive act to be done by the seller in performance of the contract. Secondly, it is impossible to find in this correspondence an agreement to a change of ownership before the time of shipment. The letters, especially those of 27th August and 14th September, which are particularly relied on by the plaintiff, do not contain any provision or implication of any earlier change of ownership. Thirdly, there is no actual or constructive delivery; no suggestion of the seller becoming a bailee for the buyer. Fourthly, there is no suggestion of the goods being at the buyer's risk at any time before shipment; no suggestion that the buyer should insist on the seller arranging insurance for them. Fifthly, the last two acts to be performed by the seller, namely, sending the goods to Liverpool and having the goods shipped on board, were not performed.

Therefore, my decision that the *prima facie* inference which one would have drawn from the contract is that the property was not to pass at any time before shipment, is in my view not displaced by the subsequent correspondence between the parties. It follows, therefore, that there was no appropriation of these goods and therefore the action fails.

---

40 (1857), 26 L.J.Q.B. 296.
41 (1859), 4 H. & N. 402.

Healey v. Howlett & Sons

(1917), 116 L.T. 591

Where there is a contract for the sale of unascertained or future goods by description, whether the goods have been "unconditionally appropriated to the contract" for the purpose of s. 18, r. 5(1) will depend on the circumstances.

The seller contracted to sell to the buyers 20 boxes of mackerel f.o.r. Valentia, Co. Kerry. The boxes were placed on rail, but were not marked with the buyers' name. They were sent to Holyhead along with 170 other boxes for delivery to other customers. When the fish arrived at Holyhead, the railway company allotted 20 boxes out of the 190 boxes to the buyers, who found that they were not in merchantable condition. The seller sued for the price of the goods on the ground that the property had passed under s. 18, r. 5(1), since the goods had been appropriated to the contract when they were placed on rail at Valentia.

Held, by the King's Bench Division, that the action failed. There had been no appropriation, for none of the 190 boxes had been marked with the buyers' name so as to distinguish them from the remainder.

RIDLEY, J. (at page 592)

This case raises an interesting point. The contract was for 20 boxes of hard bright mackerel, the order being sent from Billingsgate by the defendants and accepted by the plaintiff at Valentia, Co. Kerry. When the order was received the fish were put on rail at Valentia. The 20 boxes intended for the defendants were not marked with their name, but were consigned together with 170 others to the plaintiff's order at Holyhead. After they had been put on rail, an invoice was sent by the plaintiff to the defendants having upon it the words "At sole risk of purchaser after putting fish on rail here". I do not see how those words can form part of the contract, and I cannot so treat them.

The fish were delayed *en route*. The practice was that at Holyhead fish sent by the plaintiff were appropriated by the railway company acting as his agents to the purchasers for whom they were intended. The plaintiff, however, says and the Judge of the City of London Court has held that the mere placing on rail at Valentia amounts to an appropriation so as to put the risk on the defendants. It was said to have been appropriation within the principle of the authorities which establish that where there is a contract for the sale of goods which are not specific, the property passes as soon as there has been an appropriation of particular goods to the contract. I think it is clear on the authorities that goods become the property of a consignee as soon as they are marked off by some distinct act as his and not the sellers, and are delivered to the carrier as agent to complete delivery to the purchaser. Here, however, out of a large number of boxes only a portion were to belong to the defendants, and none had been marked off. I know of no case where it has been held that because all the parcels are meant to be divided between three separate purchasers there is an appropriation of them all to the risk of the purchasers when it is impossible to say at whose risk any one of the boxes could be. Had there been appropriation at Valentia in the present case, some process of allotment would have to be adopted in order to decide where the loss was to fall if a portion of the goods disappeared and another arrived safely. Suppose half the boxes had been lost at sea, who could say whether they were those of the defendants or of one or more of the other purchasers? The name of the consignee should have been placed on the boxes. . . .

In the present case there are insuperable objections to holding that the property has passed. It would be impossible to say which consignee must bear the loss caused by the deterioration of any particular boxes of the mackerel.

The essence of the authorities which decide that the appropriation of goods to the contract by delivery to the carrier at the beginning of the transit may be sufficient to pass the property is that it should be known to whom the goods are appropriated, and not that the question as to who is to bear any loss that may happen should be open to any discussion or be determined by accident.

Pignataro *v.* Gilroy & Son

(1919), 120 L.T. 480

Where there is a contract for the sale of unascertained or future goods by description, an "unconditional appropriation" of them to the contract by the seller with the assent of the buyer will pass the property in them to the buyer under s. 18, r. 5(1).

The sellers sold 140 bags of rice to the buyer, and on 28th February, 1918, gave him a delivery order for 125 bags so that he could obtain delivery of this quantity at Chambers Wharf, and said that the remaining 15 were available for collection at the sellers' warehouse in Long Acre, and asked the buyer to take them away. The buyer did nothing until 25th March, when he sent someone to collect the 15 bags from the warehouse, only to find that they had been stolen a little while before. The buyer then brought an action for non-delivery.

Held, by the King's Bench Division, that the sellers had appropriated the goods to the contract with the implied assent of the buyer, and therefore the property had passed to the buyer under s. 18, r. 5(1). Accordingly the goods were at the risk of the buyer, and the sellers were not liable for their non-delivery.

ROWLATT, J. (at page 480)

On the sale of the 140 bags of rice it became the duty of the vendors under the contract to appropriate them to the purchaser from their general stock. If such appropriation were assented to, either expressly or implied, by the purchaser, the property would pass, and upon this would turn the whole question of the risk of loss, which must be borne by one or other of the parties if the goods were lost, damaged, or stolen while in the possession of the vendors. When the sellers received the purchaser's cheque for the goods and were asked for the delivery order, it was right and proper for them to appropriate and place at the disposal of the purchaser the goods for which he had thus paid, in order to effectuate its delivery, or its equivalent, concurrently with the receipt of the money. This the defendants did; and they sent a delivery order to the plaintiff authorising him to obtain delivery of the 125 bags at Chambers Wharf. As to the 15 bags which were not at the wharf, but at the defendants' warehouse in Long Acre, the defendants told the plaintiff they were ready for him to take delivery of them, and asked that they should be taken away. If the plaintiff had replied, saying he would remove the goods, the case would have been precisely the same as *Rohde* v. *Thwaites*.[42] In that case there had been a sale of 20 hogsheads of sugar; four were delivered to and accepted by the purchaser. The vendor filled up and appropriated to the purchaser 16 other hogsheads, and informed the purchaser that they were ready and desired him to take them away. The purchaser replied that he would do so as soon as he could. It was held that the appropriation having been made by the vendor, and assented to by the purchaser, the property in the 16 hogsheads had passed to the purchaser; and that their value might be recovered under a contract for goods bargained and sold. The plaintiff in the present case, however, did nothing for a month, and the question was what was the effect of this inaction. If the goods were of the quality required, it was difficult to see how the plaintiff could have dissented from the appropriation on this ground, unless there happened to be some bags inferior to those he had inspected. He could not object either to the place from which he was required to fetch the bags, inasmuch as he had already inspected the rice lying at those premises at the time, and for the purpose of this very contract. At any rate no objection at all was taken on any of these possible grounds. Yet it was obvious that, if the purchaser was to make any objection, he must do so promptly. He was not entitled to place upon the vendors the risk involved in the continued possession of these goods appropriated to him, nor to prolong the incumbrance of the vendors' premises. As he chose to say nothing for a whole month in response to an appropriation provoked by his own letter, and of which he had been informed, in the opinion of the Court, this came to precisely the same thing as if he had written to say that he would remove them, but without doing so.

---

[42] (1827), 6 B. & C. 388.

Wardar's (Import & Export) Co. Ltd. *v.* W. Norwood & Sons Ltd.

[1968] 2 All E.R. 602

When goods are in the possession of a third party, they are "unconditionally appropriated" to the contract for the purpose of s. 18, r. 5(1) when he acknowledges that he holds them on the buyer's behalf.

The sellers sold to the buyers 600 cartons of frozen ox kidneys, part of a consignment of 1,500 lying in cold store in the possession of a third party. The buyers' carrier took delivery the next day. When he arrived at 8 a.m., he found 600 cartons standing on the pavement on bogies awaiting his arrival. He handed over a delivery order to an official employed by the third party, and this was accepted by the official. Loading the meat into the carrier's refrigerated lorry was completed by 12 noon, and by that time much of the meat was thawing. The carrier did not turn on the refrigerating machinery in his lorry until 10 a.m. and it did not become effective for three hours. On arrival at the buyers' premises the meat was condemned as unfit for consumption. The sellers contended that the property in the meat had passed to the buyers under s. 18, r. 5(1), and that the loss fell on the buyers.

Held, by the Court of Appeal, that the property had passed under s. 18, r. 5(1) because there had been an "unconditional appropriation" of the goods to the contract. When goods were in the possession of a third party, appropriation occurred when he acknowledged that he held them on the buyers' behalf. When the carrier handed over the delivery order to the official employed by the third party, and this had been accepted, the acknowledgment required had been made. Accordingly, the risk of deterioration passed at that time under s. 20.

SALMON, L.J. (at page 605)

It is unnecessary to decide the point whether there was an unconditional appropriation to the contract at the moment when the goods were put on to the pavement, which is perhaps fortunate, because we do not know precisely when that was; but in my view there can be no doubt that there was a clear, unconditional appropriation when the delivery order was handed over in respect of the goods which had been deposited on the pavement for loading. There is certainly no evidence that they were not then of merchantable quality. It would seem from the evidence of Mr McBeath, the driver of the lorry, that at some stage the porters wished to take a tea-break. The driver was apparently concerned at the goods being left standing on the pavement, but he was told, according to his evidence, that the tea-break would take only five minutes. It appears that it took about an hour; and it was after the tea-break, according to Mr McBeath that he first noticed that some of the cartons were dripping, which would be a strong indication that the goods had by then started to deteriorate. Meantime, however, a good many of the cartons—we do not know how many—had already been loaded into the lorry. Since, however (as I think), the goods were appropriated to the contract when the delivery order was handed over and accepted in respect of the goods standing on the pavement, any deterioration that occurred thereafter was at the risk of the buyers.

Philip Head & Sons Ltd. *v.* Showfronts Ltd.

[1970] 1 Lloyd's Rep. 140

Where there is a contract for the sale of unascertained or future goods by description, whether the goods are in a "deliverable state" for the purpose of s. 18, r. 5(1) will depend on the circumstances.

The plaintiffs were housefurnishers and had been employed by the defendants to provide and lay some carpets in a suite of offices. The bales containing the carpets were despatched by the manufacturers and arrived at the premises on 21st, 22nd and 23rd February, 1967, and the plaintiffs' agent signed for them. Some of the rooms were immediately carpeted by the plaintiffs, but in order to cover a large room various lengths of the carpet which arrived on 23rd February required to be stitched together, so they were sent off to the stitchers on that day. They arrived back at 4.30 p.m., and were seen by the employees of the plaintiffs' agent on 25th February. When he arrived on 26th February, they could not be found. The plaintiffs contended that the property in the carpet had passed to the defendants under s. 18, r. 5(1), that the defendants were therefore liable to them for the price, and that the risk had passed to the defendants under s. 20 of the Act.[43] The defendants repudiated liability on the ground that the property had not passed because the carpet was not in a "deliverable state".[44]

Held, by the Queen's Bench Division, that the carpet was not in a "deliverable state", and that the action failed.

MOCATTA, J. (at page 143)

The problem here is, I think, however, whether it can be said that carpeting in a deliverable state was unconditionally appropriated to the contract. That phrase is defined in s. [61(5)] of the statute as follows:

"Goods are in a 'deliverable state' within the meaning of this Act when they are in such a state that the buyer would under the contract be bound to take delivery of them".

There is not much assistance in the authorities as to the meaning of this phrase. It is, however, both interesting and, I think, helpful to read a passage from an opinion of Lord BLACKBURN in *Seath* v. *Moore*,[45] in which many of the points subsequently codified in the Sale of Goods Act . . ., including some of the problems which I have to deal with here, are discussed. It is true that that case was one dealing with problems arising out of a shipbuilding contract, but in this particular passage Lord BLACKBURN is purporting to state the relevant principles of English law in general terms. He stated in relation to the passing of property:[46]

---

[43] For the passing of risk, see pp. 51, 52, *post*.
[44] The defendants' contention that the contract was one of labour and of the sale of materials, and that therefore the Sale of Goods Act did not apply to it, was rejected by MOCATTA, J.: [1970] 1 Lloyd's Rep. 140, at p. 143.
[45] (1886), 11 App. Cas. 350.
[46] *Ibid.*, at p. 370.

"It is essential that the article should be specific and ascertained in a manner binding on both parties, for unless that be so, it cannot be construed as a contract to pass the property in that article. And in general, if there are things remaining to be done by the seller to the article before it is in the state in which it is to be finally delivered to the purchaser, the contract will not be construed to be one to pass the property till those things are done.

"But it is competent to parties to agree for valuable consideration that a specific article shall be sold, and become the property of the purchaser as soon as it has attained a certain stage: though if it is part of the bargain that more work shall be done on the article after it has reached that stage, it affords a strong *prima facie* presumption against its being the intention of the parties that the property should then pass. I do not examine the various English authorities cited during the argument. It is, I think, a question of the construction of the contract in each case at what stage the property shall pass; and a question of fact in each case whether that stage has been reached".

I find that passage to give valuable guidance here.

I have described as best I can the state of the carpeting subsequently stolen at the time that it came back to these premises after having been stitched up; it was plainly a heavy bundle, very difficult to move. Although I have determined that this was a contract to which the Sale of Goods Act . . . applied, nevertheless an important feature of it was undoubtedly the laying of the carpeting following on the planning. It seems to me that one has to consider—in each case it is a case of fact—where there is work to be done in relation to the article sold before the contractual obligations of the sellers are completed, what is the relevant importance of that work in relation to the contract when deciding whether the property has passed and in particular whether the article or goods in question is or are at a particular moment of time in a deliverable state under s. 18, r. 5(1). I think one is entitled to apply everyday common sense to the matter; a householder, for example, purchasing carpeting under a contract providing that it should be delivered and laid in his house, would be very surprised to be told that carpeting, which was in bales which he could hardly move, deposited by his contractor in his garage, was then in a deliverable state and his property.

I take this view because of the condition of this carpeting at the time it was stolen and the importance of the last stage in the obligations to be performed by the plaintiffs under this contract, that at the moment when this carpeting was stolen, it had not been unconditionally appropriated to the contract in a deliverable state, and accordingly, in my judgment, the property had not passed at the moment that the carpeting was stolen. In those circumstances the plaintiffs' case must fail.

(4) TRANSFER OF RISK

Demby Hamilton & Co. Ltd. *v.* Barden (Endeavour Wines Ltd., Third Party)

[1949] 1 All E.R. 435

By s. 20(2): "*. . . where delivery has been delayed through the fault of either buyer or seller the goods are at the risk of the party at fault as regards any loss which might not have occurred but for such fault*".

The sellers agreed to supply 30 tons of apple juice, delivery to be made in weekly truckloads. They crushed the last apples which they had for crushing that season, and put the juice in casks. Delivery would have been completed by February, 1946, but in December, 1945, they were asked by the buyer to hold up delivery. They did so, and then delivered some more of the juice in January and April, 1946, but the buyer would accept no more after that date. By November, 1946, the remainder of the juice had gone bad.

Held, by the King's Bench Division, that under s. 20, the loss fell on the buyer, because the delivery had been delayed through his fault, and the loss would not otherwise have occurred.

SELLERS, J. (at page 436)

The first question which arises is whether the sellers are entitled to recover . . . by reason of the provisions of s. 20 of the Sale of Goods Act. . . . It would appear that [s. 20(2)] has not so far called for consideration in the Courts. . . . I am not going so far in this case as to say that I place the onus on the buyer to show that the loss did not occur or might not have occurred. I think that all the facts and circumstances have to be looked at in very much the same way as a jury would look at them in order to see whether the loss can properly be attributed to the failure of the buyer to take delivery of the goods at the proper time. . . . The first requirement of the [sub-section] in question is that delivery has been delayed through the fault of the buyer. I am satisfied on the facts in the present case that a good delivery, which would have avoided all loss, was delayed through the fault of the buyer. . . . The next requirement of the [sub-section] is that, where delivery has been delayed through the fault of the buyer, the goods are at the risk of the party in fault "as regards any loss which might not have occurred but for such fault". The goods referred to there must be the contractual goods which have been assembled by the seller for the purpose of fulfilling his contract and making delivery. The goods may have been defined goods, goods manufactured for the purposes of delivery, or goods which had been acquired by the seller from somebody else for the purpose of fulfilling his contract. It does not seem to me that the Act requires to be construed in any narrow sense. The real question is whether the loss which has accrued was brought about by the delay in delivery, and that must have regard to the goods which were there to be delivered. Different circumstances may arise in different cases.

It may be that the seller was in a position to sell the goods elsewhere and acquire other goods for the postponed time of delivery, and if he does not do so and there is some loss in the meantime, the responsibility for the loss would be held to fall upon him. Again, there may be cases (and I think this is one of them) where the seller has his goods ready for delivery and has to keep them ready for delivery as and when the buyer proposes to take them. In the present case the position is clear. The casks of apple juice which were not accepted were manufactured at the time of the contract, and the contract required that delivery should be in accordance with sample. It would have been very difficult to have obtained goods which complied with the sample unless the apples had all been crushed at the same time. They would have had to be apples from the same district and the juice from them, when obtained, would have had to be of the same maturity. The condition of apples changes. They may be unripe at one time and too ripe at another. The 30 tons of juice were goods which the sellers rightly and reasonably kept for the fulfilment of their contract. These were the last apples which the sellers had that season for crushing, and, therefore, the goods in question were goods which the sellers had awaiting delivery in fulfilment of their contract with the buyer. I have to ask myself whether this loss might not have occurred but for the fault of the buyer. I am satisfied that it would not have occurred but for his fault.

C. TRANSFER OF TITLE

(1) SALE BY PERSON NOT THE OWNER

Heap v. Motorists Advisory Agency Ltd.

[1922] All E.R. Rep. 251

By s. 21(1): ". . . *Where goods are sold by a person who is not their owner, and who does not sell them under the authority or with the consent of the owner, the buyer acquires no better title to the goods than the seller had, unless the owner of the goods is by his conduct precluded from denying the seller's authority to sell". Whether he is so precluded is a matter of fact in each case.*

Heap, a motor engineer, was induced by North to allow him to drive away his car to show it to Hargreaves, a potential customer. In fact, there was no such person as Hargreaves. North used the car for a few weeks, and then sold it to the Motorists Advisory Agency Ltd. Heap claimed its return from the company. But the company maintained that it had a good title under s. 21(1).

Held, by the King's Bench Division, that the action succeeded, for Heap was not precluded (under s. 21) by his conduct from denying North's authority to sell. Negligence in order to give rise to a defence under this section meant more than mere carelessness on the owner's part, and must amount to a disregard of his obligations towards the person setting up the defence.

LUSH, J. (at page 255)

It follows that the plaintiff should succeed unless the defendants can bring themselves within some statutory provision giving them a defence to the action. I will deal with the defences in order. It was said first that s. 21(1) of the Sale of Goods Act . . . afforded a defence. That sub-section provides that where goods are sold by a person who is not the owner, and who does not sell them under the authority or with the consent of the owner, the buyer acquires no better title than the seller had

> "unless the owner of the goods is by his conduct precluded from denying the seller's authority to sell".

The defence founded on that sub-section is raised in these circumstances. North having got the car, used it in order to go to the premises of a well-known firm of motor engineers who employed him for a time as an agent to sell cars of theirs if he could. North appears then to have become acquainted with a man named Cory who was also employed by the firm. North seems to have thought it likely that the defendants who are themselves dealers in motor cars, might buy this car, but, apparently for reasons of prudence, instead of going to the defendants himself he got Cory to approach them. Cory, as to whom nothing is known either for him or against him, and has gone where nobody can find him, went to the defendants, told them that North had this car, which he was able to show them, for sale at the very low price of £110, and asked them to buy it. I need not for the moment consider whether the defendants dealt with Cory or with North, I need only now say that they ultimately bought the car. On the assumption that for this purpose North was the seller of the car to the defendants, it is said that the plaintiff by his conduct is estopped from denying North's authority to sell to them. I cannot follow the argument that was addressed to me on behalf of the defendants on this part of the case. It is true that the plaintiff was very trustful in parting with the possession of the car, and in letting North go on using the car without accounting for the price. He was not so careful as he should have been in his own interest, but that does not mean that he was negligent in the sense that he broke some duty that he owed to the defendants. Negligence, in order to give rise to a defence under this section in question must be more than mere carelessness on the part of a person in the conduct of his own affairs, and must amount to a disregard of his obligations towards the person who is setting up the defence. There is, in my opinion, no evidence to show that the plaintiff was negligent in that sense and to justify the defence that he is precluded from denying the seller's authority to sell.

(2) Market Overt

Hargreave *v.* Spink

(1892), 65 L.T. 650

By s. 22(1): "Where goods are sold in market overt, according to the usage of the market, the buyer acquires a good title to the goods provided he buys them in good faith and without notice of any defect or want of title on the part of the seller".

The plaintiff was the owner of some jewellery which was stolen from her. It was sold in a showroom above their shop in the City of London to the defendants who were jewellers.

Held, by the Queen's Bench Division, that the defendants did not obtain a good title to the jewellery, for the goods had not been sold in market overt,[47] since the sale had not taken place in the defendants' shop.

Held (*obiter*), that in any event the market overt rule did not apply in the case of a sale *to* a shopkeeper.[48]

WILLS, J. (at page 650)

The plaintiff, a married lady, was the owner of a quantity of jewellery which was stolen from her. The defendants are silversmiths and jewellers. They bought the jewellery *bona fide* from a person who brought it to their business premises for sale and under circumstances which entitle them to keep the stolen property if the sale to them was made in market overt, and it is only right to say that upon learning by an advertisement that the property had been stolen they gave immediate information to the plaintiff of every circumstance connected with their purchase. No prosecution has taken place. The plaintiff now sues for the return of the jewels. The defendants' place of business is within the City of London. It consists (*inter alia*) of a shop, in the ordinary acceptation of the term, with a shop window in which goods are exposed for sale, and there is the ordinary means of access from the shop to the street by a door by which any person can enter. Behind the counter is a door out of the shop opening upon the foot of a staircase which leads to a showroom on the first floor. The person who brought the jewellery for sale explained her business, and was thereupon taken behind the counter and into the upper room where the purchase by the defendants was effected. Out of London the shop itself would not be market overt, but by the custom of London:

"every shop in which goods are exposed publicly to sale is market overt for such things as the owner professes to trade in";

---

[47] This case was decided under the Common Law, but the principle remains the same under s. 22 of the Sale of Goods Act. 1979 In April, 1966, the Law Reform Committee in their 12th Report (Transfer of Title to Chattels) (Cmnd. 2958) recommended in par. 33 that "Section 22 of the Sale of Goods Act . . . should be repealed and replaced by a provision enabling a person who buys in good faith by retail at trade premises or at a public auction to acquire a good title".
[48] This point was later expressly decided in *Ardath Tobacco Co. Ltd.* v. *Ocker* (1931), 47 T.L.R. 177.

those are the words in which Sir Wm. BLACKSTONE states the custom (2 Bl. 449).
Lord COKE says: "Every shop in London is a market overt for such things only which
by the trade of the owner are put there to sale"; and he adds, "when I was Recorder of
London, I certified the custom of London accordingly" (*The Case of Market Overt*[49]).
If, therefore, the sale had been by the defendants and in the shop itself, there could
have been no doubt. In the present case, however, the sale was effected in the showroom upstairs to which access could only be obtained by the permission and invitation
of the defendants, and which was as essentially a private place as any convenient room
in a private house. It seems to me that by no reasonable stretch of language can the
showroom, to be approached only by passing behind the counter in the shop, and with
the permission of the defendants or of their servants in the shop, be called a shop. A
showroom of this description and so appropriated is certainly not in ordinary parlance
a shop, and I see no reason for such an extension, if I should not more properly say
perversion, of the natural and ordinary meaning of the word. It is impossible, upon a
careful perusal of the scanty authorities upon the subject, not to see that there is a
certain element of publicity required in the transaction to bring it within the principle
of a sale in market overt. Lord COKE, in the case referred to, says that the reason of
the case is common to the custom of London, and to the general law of the land as to
market overt. The market, to be a market overt, must be an open, public, and legally
constituted one (*Lee* v. *Bayes*[50]). The shop in London must be one in which goods are
openly sold; that is, as I take it, where they are sold in the presence and sight of any
one of the public who may come into the shop upon legitimate occasion. The keeping
[of a] shop is an invitation to anyone who chooses to come to deal with the shopkeeper
to enter. No one could be said to be a trespasser who came in with the *bona fide* intention
of buying the wares exposed for sale. In the case of a showroom situated as that in the
present case there is no such invitation, and it is very certain that no one would be
allowed to go behind the counter and up the stairs unless permission was specially
given, or he was an *habitué* of the place, and had a general permission to go there.
Such a distinction is, as it seems to me, entirely in consonance with the authorities.
BLACKSTONE speaks of a shop wherein goods are exposed publicly for sale. Lord
COKE says:

> "If the sale had been openly in the shop so that anyone who stood or passed by the shop
> might see it there, it would change the property";

and again,

> "If the sale be in the shop of a goldsmith, either behind a hanging, or behind a cupboard
> upon which his plate stands, so that one who stood or passed by the shop would not see it,

---

[49] (1596), 5 Co. Rep. 83b.
[50] (1856), 18 C.B. 599, *per* JERVIS, C.J., at p. 601.

it would not change the property. So if the sale be not in the shop but in the warehouse or other place of the house, it would not change the property, for that is not in market overt".

In the report of the same case in Cro. Eliz. 454 it is said: "If the sale be in a back shop or other place not open, no property passes". The same case is rather more fully reported in Sir Francis Moore's Reports, where it is said:

> "Where a shop contains an outer room and an inner room, the sale in the inner room does not alter the property. So where a curtain is drawn in the shop, the sale made in such a shop in that part which is more remote from the street, provided that the curtain is between the place where the sale is made and the street, it is not a good sale to alter the property as against the owner".[51]

"A sale in market overt", says MANSFIELD, C.J., in *Hill* v. *Smith*,[52] "requires that the commodity should be openly sold and delivered in the market". In *Lyons* v. *De Pass*[53] the question put to the jury was, whether the place of sale was an "open shop". An "open shop" is the expression used by CRESSWELL, J., in *Lee* v. *Bayes*.[54] Shops, it is true, are not now exactly what they were structurally, and in many other respects, in the time of Queen Elizabeth. But the distinction between the "back shop or other place not open" and the regular shop to which any respectable person would be admitted as a matter of course is as sharp now as then, and the showroom upstairs with the approach I have described seems to me to answer precisely to the description of a "place not open". I think, therefore, that the sale in the present case did not alter the property, and the plaintiff is entitled to succeed. This view makes it unnecessary to decide the question whether a shop in London is a market overt for goods of a class usually bought therein as well as sold, a question of considerable difficulty. The custom as stated by Lord COKE is that the shop is market overt for such things only which by the trade of the owner are "put there to sale". BLACKSTONE says "every shop in which goods are exposed publicly to sale is market overt for such things only as the owner professes to trade in", i.e., the owner of the shop. When a casual person having jewellery for sale goes into a jeweller's shop to sell it if he can to the jeweller, it seems to me that his goods so offered for sale to the one person who is carrying on the business in that shop are neither "put there to sale", nor "exposed publicly to sale"— expressions which seem to me to point to goods placed in the shop by or with the consent of the shopkeeper for sale to all comers prepared to buy. . . .

It can hardly be doubted that in early times when the custom grew up as in later times a shop was very much more often used by the shopkeeper for selling only, and that there would not be many trades, except a goldsmith's, where goods would be at all

---

51 (1596), Moore, K.B. 360, *sub nom. The Bishop of Worcester's Case.*
52 (1812), 4 Taunt. 520, at p. 533.
53 (1840), 11 Ad. & El. 326.
54 (1856), 18 C.B. 599, at p. 601.

likely to be brought to the shop and there purchased by the shopkeeper. The custom is a general one applicable to all sorts of shops, and it might therefore be expected naturally to deal only with a state of things common to at least the great majority of shops. Sales effected in a shop to a shopkeeper seem to me to stand upon a footing differing in many substantial respects from sales by the shopkeeper, and some of the reasons which have been given to explain how the doctrine of market overt grew up certainly do not apply with the same force to the case of sales to the shopkeeper as they do to the case of sales by the shopkeeper. The circumstances of this case afford a good illustration of some of these differences. A sale by a shopkeeper is a sale by a person who can be found if wanted, and about whom inquiries can be made having a certain more or less permanent status of some degree, often a very high degree, of substantiality and respectability; he stands upon a very different footing from a casual and unknown person who comes into the shop. The inclination of my opinion is certainly against such an extension of the custom as the defendants contend for.

Reid *v*. Commissioner of Police of the Metropolis

[1973] 2 All E.R. 97

Even where a person buys in good faith in market overt during the usual hours at which the market is open, he will not get a good title to them under s. 22(1), unless the sale takes place between sunrise and sunset.

Reid's candelabra were stolen in 1969. In 1970 Cocks bought them in good faith at the New Caledonian Market, Southwark, during the usual market hours (i.e., from 7 a.m. onwards). When Reid claimed the goods from him, Cocks contended that he had acquired a good title under s. 22(1).

Held, by the Court of Appeal, that Reid was entitled to the goods, for Cocks could not rely on s. 22(1) because the sale had taken place before sunrise (i.e., before 8.19 a.m. on the day in question), and only sales between sunrise and sunset were protected by the section even though the goods had been bought during normal market hours.

Lord Denning, M.R. (at page 99)

He said that a sale in market overt did not destroy the title of the true owner unless it was made between sunrise and sunset. And here it was before sunrise. It was in the half-light before the sun's rim rose above the horizon.

To solve this question we have to go back to the works of Sir Edward Coke. In 1596 there was an important case about market overt;[55] Coke reported it. He afterwards expounded the law of market overt in his Institutes.[56] He first stated the rule of the Common Law which was, he said:

---

[55] *Market Overt Case* (1596), 5 Co. Rep. 83b.
[56] (1642), Vol. 2, pp. 713-714.

". . . that all sales and contracts of any thing vendible in Faires or Markets overt, should not be good onely between the parties, but should bind those that right had thereunto. But this rule hath many exceptions".

COKE then set out 12 exceptions. The only one material for our purpose is No. 11, which says:

"The sale must not be in the night, but between the rising of the Sun, and the going downe of the same: for he that hath a Faire or Market, either by grant or prescription, hath power to hold it *per unum diem, seu duos, vel tres dies*, &c., where (*dies*) is taken for *dies solaris*; for if it should be taken for *does naturalis*, then might the sale be made at midnight. And yet the sale that is made in the night is good between the parties, but not to bind a stranger that right hath".

Counsel sought to suggest that this exception was based on the interpretation of the word "*dies*" in a grant of a franchise of a market. He argued that, when there was a statutory or other market, the sale was good as against the true owner if it was made in the *usual hours*, but bad if it was made "not at the usual hours". He quoted Sir William BLACKSTONE in his Commentaries[57] for that proposition.

I think we should follow the words of Sir Edward COKE rather than those of Sir William BLACKSTONE. In the first place, COKE is supported by very good authority. He himself refers in the margin to the Entrees of William Rastell. These were printed in 1596 and were based on "good Presidents" (*sic*). Under the heading "Faires &c Markets" William Rastell says[58] that a sale in open market, in order to bind the true owner, must be made '*ab ortu solis usque ad eius occasu*', that is, between the rising of the sun and the going down of the same. In the second place, in the *Market Overt Case*[59] the Judges laid emphasis on the need for the goods to be openly on sale in a *place* where those who stand or pass by can see them. Thus, when a thief stole a silver basin and ewer belonging to the Bishop of Worcester and they afterwards appeared on sale in a scrivener's shop in London, the purchaser got no title: because people go to a scrivener's shop for pen and paper, not for gold or silver plate. Sir Edward COKE said:[60]

"But if the sale had been openly in a goldsmith's shop in London, *so that anyone who stood or passed by the shop might see it*, there it would change the property. But if the sale be in the shop of a goldsmith, either behind a hanging, or behind a cupboard upon which his plate stands, *so that one that stood or passed by the shop could not see it*, it would not change the property: so if the sale be not in the shop, but in the warehouse, or other place of the house, it would not change the property, for that is not in market overt, and *none would search there for his goods*".

---

[57] (1766), Vol. 2, p. 450.
[58] At p. 347.
[59] (1596), 5 Co. Rep. 83b.
[60] *Ibid.*

If such be the requirements as to *place*, a similar requirement may be expected as to *time*. The goods should be openly on sale at a *time* when those who stand or pass by can see them. Thus, it must be in the day time when all can see what is for sale; and not in the night time when no one can be sure what is going on. And if in the day time, what better test can you have than between sunrise and sunset? No half-light then, but full daylight. Just as a distress, to be valid, must be made between sunrise and sunset (see *Tutton* v. *Darke*[61]), so a sale in market overt, to be valid, must be between sunrise and sunset.

Seeing that this sale was made before sunrise, Mr Cocks did not get a good title. Mr Reid, the true owner, is entitled to have the pair of Adam candelabra returned to him.

(3) Sale Under Voidable Title

Car and Universal Finance Co. Ltd. *v.* Caldwell[62]

[1964] 1 All E.R. 290

By s. 23: *"When the seller of goods has a voidable title to them, but his title has not been avoided at the time of the sale, the buyer acquires a good title to the goods provided he buys them in good faith and without notice of the seller's defect of title". In exceptional circumstances a seller is entitled to avoid a contract of sale even though he does not communicate to the other contracting party his intention to do so.*

On 12th January, 1960, the seller of a car was induced by the buyer to accept a cheque in part payment of the price. On 13th January the cheque was dishonoured on presentation, so the seller immediately informed the police and asked the Automobile Association to trace the vehicle. On 15th January the buyer sold the car to a third party.

Held, by the Court of Appeal, that in the circumstances the seller had effectively shown his intention to rescind the contract of sale, even though he had not communicated his election to do so to the fraudulent buyer. Consequently the contract was avoided on 13th January, and the buyer could not pass a good title to the third party.

---

[61] (1860), 5 H. & N. 647.
[62] This decision was followed by the Court of Appeal in *Newtons of Wembley Ltd.* v. *Williams*, [1964] 3 All E.R. 532, which is set out at p. 121, *post*, but it was there held that in similar circumstances the third party obtained a good title under the Factors Act 1889, s. 9. This section, however, was not cited to the Court in *Car and Universal Finance Co. Ltd.* v. *Caldwell* (*supra*), and, if it had been, perhaps the case might have been decided otherwise. The two decisions are difficult to reconcile. But as to the point decided in *Car and Universal Finance Co. Ltd.* v. *Caldwell* (*supra*), i.e. that a seller in exceptional circumstances need not communicate his intention to avoid a voidable contract, this would appear to be established law until it is overruled by the House of Lords. Further, the decision in *Newtons of Wembley Ltd.* v. *Williams* (*supra*) is itself not free from controversy because the Court's attention was not directed to the relationship between s. 23 of the Sale of Goods Act and s. 9 of the Factors Act 1889. In April, 1966, the Law Reform Committee in their 12th Report (Transfer of Title to Chattels) (Cmnd. 2958) stated in par. 16: "We think that unless and until notice of the rescission of the contract is communicated to the other contracting party, an innocent purchaser from the latter should be able to acquire a good title. No doubt this will mean that the innocent purchaser will do so in the great majority of cases since it will usually be impracticable for the original owner of the goods to communicate with the rogue who has deprived him of them".

SELLERS, L.J. (at page 293)

An affirmation of a voidable contract may be established by any conduct which unequivocally manifests an intention to affirm it by the party who has the right to affirm or disaffirm. Communication of an acceptance of a contract after knowledge of a fundamental breach of it by the other party or of fraud affecting it is, of course, evidence establishing affirmation but it is not essential evidence. A party cannot reject goods sold and delivered if he uses them after knowledge of a right to reject, and the judgment[63] cites a case[64] where an instruction to a broker to re-sell was sufficient affirmation of the contract in question even though that conduct was not communicated. It may be said that a contract may be more readily approved and accepted than it can be terminated where a unilateral right to affirm or disaffirm arises. The disaffirmation or election to avoid a contract changes the relationship of the parties and brings their respective obligations to an end, whereas an affirmation leaves the contract effective though subject to a claim for damages for its breach. Where a contracting party could be communicated with, and modern facilities make communication practically world-wide and almost immediate, it would be unlikely that a party could be held to have disaffirmed a contract unless he went so far as to communicate his decision so to do. It would be what the other contracting party would normally require and unless communication were made, the party's intention to rescind would not have been unequivocal, or clearly demonstrated or made manifest. But in circumstances such as the present case the other contracting party, a fraudulent rogue who would know that the vendor would want his car back as soon as he knew of the fraud, would not expect to be communicated with as a matter of right or requirement and would deliberately, as here, do all he could to evade any such communication being made to him. In such exceptional contractual circumstances, it does not seem to me appropriate to hold that a party so acting can claim any right to have a decision to rescind communicated to him before the contract is terminated. To hold that he could would involve that the defrauding party, if skilful enough to keep out of the way, could deprive the other party to the contract of his right to rescind, a right to which he was entitled and which he would wish to exercise as the defrauding party would well know or at least confidently suspect. The position has to be viewed, as I see it, between the two contracting parties involved in the particular contract in question. That another innocent party or parties may suffer does not in my view of the matter justify imposing on a defrauded seller an impossible task. He has to establish clearly and unequivocally that he terminates the contract and is no longer to be bound by it. If he cannot communicate his decision, he may still satisfy a Judge or jury that he had made a final and irrevocable decision and ended the contract.

---

63 Of Lord DENNING, M.R., in the Court below: [1963] 2 All E.R. 547, at p. 550.
64 Re Hop and Malt Exchange and Warehouse Co., ex parte Briggs (1866), L.R. 1 Eq. 483.

I am in agreement with the Master of the Rolls, who asked:[65]

"How is a man in the position of defendant ever to be able to rescind the contract when a fraudulent person absconds as Norris did here?"

and answered [66] that he can do so

"if he at once, on discovering the fraud, takes all possible steps to regain the goods, even though he cannot find the rogue nor communicate with him".

The plaintiffs contended that in *Scarf* v. *Jardine*[67] Lord BLACKBURN laid it down that election to avoid a contract is not completed until the decision has been communicated to the other side "in such a way as to lead the opposite party to believe that he has made the choice", and they relied on the many works of authority[68] which state that where a right of election exists, there has to be communication. *Scarf* v. *Jardine*[69] is a very different case from the present. It is so well known and so often cited that it does not call for analysis. In that case Lord BLACKBURN and, in the various works referred to, the authors had not in mind in enunciating a general principle the circumstances and the arguments which have arisen in the present case. Even in the light of this statement of the law it was conceded—and rightly so—that if the defendant could have found the car and had re-taken it without the knowledge of the buyer, but before resale to an innocent purchaser, the contract would have been at an end and the title restored to the defendant. Such an act would have been an unequivocal act of election to disaffirm the contract.

In the case of an innocent misrepresentation in circumstances which would permit the party misled to rescind, the other party would not deliberately avoid communication (for that would seem to negative innocence) and circumstances would be rare where communication could not be readily made in one way or another. If communication was possible, it is difficult to see how there could be rescission without communication and the inference would be that the contracting parties required communication of termination. Special circumstances may arise and call for future consideration but I do not think that the plaintiffs' comparison in argument between innocent and fraudulent misrepresentation invalidates the learned Master of the Rolls' judgment. It has to be recognised that in transactions such as this where fraud intervenes, some innocent party may have to suffer and it may well be that legislation is overdue to do justice between the victims of fraud and to apportion in some way the loss. But in the present case I can see nothing unjust in the loss falling on the

---

[65] [1963] 2 All E.R., at p. 550.
[66] *Ibid.*, at p. 550.
[67] (1882), 7 App. Cas. 345, at p. 361.
[68] Kerr, W. W., *Law of Fraud and Mistake*, 7th Edn. (1952), p. 530; Benjamin on Sale (8th Edn. 1950), p. 441; Pollock, Sir F., *Principles of Contract*, 13th Edn. (1950), p. 467.
[69] *Supra.*

G. & C. Finance Corporation Ltd. (against whom the plaintiffs can claim redress) who made the minimum inquiries, who bought a car which apparently they never saw and hired it out to a man of whose existence and identity they did not know and who may well have been fictitious, rather than that the loss should fall on the defendant who acted immediately and did all in his power to retract the transaction.

I would dismiss the appeal on this issue and that is sufficient to decide the appeal in the defendant's favour.

(4) Disposition by Seller in Possession After Sale

Pacific Motor Auctions Pty. Ltd. _v._ Motor Credits [Hire Finance] Ltd.

[1965] 2 All E.R. 105

_By s._ 24: _"Where a person having sold goods continues or is in possession of the goods . . . the delivery or transfer by that person . . . of the goods . . . under any sale . . . to any person receiving the same in good faith and without notice of the previous sale, has the same effect as if the person making the delivery or transfer were expressly authorised by the owner of the goods to make the same". The words "continues . . . in possession" refer to the continuity of physical possession regardless of any private transactions between the seller and original buyer which might alter the legal title under which the possession was held._

Motor Credits (Hire Finance) Ltd. bought a number of cars from Motordom, which carried on business as car dealers, for the purpose of letting them out under hire-purchase agreements to Motordom's customers. Motordom continued in possession of them as bailees with authority to sell them. The buyers revoked Motordom's authority to sell, but on the same day Motordom sold some of the cars to Pacific Motor Auctions Pty. Ltd. which bought them in good faith. The buyers commenced proceedings claiming their return and damages for detention.

Held, by the Judicial Committee of the Privy Council, that the action failed, for Pacific Motor Auctions Pty. Ltd. had obtained a good title under s. 28(1) of the New South Wales Sale of Goods Act 1923-53,[70] for Motordom "continued in possession" of the cars. Any private transaction between the seller and the original buyer which might alter the legal title under which the possession was held, e.g., as a bailee was immaterial.

Lord Pearce (at page 112)

It is plainly right to read the section as inapplicable to cases where there has been a break in the continuity of the physical possession. . . . What is the justification, however, for saying that a person does not continue in possession where his physical possession does continue, although the title under or by virtue of which he is in

---

[70] Which corresponds to s. 24 of the (English) Sale of Goods Act 1979.

possession has changed? The fact that a person having sold goods is declared as *continuing* in possession would seem to indicate that the section is not contemplating as relevant a change in the legal title under which he possesses. For the legal title by which he is in possession *cannot* continue. Before the sale he is in possession as an owner, whereas after the sale he is in possession as a bailee holding goods for the new owner. The possession continues unchanged, but the title under which he possesses has changed. One may, perhaps, say in loose terms that a person having sold goods continues in possession as long as he is holding because of, and only because of, the sale; but what justification is there for imposing such an elaborate and artificial construction on the natural meaning of the words? The object of the section is to protect an innocent purchaser who is deceived by the vendor's physical possession of goods or documents and who is inevitably unaware of legal rights which fetter the apparent power to dispose. Where a vendor retains uninterrupted physical possession of the goods, why should an unknown arrangement, which substitutes a bailment for ownership, disentitle the innocent purchaser to protection from a danger which is just as great as that from which the section is admittedly intended to protect him? Since the original provision under the Factors Act Amendment Act 1877 (s. 3), dealt only with the continuing in possession of documents of title to goods, it seems clear that it was intending merely to deal with the physical possession of the documents and that it did not intend that a consideration of the legal quality of the possession of the documents should have any relevance. When the Factors Act 1889 (s. 8), added continuance in possession of the goods themselves to continuance in possession of the documents, it can hardly be suggested that the word "possession" was intended to have any more esoteric meaning in relation to goods than it had in relation to documents of title. There is, therefore, the strongest reason for supposing that the words "continues . . . in possession" were intended to refer to the continuity of physical possession regardless of any private transactions between the seller and purchaser which might alter the legal title under which the possession was held.

Their Lordships do not think that such a view of the law which they believe Parliament to have intended could in practice create any adverse effect. It would mean that, when a person sells a car to a finance house in order to take it back on hire-purchase, the finance house must take physical delivery if it is to avoid the risk of an innocent purchaser acquiring title to it.

City Fur Manufacturing Co. Ltd. *v.* Fureenbond [Brokers] London Ltd.

[1937] 1 All E.R. 799

A seller "continuing in possession of the goods" can pass a good title to them under s. 24 to a bona fide *purchaser for value even though they are actually in the possession of the seller's agent.*

Herman purchased a quantity of skins from Lampson & Co. Ltd., a firm of brokers, but did not pay for them. He sold them to the plaintiffs, but the goods remained in the brokers' warehouse. The plaintiffs gave him a bill of exchange in payment of the price so that he could pay off his debt to the brokers and arrange for the brokers to deliver the goods to them. Instead he pledged the goods with the defendants.

Held, by the King's Bench Division, that the defendants obtained a good title under s. 24 for Herman was a seller in possession of the goods. It was not necessary for him to be in *personal* possession of them. Possession by his agents—Lampson & Co. Ltd.—was sufficient.

BRANSON, J. (at page 800)

One Herman, bought certain lots of furs at a sale which was held on 10th February by Messrs Huth. He bought seven parcels, and Messrs Huth, who were acting as brokers and auctioneers between purchasers and the owners of the goods at this sale, rendered to Herman under date 10th February a broker's contract note showing that they had that day bought for him at this public sale the seven parcels of goods in question. Having become the purchaser of the goods, Herman did not desire to pay for them all at once. The prompt day was 4th March, by which time the sellers had to be paid, and by which time Herman ought to have paid for the goods, but not intending to pay for them all by that time, he availed himself of a practice which exists among the auctioneers and brokers in the fur trade, under which the broker pays the vendor upon the prompt day, and, subject to such arrangements as he may make or care to make with the purchaser, he advances part of the purchase price for the purchaser, who is thus enabled to delay payment for a certain time. In the meantime the auctioneers hold the goods in the warehouse subject to the payment by the purchaser of the amount which they have advanced on his behalf in order to satisfy the vendor. That was the position as between Herman and Messrs Huth, who subsequently became C. M. Lampson & Co. Ltd.

In the meantime, on 2nd March, Herman sold certain of these skins to the plaintiffs and received in payment for them bills of exchange payable in July and August. Some of the goods so sold were taken up, and no question arises about them; but the rest of the goods remained in the warehouse of C. M. Lampson & Co. Ltd., subject to the arrangement which I have already detailed.

On 1st July, Herman made a further sale of the rest of the skins to the plaintiffs, and again got a bill of exchange in payment for them. Herman persuaded the plaintiffs to give to him that bill of exchange upon the representation that he would use it to clear the skins of the amount which he owed to Lampsons, so that the plaintiffs could get delivery of them on presentation of the delivery orders to Lampsons; but he did not do it. Instead of doing it, he went to the defendants and explained to them that he wanted to borrow money on these skins, which were his property, lying in Lampson's warehouse subject to a claim by Lampsons of £178; he got the defendants to advance him the money to pay off Lampsons in order that the skins might be delivered by Lampsons to the defendants and held by the defendants as pledges for the amount that they had advanced, or that they were going to advance, to Herman. The transaction was carried out. The defendants drew a cheque on 21st August in favour of C. M. Lampson & Co. Ltd., for £178 0s. 6d., and that cheque was cleared upon 22nd August. Upon that date, therefore, Lampsons had been paid all that they were entitled to get in respect of these skins and they held the skins to the order of Herman. But Lampsons, quite rightly, would not deliver the goods to the defendants until a proper order from Herman was produced and shown to them. That was done, and acting upon that order they delivered the skins to the defendants, who now hold them, and claim to do so as pledges against the £178 which they have advanced to Herman.

The plaintiffs allege that the skins are theirs, having passed to them by virtue of the two contracts of sale of 2nd March and 1st July, and they say: "We have paid for these skins and they are our property", and so they are; but the question is whether, by virtue of the Sale of Goods Act, s. [24], the defendants are or are not entitled to hold the skins as though the delivery to them had been expressly authorised by the plaintiffs. That, I think, depends upon whether, in the circumstances of this case, the defendants bring themselves within the language of s. [24] of the Act. I think they do. The section says: "Where a person having sold goods"—that is, Herman—"is in possession of the goods"—[counsel] says that Herman, if not all through, at all events after 22nd August, was in possession of these goods; and that depends upon what is the true interpretation to be put upon the word "possession". I think it is perfectly plain by a reference to the Factors Act 1889, s. 1(2), that it is sufficient in that Act that possession is possession by another person on behalf of the person whose possession is material, and I see no reason why the same kind of construction should not be put upon the words "in possession of the goods" in s. [24] of the [Sale of Goods] Act . . ... Possession by an agent, possession by a warehouseman or mercantile agent, is a perfectly well known form of possession in the business world, and I can see no reason for confining the meaning of it to personal possession or actual possession of the person who has sold the goods. These goods, until Herman sold them to the plaintiffs, were Herman's goods. They were in possession of Lampsons subject to this arrangement under which at any moment Herman could get them by paying that which he owed upon the goods, and I think it would be true to say that they were in his possession from the beginning, because they were held for him or upon his behalf by Lampsons. It is true that that was subject to his discharging his part of the bargain by virtue of which they were being so held, but none the less, they were held on his behalf. At any moment, as I say, he could pay the £178, and then they would deal with the goods as he ordered; but at all events when they had got his £178 on 22nd August, they held the goods for him and subject to his control, and upon his behalf, and I think that he was a person having possession of the goods which he had sold the plaintiffs. [Section 24] is therefore satisfied.

Worcester Works Finance Ltd. *v.* Cooden Engineering Co. Ltd.

[1971] 3 All E.R. 708

Where a seller of goods continues in possession of the goods after a sale, and then allows a person from whom he has bought them on another occasion in exchange for a "dud" cheque to retake possession of them, that person gets a good title to them under s. 24 if he acts in good faith and without notice of the other sale, for the retaking of possession with consent amounts to a "delivery" of the goods within the meaning of that sub-section.

The defendants sold a car to Griffiths, a car dealer, in June, 1966, for £525, and received a cheque in payment. Griffiths took delivery of the car, and sold it to the plaintiffs for £450. The plaintiffs let it out to Millerick under a hire-purchase agreement. Millerick never took possession of it, and it still remained in Griffiths' possession. Griffiths kept up the hire-purchase payments to conceal the fraud, but later stopped doing so. In August his cheque in favour of the defendants was dishonoured, so, with his consent, they retook possession of the car. The plaintiffs discovered what had happened, and claimed the car from them. But the defendants contended that they had a good title to it under s. 24, for Griffiths was a person "who, having sold goods, remained in possession of them", their retaking of the car with his consent amounted to a "delivery" of them within the meaning of that sub-section, and they had received the car in good faith and without notice of the previous sale to the plaintiffs.

Held, by the Court of Appeal, that this contention succeeded, and that the defendants had a good title.

LORD DENNING, M.R. (at page 711)

The question is whether Mr Griffiths comes within the following words. Was he a person who "continues or is in possession of the goods"? The material word here is "continues". The words "or is" have been explained in a New Zealand case of

Mitchell v. *Jones*,[71] which was approved by the Privy Council in *Pacific Motor Auctions Pty. Ltd.* v. *Motor Credits (Hire Finance) Ltd.*[72] They refer only to a case where the person who sold the goods had not got the goods when he sold them, but they came into his possession afterwards. Those words "or is" do not apply to this case because Mr Griffiths, at the time when he sold the car to Worcester Finance, was already in possession of it. The only relevant word is therefore "continues". Was Mr Griffiths a person who, having sold goods, "continues . . . in possession of the goods"?

Counsel for Worcester Finance submits that the words "continues in possession" mean continues in *lawful* possession. He says that, after Mr Griffiths sold the car to Worcester Finance, he ought to have delivered it to the hirer Mr Millerick; and that, by retaining it himself, he retained it unlawfully; and he was, *vis-à-vis* Worcester Finance, a trespasser. He was in possession of it without their consent at all. In support of his contention counsel relied on two cases: *Staffs Motor Guarantee Ltd.* v. *British Wagon Co. Ltd.*[73] applied in this Court in *Eastern Distributors Ltd.* v. *Goldring (Murphy, Third Party)*.[74] In those cases it was held that the words "continues in possession" mean continues in possession as seller and not as bailee; and accordingly, if the person who had sold goods continued in possession as a bailee, he did not "continue in possession" within the meaning of the section. But those cases are no longer good law. They were disapproved by the Privy Council in *Pacific Motor Auctions Pty. Ltd.* v. *Motor Credits (Hire Finance) Ltd.*,[75] and, although decisions of the Privy Council are not binding on this Court, nevertheless when the Privy Council disapprove of a previous decision of this Court, or cast doubt on it, then we are at liberty to depart from the previous decision. I am glad to depart from those earlier cases and to follow the Privy Council. The words "continues . . . in possession" refer to:[76]

> "the continuity of physical possession regardless of any private transaction between seller and purchaser which might alter the legal title under which the possession was held".

This is how Lord PEARCE put it. It does not matter what private arrangement may be made by the seller with the purchaser—such as whether the seller remains as bailee or trespasser, or whether he is lawfully in possession or not. It is sufficient if he remains continuously in possession of the goods that he has sold to the purchaser. If so, he can pass a good title to a *bona fide* third person, and the original purchaser will be ousted. But there must be a continuity of physical possession. If there is a substantial break in the continuity, as for instance, if the seller actually delivers over

---

71 (1905), 24 N.Z.L.R. 932.
72 [1965] 2 All E.R. 105, P.C. See p. 62, *ante*.
73 [1934] All E.R. Rep. 322.
74 [1957] 2 All E.R. 525, C.A.
75 *Supra*.
76 [1965] 2 All E.R. 105, at p. 114.

the goods to a purchaser who keeps them for a time, and then the seller afterwards gets them back, then the section might not apply. Applying these principles it is plain that Mr Griffiths was a person who, having sold goods to Worcester Finance, "continued . . . in possession" of them until the time when they were retaken by Cooden.

The next question is whether the retaking by Cooden was "the delivery or transfer" by Mr Griffiths of the goods to Cooden under a "disposition" thereof. Mr Griffiths did not actually deliver or transfer the car to Cooden. But he acquiesced in their retaking it. That was, I think, tantamount to a delivery or transfer by him. But was it under a "disposition" thereof? Counsel for Worcester Finance argued that there was no disposition here; there was, he said, only a retaking by Cooden. To my mind the word "disposition" is a very wide word. In *Carter* v. *Carter*[77] STIRLING, J., said that it extends "to all acts by which a new interest (legal or equitable) in the property is effectually created". That was under an entirely different statute, but I would apply that wide meaning in this section. When Cooden retook this car (because the cheque had not been met), there was clearly a transfer back to them of property in the goods. They would not thereafter be able to sue on the cheque. By retaking the goods they impliedly gave up their remedy on the cheque. That retransfer of the property back to Cooden was a "disposition" within the section.

The last question is whether at the time when Cooden retook the car, they received "the same in good faith and without notice of the previous sale", i.e., without notice of the sale by Mr Griffiths to Worcester Finance. The word "notice" here means actual notice, that is to say, knowledge of the sale or deliberately turning a blind eye to it. Our commercial law does not like constructive notice. It will have nothing to do with it. I am quite clear that Cooden acted in good faith without notice of the sale to Worcester Finance. They had sold a car and been given a dud cheque for it; and were just retaking it. So all the requisites of s. [24] are satisfied. The retaking by Cooden has the same effect as if it was expressly authorised by Worcester Finance. It is equivalent to a transfer by Mr Griffiths back to Cooden with the express authority of the finance company. So Cooden acquired a good title to the car.

This result is consonant with the object of s. [24]. Worcester Finance did not see the car at all. They did not take possession of it. They simply received documents from the dealer, Mr Griffiths, and handed out money to him. They relied on his honesty. He was dishonest. He got £450 out of them by a trick. In contrast, Cooden actually had possession of the car, sold it to Mr Griffiths and, when his cheque was dishonoured, they retook it. Plainly as a matter of commercial good sense the title should remain in

---

[77] [1896] 1 Ch. 62.

Cooden and not in Worcester Finance. Cooden are protected by s. [24]. The car is theirs.

MEGAW, L.J. (at page 714)

The second point raised by counsel for the plaintiffs is as to the meaning of the words, again in s. [24], "delivery or transfer . . . of the goods . . . under any . . . disposition thereof . . .". It is said by counsel for the plaintiffs, that "disposition" in that context must mean something more than a mere transfer of possession. That is plainly right. "Disposition" must involve some transfer of an interest in property, in the technical sense of the word "property", as contrasted with mere possession. In the present case, however, I have no doubt that what happened is properly described as a delivery of the goods under a disposition thereof in that sense. The cheque which Mr Griffiths had given for this motor car had been presented by the defendants to their bank and had been dishonoured more than once. The cheque finally came back on 26th July, 1966, the defendants' account being again debited by the bank because of the refusal of the cheque. Three weeks later the defendants took repossession of the car, having first telephoned and said that they were proposing so to do. After repossession had been taken, the car having been given up voluntarily by Mr Griffiths following on the call made on him after the telephone conversation, I have no doubt whatever that the effect in law of that taking, the repossession, was that the interest in property in the car reverted to the defendants. It was not, in law, a mere transfer of possession. It was a transfer of the goods under a disposition in the true sense of the word. It does not matter whether or not the parties to the transaction realised its legal effect. If thereafter the defendants had sought to sue Mr Griffiths on the cheque, they would have been met by the completely unanswerable defence by Mr Griffiths: "You [the defendants] have waived your right to sue on that cheque in consideration of my surrender to you of my interest in the car". That is a disposition.

The third and last point taken by counsel for the plaintiffs is that s. [24] of the Sale of Goods Act 1893 is of no avail to the defendants unless it can be shown that what was done by them was done in good faith and without notice of the previous sale. Let it be assumed for present purposes that counsel for the plaintiffs is right in his submission that the onus of proof of absence of notice of a previous sale rests on the defendants. In my view there was evidence on which the Judge was entitled to come to the conclusion to which he did come, that there was at the relevant time no notice on the part of the defendants of the previous sale. Since there was evidence on which the Judge was entitled to reach that conclusion, I see no ground for interference by this Court.

(5) Disposition by Buyer in Possession After Sale

Percy Edwards Ltd. *v.* Vaughan

(1910), 26 T.L.R. 545

Where a person has obtained goods on approval and the property in them has not passed to him, he is not a person who has "agreed to buy" them within the meaning of s. 25(1), and accordingly he cannot give a third party a good title to them under that sub-section.

> On 2nd October, 1909, the plaintiffs, who were jewellers, allowed a Mr de Meulemeester to take away a necklace on approval. The evidence showed that it was the intention of the parties that the property in the necklace was not to pass except on payment of cash on or before 18th October. On 13th October he pledged the necklace with the defendant. The plaintiffs claimed that they were entitled to its return, but the defendant contended (*inter alia*) that the pledge was valid under s. 25(1) because Mr de Meulemeester was a person who had "agreed to buy" goods within the meaning of that sub-section.
>
> *Held*, by the Court of Appeal, that Mr de Meulemeester was not such a person, and could therefore not pass a good title to the defendant.

Cozens-Hardy, M.R. (at page 546)

It was argued that the case was within s. 18 of that Act; s. 18 must be read with s. 17, which provided:—"Where there is a contract for the sale of specific or ascertained goods the property in them is transferred to the buyer at such time as the parties to the contract intend it to be transferred". By s. 18 rules for ascertaining the intention of the parties are given, and r. 4 was:—"When goods are delivered to the buyer on approval or 'on sale or return' or other similar terms, the property [in the goods] passes to the buyer: (a) when he signifies his approval or acceptance to the seller or does any other act adopting the transaction". This much at least was clear from the evidence, that if de Meulemeester had come back on Monday, 18th October, with the cash, he would have been entitled to the necklace, and if he did not bring the cash, he ought to have brought back the necklace to the plaintiffs; and really the only question for decision was whether there was an intention expressed in the contract that the property should not pass except for cash (as as to take it out of the operation of s. 18, r. 4), and on this point there were the answers to questions 1 and 2 which had been given by the jury. If there was evidence to support these findings, then the property in this necklace did not pass except on a payment of cash on or before 18th October. The evidence and the very careful summing up of the learned Judge had all been read to this Court, and in giving judgment Hamilton, J., said he could not say there was no evidence to go to the jury of such a contract as their answers 1, 2 and 5 affirmed, and this Court could not say there was no such evidence, and consequently the case fell within *Weiner* v. *Gill*,[78] and the property in the necklace had not passed out of the plaintiff, and he was entitled to recover it from the [defendant]. Speaking for himself, he (the Master of the Rolls) was not prepared to say that there was no evidence to go to the jury on this point, and that being so their findings could not be disturbed, and this appeal must be dismissed with costs. A transaction on sale or return was not a case where a person was in possession under an agreement to buy within s. 25 of the Sale of Goods Act . . . , and that section did not help the [defendant].

Cahn *v*. Pockett's Bristol Channel Steam Packet Co. Ltd.

(1899), 80 L.T. 269

Where the seller sends the buyer a bill of lading together with a bill of exchange for his acceptance, the buyer, if he does not accept the bill of exchange, should return the bill of lading to the seller, as required by s. 19(3), but, if he transfers it for value to a third party who acts in good faith, the third party acquires a good title under s. 25(1).

Steinmann & Co. sold Pintscher 10 tons of copper to be delivered at Rotterdam, shipped them on a vessel owned by the defendants and sent Pintscher a bill of lading for his acceptance. Pintscher never accepted the bill of exchange, but kept the bill of lading and endorsed it to the plaintiff to whom he sold the goods. Steinmann & Co. purported to stop the goods in transit because they had not been paid and Pintscher was insolvent. The defendants refused to deliver the goods to the plaintiff, so he brought an action against them for non-delivery, contending that he had obtained a good title to them under s. 25(1) of the Sale of Goods Act, for Pintscher was in possession of the bill of lading with the consent of Steinmann & Co., even though he had not returned it to them, as required by s. 19(3) of the Act, on failing to accept the bill of exchange.

Held, by the Court of Appeal, that the plaintiff's contention succeeded and that he had acquired a good title.

SMITH, L.J. (at page 272)

Did Pintscher obtain the actual custody of it with the consent of Steinmann & Co.? In my judgment the words of the Act mean actual, physical, custody. After consideration, the only answer I can give to this question is that the bill of lading was obtained by Pintscher from Steinmann & Co., and was in his actual custody with the consent of Steinmann & Co. It is, however, argued that what Lords WESTBURY and CAIRNS said in *Shepherd* v. *Harrison*[79] shows that I am wrong, but I do not think so. What those noble and learned Lords were dealing with was the passing of property in goods contained in a bill of lading to a purchaser, he not accepting the draft accompanying the bill of lading. We have nothing to do in this case with the passing of property to

---

[78] [1906] 2 K.B. 574.
[79] (1871), L.R. 5 H.L. 116.

Pintscher. That no property passed to Pintscher in the copper cannot be doubted, but this is not the question. Lord WESTBURY in that case, speaking of the letter sent with the bill of lading and the bill of exchange, said that the meaning of the transaction, though it was not in writing, clearly was: "Remember you are not to possess yourselves of the bill of lading, until you have accepted the bill of exchange". And Lord CAIRNS said: "I do not believe there is a merchant in England that would have had any doubt that the meaning of that", i.e., sending the bill of lading and draft together, "was: You shall have the bill of lading when you accept the bill of exchange". And further on he says: "I hold it to be perfectly clear that when a cargo comes in this way, protected by a bill of lading and a bill of exchange, it is the duty of those to whom the bill of lading and the bill of exchange are transmitted in a letter, either to approbate or to reprobate entirely and completely, then and there. . . . I therefore think that when one merchant in this country sends to another, under circumstances like the present, a bill of lading and a bill of exchange, it is not at all necessary for him to say in words: We require you to take notice that our object in enclosing these bills of lading and bills of exchange is that before you use the bills of lading you shall accept the bills of exchange". It seems to me that the noble and learned Lords clearly state that before the draft is accepted the buyer is not to use the bill of lading, and if he does so, it is a clear breach of his duty to his seller, and in such circumstances no property passes to the buyer. But this does not cover the present question, which is: Did Pintscher obtain the actual custody of the bill of lading—that is, of the thing itself— with Steinmann & Co.'s consent? The noble and learned Lords were not dealing with the effect of the Factors Acts, which was not before them and with which they had nothing to do. I agree that it was Steinmann & Co.'s intention that Pintscher was not to use the bill of lading unless and until he accepted the draft, but the bill of lading was none the less in Pintscher's actual custody with Steinmann & Co.'s consent before he had accepted the draft. The Legislature when it passed the Sale of Goods Act . . . , by s. 19, sub-s. 3, enacted what had been held by the House of Lords in *Shepherd* v. *Harrison*,[80] and nothing more, the Act being an Act to codify the law.

ROMER, L.J. (at page 276)

Section 25, sub-s. [1], of the Sale of Goods Act . . . applies if Pintscher obtained possession of the bill of lading with the consent of Steinmann & Co. Now, "possession" in that context means, I think, "actual custody": (see the definition of "possession" in s. 1, sub-s. 2, of the Factors Act 1889). The question therefore becomes narrowed to one of consent. On that question I have come to the conclusion that Steinmann & Co. did consent to Pintscher's obtaining the custody of the bill of lading. No doubt

---

[80] *Supra.*

Steinmann & Co. contemplated that Pintscher would on receipt of the bill of lading accept the bill of exchange drawn for the price of the goods. And when Pintscher declined to accept the bill of exchange, he ought not to have dealt with the bill of lading. But I do not think this is a case where the owners of the bill of lading made it a condition precedent to its custody being obtained by Pintscher that the bill of exchange should be accepted, so that if the bill of exchange was not accepted, it was not the intention of Steinmann & Co. that Pintscher should obtain the custody of the bill of lading. I think the circumstances negative that view. It appears to me that Steinmann & Co. did intend and consent that the bill of lading and the bill of exchange should both come into the actual custody of Pintscher, though after Pintscher obtained that custody he had certain duties to discharge as between him and Steinmann & Co. with regard to both documents. Steinmann & Co., in short, consented that Pintscher should obtain the custody of the bill of lading, though they did not consent that Pintscher should use the bill of lading after it came into his custody before accepting the bill of exchange: (see the observations of Lord CAIRNS in *Shepherd* v. *Harrison*[81]). It follows that Pintscher was for the purposes of this case in the position of a mercantile agent having possession of the bill of lading with the consent of the owner. And accordingly s. 2 of the Factors Act 1889 applies, and the plaintiff obtained a good title to the goods. For under the circumstances of this case it cannot, in my opinion, be successfully contended by Steinmann & Co. that the transaction between Pintscher and the plaintiff was not a "disposition of the goods" within the meaning of that phrase as used in s. 2, sub-s. 1, of the last-named Act.

D. PERFORMANCE OF THE CONTRACT

(1) DELIVERY OF WRONG QUANTITY

Behrend & Co. Ltd. *v*. Produce Brokers' Co. Ltd.

[1920] All E.R. Rep. 125

By s. 30(1): "*Where the seller delivers to the buyer a quantity of goods less than he contracted to sell, the buyer may reject them, but if the buyer accepts the goods so delivered he must pay for them at the contract rate*".

The sellers, under two separate contracts of sale, agreed to deliver in London two parcels of cotton seed—one containing 176 tons and the other 400 tons. When the ship carrying them arrived in London, the buyers obtained delivery of 15 tons of one parcel and 22 tons of the other. The vessel then proceeded to Hull to unload another cargo, and returned to London a fortnight later. The buyers paid for the goods actually delivered, but refused to accept the remainder when the ship came to London on the second occasion.

---

[81] *Supra.*

Held, by the King's Bench Division, that they were entitled to do so under s. 30(1) of the Sale of Goods Act for they were entitled to delivery of the whole of both parcels once the vessel had commenced to discharge.

BAILHACHE, J. (at page 128)

In this case the sellers, by two contracts of sale, and in the events which happened, bound themselves to the buyers to deliver in London, on the steamship *Port Inglis*, to the buyers' craft alongside, two separate parcels of cotton seed, one of 176 tons and the other of 400 tons. The buyers, on their part, had to pay for these parcels against shipping documents, and to send craft to receive the goods. The buyers fulfilled both these obligations, and received from the *Port Inglis* some 15 tons of one parcel and 22 tons of the other. When these had been delivered, it was discovered that the rest of the seed was lying under cargo for Hull, and the *Port Inglis* stopped delivery and left for that port, promising to return and deliver the rest of the seed. She returned in about a fortnight's time, and the seed was tendered to the buyers, but they had meantime informed the sellers that they regarded the departure of the *Port Inglis* with the remainder of their seed on board as a failure to deliver and a breach of contract. They kept so much of the seed as had been delivered to them, and demanded repayment of so much of the contract price as represented the seed undelivered. The umpire has decided in favour of the buyers, and I am asked to say whether he was right.

Everything depends upon whether the departure of the *Port Inglis* for Hull with the greater part of both parcels of seed on board was a failure to deliver, notwithstanding the promise to return and complete delivery. Both contracts between the parties are in the same terms, and neither has any express provision on the subject. In my opinion, the buyer under such a contract, and where each parcel of goods is indivisible, as here, has the right to have delivery on the arrival of the steamship, not necessarily immediately or continuously; he must take his turn, or the goods may be so stowed that other goods have to be discharged before the whole of the buyer's parcel can be got out. To such delays and others which may occur in the course of unloading the buyer must submit, but in the absence of any stipulation to the contrary the buyer, being ready with his craft, is entitled to delivery of the whole of an indivisible parcel of goods sold to him for delivery from a vessel which has begun delivery to him before she leaves the port to deliver goods elsewhere. If this is so, the rest of the case is covered by s. 30 of the Sale of Goods Act, and the buyer can either reject the whole of the goods, including those actually delivered, in which case he can recover the whole of his money or he may keep the goods actually delivered and reject the rest, in which case he must pay for the goods kept at the contract price, and he can recover the price paid for the undelivered portion: see *Devaux* v. *Conolly*.[82] I think that the award is right.

---

[82] (1849), 8 C.B. 640.

Shipton, Anderson & Co. *v.* Weil Brothers & Co. Ltd.

(1912), 106 L.T. 372

By s. 30(2): *"Where the seller delivers to the buyer a quantity of goods larger than he contracted to sell, the buyer may accept the goods included in the contract and reject the rest, or he may reject the whole". This section, however, is subject to the application of the "de minimis" rule.*

The sellers agreed to sell to the buyers a cargo of wheat described as "4,500 tons, 2% more or less", and were given an option to tender another 8% if the sellers thought fit. This would in all have amounted to a maximum of 4,950 tons. The sellers, however, tendered a quantity of 4,950 tons 55 lb., though they made no attempt to charge the buyers with the cost of the 55 lb.

Held, by the King's Bench Division, the difference of 55 lb. was so trivial as to be insignificant, and accordingly the *de minimis* rule applied, and the buyers were not allowed to reject under s. 30(2).

LUSH, J. (at page 375)

The second question is this: "Whether if they were only entitled to calculate the 8% on the 4,500 tons"—which is in my view the real position—"the excess so in fact tendered was so trifling as not to amount to a breach of the said contract". Now the excess quantity is trifling, so trifling that it is quite impossible to suppose that any business man would regard it as in any way affecting the quality of the contract or as making the contract any the more or any the less an advantageous contract to enter into. It is an excess of 55 lb. in a total cargo of 4,500 tons; approximately it is an excess of 1 lb. in every 100 tons tendered. If you consider the excess in pounds, shillings, and pence it seems more trifling still. It is an excess of 4s. in a contract price of over £40,000, or putting it again in still plainer figures an excess of 1s. in £10,000. Mr Maurice Hill and Mr Leck, however, say that that is an excess which by law entitles the buyer to reject, and they rely upon s. 30 of the Sale of Goods Act . . . That section says:

"Where the seller delivers to the buyer a quantity of goods larger than he contracted to sell, the buyer may accept the goods included in the contract and reject the rest, or he may reject the whole".

They contend, as they must, to be consistent, that any excess that can be measured in weight or in currency would have this effect. If it is 1s. instead of 4s., if it is 6d., if it is anything that you can measure in a contract price of £40,000, that is fatal, and there is a discrepancy between the contract and the tender which is vital. I asked if there was any authority for such a contention, and I was referred to the case of *Tamvaco* v. *Lucas.*[83] The difference between the contract quantity and the shipped

---

[83] (1859), 1 E. & E. 581.

quantity was no doubt not very large in that case, and it was undoubtedly held that the tender was a bad tender, because there had been an excess, but I will point out that as far as I can gather from the arguments and from the judgment the question was not raised which is raised in this case—viz., can you have an excess so trivial that it is not in substance an excess at all? It was dealt with on the footing that there had been in fact an excessive tender, and the question was whether in the circumstances in that case the buyer could or could not reject. I do not think that that case can be relied upon as an authority for Mr Maurice Hill's proposition, which, as I have said, is, that any excess, if once you can measure it and put it into pounds, shillings, and pence, or put it into weight, is of itself necessarily in law an excess which makes the tender bad. I have succeeded in finding a case which I think is more in point. It is true that the actual point was not decided because it was not necessary to decide it, but there was a *dictum* of BIGHAM, J., in that case which exactly in my opinion applies to this case. The case I refer to is *Harland and Wolff Ltd.* v. *Burstall and Co.*[84] In that case there was a smaller quantity delivered than the contract quantity, the shortage amounting to 30 loads out of 500; of course, a very different proportion to this; and BIGHAM, J., held that there was a deficiency there which did entitle the buyers to reject. In giving judgment he said:[85]

> "Of course, in carrying out a commercial contract such as this some slight elasticity is unavoidable; no one supposes that the delivery is to be within a cubic foot of the named quantity, but it must be substantially of the quantity named; and in my judgment 470 loads is not substantially 500".

I think that the question is this: has there been a substantial departure from the contract? As I pointed out during the arguments, the right to reject is founded upon the hypothesis that the seller was not ready and willing to perform, or had not performed his part of the contract. The tender of a wrong quantity does evidence an unreadiness and unwillingness, but that, in my opinion, must mean an excess or deficiency in quantity which is capable of influencing the mind of the buyer. This excess is not. I agree that directly the excess becomes a matter of possible discussion between reasonable parties, the seller is bound to justify what he has done under the contract, but the doctrine *de minimis* cannot, I think, be excluded merely because the statute refers to the tender of a smaller or larger quantity than the contract quantity as entitling a buyer to reject.

I wish to add this: The reason why an excess in tender entitles a buyer to reject is that the seller seeks to impose a burden on the buyer which he is not entitled to impose.

---

[84] (1901), 6 Com. Cas. 113.
[85] *Ibid.*, at p. 116.

That burden is the payment of money not due. It is, *prima facie*, no burden on the buyer to have 55 lb. more than he wanted offered to him, and there is nothing to suggest that the sellers here would have ever insisted or thought of insisting upon payment of the 4s. over the £40,000. The sellers' original appropriation was, as I have pointed out, within the quantity, accepting Mr Maurice Hill's contention, which, as I have said is the right one, as to the meaning of the quantity clause. The 55 lb. appears when they have converted the quantity shipped from kilos into tons. It only appears in the provisional invoice, and the buyers rejected, as I have said, before they actually received the document. If the sellers had expressly or impliedly insisted upon payment of the 4s. and asserted their view of the contract, and insisted on the right to have it agreed to, the case would have been different, but nothing of that kind can be supposed to have taken place here.

For these reasons I think that the second question must be answered in the affirmative.

Ebrahim Dawood Ltd. *v*. Heath (Estd. 1927) Ltd.

[1961] 2 Lloyd's Rep. 512

By s. 30(4): "*Where the seller delivers to the buyer the goods he contracted to sell mixed with goods of a different description not included in the contract, the buyer may accept the goods which are in accordance with the contract and reject the rest, or he may reject the whole*".

The sellers agreed to sell to the buyers 50 tons of galvanised steel sheets "assorted over six, seven, eight, nine and 10 feet long". The buyers paid the whole of the purchase price in advance. When the sheets arrived, it was discovered that the whole of the 50 tons consisted of six-foot lengths. The buyers claimed that under s. 30(4) they were entitled to accept one-fifth of the consignment, and to recover four-fifths of the purchase price as money paid on a consideration which had wholly failed.

Held, by the Queen's Bench Division (Commercial Court), that they were entitled to do so, and that they were not restricted to claiming damages alone.

McNair, J. (at page 518)

The next point is whether the plaintiffs' right to recover the money which they have paid in advance . . . in respect of four-fifths of the contract weight, which was . . . not delivered in accordance with the contract, stands as a claim to recover the money as paid to the use of the plaintiffs, or paid for a consideration which has wholly failed. The contrary view is that the remedy only stands in damages so that if . . . the market price at the time of the delivery conformed to £70 against the contract price of £73 10s. 0d., there would be recovered on this argument only £70 per ton, leaving a profit of £3 10s. 0d. in the pockets of the seller.

Oddly enough . . . there is no express decision as to the nature of the right of recovery of money paid in advance where the buyer elects to operate s. [30(4)], and take part of the goods which are in accordance with the contract, and reject the balance. There is abundant authority on a very similar stipulation arising under s. 30(1). . . .

Now there are cases where the payment of the contract price has been made in advance for a total contracted number of articles, and there has then been failure by the seller to deliver the whole of these contracted quantities. In those circumstances, it is clear on the authority to which I shall refer in a moment, that the buyer's right of recovering so much of the purchase price as relates to the quantity short delivered, is a right to recover money paid to his use or money paid for a consideration which has wholly failed.

The modern case on that topic is the decision of BAILHACHE, J., in the case of *Behrend & Co. Ltd.* v. *Produce Brokers' Co. Ltd.*,[86] where there had been a short delivery of cotton-seed. The buyers kept so much of the seed as had been delivered to them and demanded repayment of so much of the contract price as represented the seed undelivered. After discussing how this right to take part is to be exercised, the learned Judge says:[87]

> "If this is so, the rest of the case is covered by s. 30 of the Sale of Goods Act, and the buyer can either reject the whole of the goods, including those actually delivered, in which case he can recover the whole of his money; or he may keep the goods actually delivered and reject the rest, in which case he must pay for the goods kept at the contract price, and he can recover the price paid for the undelivered portion".

I think it is quite plain on [the] authorities, at any rate, when one is considering the recovery of money under s. 30(1), that a short delivery has been made. The claim is quite clearly a claim for recovery of money had and received. The same principle seems to me also to be applicable to a case under sub-s. [(4)]. There, too, payment of the price has been made in advance, and part of the goods delivered are properly rejected. The buyers' right to recover that part of the purchase price which relates to the goods so properly rejected, is clearly a right of the same nature, namely, the right to recover money for a consideration which has wholly failed and which, accordingly, must be regarded as money paid to the buyers' use.

---

[86] [1920] All E.R. Rep. 125, p. 73, *ante*.
[87] *Ibid.*, at p. 128.

(2) INSTALMENT DELIVERIES

Maple Flock Co. Ltd. *v.* Universal Furniture Products (Wembley) Ltd.

[1933] All E.R. Rep. 15

By s. 31(2): "Where there is a contract for the sale of goods to be delivered by stated instalments, which are to be separately paid for, and the seller makes defective deliveries in respect of one or more instalments . . . it is a question in each case depending on the terms of the contract and the circumstances of the case whether the breach of contract is a repudiation of the whole contract or whether it is a severable breach giving rise to a claim for compensation but not to a right to treat the whole contract as repudiated".

The sellers agreed to supply the buyers with 100 tons of flock by instalments. The first 15 deliveries of $1\frac{1}{2}$ tons each were satisfactory, but when a sample was analysed, the 16th delivery was found to contain considerably more parts of chlorine in it than was allowed under the contract. There was no reasonable probability that any future deliveries would be defective, and four later deliveries which were made were satisfactory. The buyers sought to repudiate the contract.

Held, by the Court of Appeal, that they were not entitled to do so, for under s. 31(2) the defective delivery did not amount to a repudiation by the sellers of the whole contract.

LORD HEWART, C.J. (at page 17)

The decision of this case depends on the true construction and application of s. 31(2) of the Sale of Goods Act . . .. That sub-section was based on decisions before the Act, and has been the subject of decisions since the Act. A contract for the sale of goods by instalments is a single contract, not a complex of as many contracts as there are instalments under it. The law might have been determined in the sense that any breach of condition in respect of any one or more instalments would entitle the party aggrieved to claim that the contract has been repudiated as a whole; or, on the other hand, the law as established might have been that any breach, however serious, in respect of one or more instalments, should not have consequences extending beyond the particular instalment or instalments or affecting the contract as a whole. The sub-section, however, which deals equally with breaches either by the buyer or by the seller, requires the Court to decide on the merits of the particular case what effect (if any) the breach or breaches should have on the contract as a whole. . . . With the help of [the] authorities[88] we deduce that the main tests to be considered in applying the sub-section to the present case, are, first, the ratio quantitatively which the breach bears to the contract as a whole, and secondly, the degree of probability or improbability that such a breach will be repeated. On the first point, the delivery complained

---

[88] *Mersey Steel & Iron Co. Ltd.* v. *Naylor, Benzon & Co.* (1884), 9 App. Cas. 434; *Freeth* v. *Burr* (1874), L.R. 9 C.P. 208; *Hoare* v. *Rennie* (1859), 5 H. & N. 19; *Millar's Karri & Jarrah Co.* (1902) Ltd. v. *Weddel, Turner & Co.* (1908), 100 L.T. 128; *Robert A. Munro & Co. Ltd.* v. *Meyer*, [1930] 2 K.B. 312.

of amounts to no more than $1\frac{1}{2}$ tons out of a contract for 100 tons. On the second point, our conclusion is that the chance of the breach being repeated is practically negligible. We assume that the sample found defective fairly represents the bulk; but bearing in mind . . . that the breach was extraordinary and that the sellers' business was carefully conducted, bearing in mind also that the sellers were warned, and that the delivery complained of was an isolated instance out of 20 satisfactory deliveries actually made both before and after the instalment objected to, we hold that it cannot be reasonably inferred that similar breaches would occur in regard to subsequent deliveries. . . . There may, indeed, be . . . cases where the consequences of a single breach of contract may be so serious as to involve a frustration of the contract and justify rescission, or, furthermore, the contract might contain an express condition that a breach would justify rescission, in which case effect would be given to such a condition by the Court. But none of these circumstances can be predicated of this case. We think the deciding factor here is the extreme improbability of the breach being repeated, and on that ground, and on the isolated and limited character of the breach complained of, there was, in our judgment, no sufficient justification to entitle the [buyers] to refuse further deliveries as they did.

(3) Buyer's Right of Examining the Goods

Saunt *v.* Belcher & Gibbons Ltd.

[1920] All E.R. Rep. 142

Usually the place of delivery is the place where the buyer must examine the goods.

The sellers agreed to deliver a quantity of coke to the buyers at Deptford. They knew that the buyers were going to ship it on from there to France. It would have been possible for the coke to have been inspected at Deptford, but the buyers did not do so.

Held, by the King's Bench Division, that the place of delivery, i.e., Deptford, was the place for inspection. In order to postpone the place of inspection the seller must know that the goods were being sent on to a further destination, and also the place of delivery must be unsuitable in itself or the nature or packing of the goods must make inspection at that place unreasonable.

BAILHACHE, J. (at page 143)

It is argued that, because the sellers knew that the breeze was to go to France, the place of examination and acceptance must be extended from Deptford, the place where the sellers were to deliver the goods, to France. In support of this contention, *Van den Hurk* v. *R. Martens & Co. Ltd.*[89] was cited as showing that where goods are

---

[89] [1920] 1 K.B. 850.

sold by a seller who has to deliver them at a destination which to his knowledge is not their final destination, but only a place from which there is to be a further transit, the place of inspection and acceptance is removed from the place at which the seller has to make his delivery to the place which is the ultimate destination of the goods. But that proposition is not universally true. It depends upon whether the place at which the seller has to deliver the goods, although it is not the ultimate destination of the goods, is a place where, having regard to the nature of the goods and the way in which they are packed, inspection can reasonably be had. In *Van den Hurk* v. *R. Martens & Co. Ltd.* I referred to both those points, but counsel for the buyer treats that case as an authority for his proposition that it is sufficient that the original vendor should know that the place of delivery is not the final destination of the goods. But the other point which I also stated in that case is equally essential. In *Van den Hurk* v. *R. Martens & Co. Ltd.* the goods being sodium sulphide packed in drums, I came to the conclusion that, with goods of that description, packed in that manner, when it was known that they were to be sent abroad, it was not reasonable to suppose that the drums were to be opened and the goods inspected at the place where the original vendor was to deliver. In my opinion, in order to postpone the place for inspection, it is essential that the two elements already mentioned should be present. First, the original vendor must know that the goods are going to another destination and, secondly, the place at which the original vendor is to deliver the goods must either be unsuitable in itself or the nature or packing of the goods must make inspection at that place unreasonable. Applying those two principles to the present case, I find that although the sellers knew that the goods were to go to France, yet the place at which the sellers were to deliver the goods, and the nature of the goods were such as that inspection could quite reasonably have been had at Deptford, the sellers' place of delivery.

(4) Delivery to Carrier

Thomas Young & Sons Ltd. *v.* Hobson

(1949), 65 T.L.R. 365

By s. 32(2): "Unless otherwise authorised by the buyer, the seller must make such contract with the carrier on behalf of the buyer as may be reasonable having regard to the nature of the goods and the other circumstances of the case; and if the seller omits so to do, and the goods are lost or damaged in course of transit, the buyer may decline to treat the delivery to the carrier as a delivery to himself or may hold the seller responsible in damages".

The plaintiffs were shipbreakers and sold to the defendants some electric engines from a ship which was being broken up. The engines were to be sent by rail from Sunderland to Leighton Buzzard, but the parties said nothing as to whether they were to be consigned at "owners' risk" or at the "railway company's risk". The plaintiffs sent them at "owners' risk", and on arrival the engines were found to have been seriously damaged, for they had not been firmly secured on the railway wagons on which they had been loaded. The plaintiffs claimed the price from the defendants, but the defendants refused to pay and declined to treat the delivery to the railway company as delivery to themselves on the ground that the plaintiffs had not made a reasonable contract with the railway company for the carriage of the engines, as required by s. 32(2).

Held, by the Court of Appeal, that the plaintiffs had not made a reasonable contract with the railway company, and that the defendants were not liable to pay the price.

TUCKER, L.J. (at page 366)

The evidence from the railway witnesses showed that with regard to this class of goods, which are classified as "damageable goods", there is no difference in the freight rates as between "owners' risk" and "company's risk", but before accepting such goods at company's risk they would require to inspect the packing. Mr Shroeder, the chief railway forwarding clerk at Sunderland, called by the plaintiffs, and not cross-examined, said that if suitably secured, they would be accepted at company's risk. Mr Chibnall, railway goods' agent at Leighton Buzzard, said: "We should have accepted them at company's risk if they had been properly packed by wooden battens in the wagons". Recalled, he said: "In my experience practically all machinery because of its value is sent at company's risk without any exception as far as I know".

That being the uncontradicted evidence from the railway witnesses, Mr Young, in his evidence, stated that, in the absence of specific instructions to the contrary, it was his custom to send at owners' risk. He said: "It is the general thing when consigning anything in anyone's name to put 'owners' risk' ". His invariable practice was to dispatch goods of this kind in open trucks properly secured by lashing. It is not necessary to consider what would be a reasonable contract in the case of goods secured in this manner. In the present case the plaintiffs had agreed to put the goods in box wagons, and the question is whether it was reasonable to send goods of this nature unsecured at owners' risk when they could have been sent at the same cost at company's risk, subject to inspection by the railway officials, who would, in a case like this, have required that the engines be properly secured by means of battens. We cannot think that such a requirement would have placed an unreasonable burden on the plaintiffs, and in all the circumstances we are of opinion that, on the evidence adduced at the trial, the defendants succeeded in showing that the plaintiffs had failed in their duty under s. 32(2) . . . to make such a contract with the carrier on behalf of the buyer as was reasonable having regard to the nature of the goods and the other circumstances of the case, and that the defendants were accordingly entitled to decline to treat the delivery to the railway company as delivery to them.

(5) ACCEPTANCE

Bragg *v.* Villanova

(1923), 40 T.L.R. 154

By s. 34(1): *"Where goods are delivered to the buyer and he has not previously examined them, he is not deemed to have accepted them until he has had a reasonable opportunity of examining them for the purpose of ascertaining whether they are in conformity with the contract".*

The plaintiff purchased from the defendant a quantity of Spanish walnuts f.o.b. Tarragona for delivery in England. The shipping documents arrived in England before the goods, and the plaintiff paid the price. When the goods arrived, the plaintiff discovered that they were not satisfactory, so claimed that he was entitled (i) to reject them under s. 34(1) for he could not be deemed to have accepted them for he had not had a reasonable opportunity of examining them for the purpose of ascertaining whether they were in conformity with the contract; and (ii) to recover the price. The defendant contended that the plaintiff had lost the right to reject the goods because he ought to have examined them at the port of shipment.

Held, by the Divisional Court of the King's Bench Division, that the right of rejection had not been lost for, in the circumstances, the plaintiff had not had a reasonable opportunity of examining the goods.

LORD HEWART, L.C.J. (at page 154)

By s. 34(1) of the Sale of Goods Act . . ., a buyer must not be deemed to have accepted goods until he had had a reasonable opportunity of examining them to see whether they conformed with the contract, and the case of *Molling* v. *Dean*[90] showed that what was reasonable must depend on the circumstances. In that case goods had been supplied by the plaintiffs in Germany to the defendants in England, the plaintiffs knowing that the defendants required the goods for sale in America. Without inspecting the goods, the defendants sent them to America, and the ultimate purchasers there found that they were not of the contract quality. It was held that in those circumstances America was the proper place for inspection. Applying the principle of that case here, the answer to the question of the arbitrator must be that the defendant had not lost the right of rejection by omitting to have the goods examined at the port of shipment.

---

[90] (1902), 18 T.L.R. 217.

Chao v. British Traders & Shippers Ltd. (N.V. Handelsmaatschappij J. Smits Import-Export, Third Party)

[1954] 1 All E.R. 779

The mere pledge of documents tendered by the seller under a c.i.f. contract does not amount to an "acceptance" of the goods within the meaning of s. 35.

(For the facts of this case see *post*, p. 152).

Held (*obiter*), by the Queen's Bench Division, that when a buyer under a c.i.f. contract deals only with the documents tendered to him, e.g., by pledging them with a bank, such an act does not amount to "an act in relation to [the goods] which is inconsistent with the ownership of the seller" within the meaning of s. 35, and does not constitute an "acceptance" of the goods.

DEVLIN, J. (at page 794)

One of the matters which was, therefore, canvassed in the course of the argument was whether the plaintiffs, by pledging the documents to their bank, as they did immediately on receipt of them, had not, in any event, dealt with the goods in such a way as to amount to an acceptance under s. 35 and had thereby lost their right to reject. On the view which I have taken, this point no longer arises. What I have to say about it is, therefore, merely *obiter dictum*, but, in view of the fact that it is a matter of some importance and that I have had considerable assistance from the researches of counsel for the defendants on the point, I think it desirable that I should state, if only so that those who may be concerned in the matter in the future may know that the problem arises and has to be solved, what I think is the right answer to it. Clearly, it would create a great deal of embarrassment and inconvenience in the ordinary forms of credit in these transactions if the normal act of pledging goods to the bank, which is done in 99 cases out of 100, meant that the buyer had lost his right to reject. Yet, on the face of it, it seems that by pledging the goods he is doing an act inconsistent with the ownership of the seller, which amounts to an acceptance under s. 35. There appears to have been no litigation on the point and no authority, probably because all parties find when this sort of point arises that it is better to leave well alone, and, as the principles in relation to this point work very well in practice, there is no reason why they should be elucidated. . . .

". . . when the goods have been delivered to him, and he does any act in relation to them which is inconsistent with the ownership of the seller . . .".

Counsel for the defendants contended that in the phrase in s. 35, the word "delivered" means physical delivery of the goods from the ship. If that were so, no dealing with the documents would be within the meaning of the section, because all such dealings would have been done before the goods had been delivered. I cannot take that view of it. I think that "delivery" means, as s. [61(1)] of the Act defines it, a "voluntary transfer of possession", and, therefore, it means transfer of possession under the contract of sale. In a c.i.f. contract the goods are delivered, so far as they are physically delivered, when they are put on board a ship at the port of shipment. The documents are delivered when they are tendered. A buyer, who, as it is convenient, takes delivery from the ship at the port of destination, is not taking delivery of the goods under the contract of sale but is merely taking delivery out of his own warehouse, as it were, by the presentation of the document of title to the goods, the master of the ship having been his bailee ever since he became entitled to the bill of lading.

I think that the true answer may be found rather differently. In *Hardy & Co.* v. *Hillerns & Fowler*[91] ATKIN, L.J., dealt with the situation, which is always a little puzzling, under a c.i.f. contract, viz., if the property passes when the documents are handed over, by what legal machinery, so to speak, does the buyer retain a right, as he undoubtedly does, to examine the goods when they arrive and to reject them if they are not in conformity with the contract? ATKIN, L.J., put forward two views for consideration. One was that, notwithstanding that the documents had been tendered, the property in the goods did not pass until the goods had been examined or until an opportunity for examination had been given. The other was that it passed, but only conditionally, at the time when the documents were tendered, and that it could be re-vested if the buyer properly rejected the goods. Counsel for the defendants said (and I think this is true) that, for the first of the two views which ATKIN, L.J., put forward, no other authority can be found, and it would, clearly, create considerable complications. If the property in the goods has not passed to him, how can the buyer pledge? It would provide a simple answer to the point had it arisen in this case, since there could not be a pledge. I think the true view is that, when the documents of title are given to the buyer, he obtains the property in the goods, subject to the condition that they re-vest if on examination he finds them not in accordance with the contract. That means that he gets only conditional property in the goods, the condition being a condition subsequent. All his dealings with the documents are dealings only with that conditional property in the goods. It follows, therefore, that there can be no dealing that is inconsistent with the seller's ownership unless the buyer deals with something more than the conditional property. If the property passed outright, not subject to any condition, there would be no ownership left in the seller with which any inconsistent act within s. 35 could be committed. If the property passes conditionally, the only ownership left in the seller is, so to speak, the reversionary interest in the property in the event of the condition subsequent operating to restore it to him. It is that reversionary interest with which the buyer must not, save with the penalty of accepting the goods, commit an inconsistent act. So long as he is merely dealing with the

---

[91] [1923] All E.R. Rep. 275, C.A.

documents, he is not purporting to do anything more than pledge the conditional property which he has got. Similarly, if he sells the documents of title, he sells the conditional property. But if, as was done in *Hardy & Co.* v. *Hillerns & Fowler*,[92] he physically deals with the goods when they have been landed and delivers them to his sub-buyer, he is doing an act which is inconsistent with the seller's reversionary interest. The seller's reversionary interest entitles him immediately on the operation of the condition subsequent, i.e., as soon as opportunity for examination has been given, to have the goods physically returned to him in the place where the examination has taken place and without being dispatched to third parties. The dispatch to a third party is an act, therefore, which interferes with the reversionary interest, but, if the view which I have expressed be the right view, neither a pledge of the goods nor a sale of documents, such as takes place on the ordinary string contract, interferes with that interest. I observe that the view expressed in *Halsbury*,[93] in the passage which I have read, seems to be that the transfer of the bill of lading to a third party would be inconsistent with s. 35. I prefer to take the view that neither of them is inconsistent for the reasons which I have given. They stand on the same level and they are both dealing merely with conditional property. It would, I think, be unsatisfactory if a Court had to decide, every time there was a string of contracts, that, as soon as the documents had been passed to the first in the string with the intention to pass title in the property, the right to reject was thereby lost. It might further be suggested that in any event, in the circumstances of this case, the buyer, having pledged the goods to a banker, was not in a position to reject, because it was his banker who exercised dominion over them by reason of the pledge. That, again, raises a question of some theoretical difficulty: Can a buyer, in effect, defeat a pledge by exercising his right of rejection? One view might be that, although the property is conditional property, i.e., subject to a condition subsequent, he cannot defeat the pledge by his own voluntary act in putting the condition subsequent into operation. The other view would be that it cannot have been contemplated that, when the buyer pledged the documents, he was intending to abandon or impair his right of rejection. It would certainly be very far from the circumstances of this case, in the course which the argument has taken, if I should express any view on that. It is merely a matter to which attention might be paid by those who are concerned with it. Obviously, the banker, in drafting his letter of credit or his instructions, can impose what condition he likes, and it may be that in those matters prevention is better than cure, at any rate, if the cure involves litigation.

---

[92] *Supra.*
[93] *Laws of England* (2nd Edn.), Vol. 29, p. 224, par. 297

E. RIGHTS OF UNPAID SELLER AGAINST THE GOODS

(1) MEANING OF "UNPAID SELLER"

J. L. Lyons & Co. *v.* May & Baker

(1923), 129 L.T. 413

Where a buyer has paid for the goods and then rightly rejects them, but continues in possession of them, he is not in the position of an "unpaid seller" within the meaning of s. 38(1). He cannot therefore claim to have a lien on them until the price has been repaid to him.

Lyons & Co. sold a quantity of citric acid crystals to Poulot, who in turn resold them to May & Baker. The goods were not of the contract quality, so Lyons & Co. agreed to take them back, and refunded the price to Poulot. Poulot gave a cheque to May & Baker, but this was dishonoured, so May & Baker claimed that they were in the position of an "unpaid seller" within the meaning of s. 38, and consequently were entitled to a lien in respect of the goods which they refused to hand over to Lyons & Co. until the price had been paid.

Held, by the King's Bench Division, that this contention failed, and that Lyons & Co. were entitled to the goods.

SHEARMAN, J. (at page 414)

In my opinion this action is well founded. It is quite clear that on the rejection of the crystals by the defendants, and also by Poulot, and the acceptance by the plaintiffs of the rejections, the property in those goods revested in the plaintiffs, apart altogether from the document given by the defendants' solicitors to Poulot. Therefore the plaintiffs had a right to demand possession of the goods from the defendants, and having made the demand for the possession of their own goods and that possession having been refused by the defendants, their right to bring an action for conversion arose. It has been contended that a buyer who has rejected goods which he has paid for, and who has not been repaid the money which he has paid for the goods, has a right to retain possession of the goods until he has received his money back, in the same way as a vendor, who has received a cheque as a conditional payment, but which has been dishonoured, has a right to stop the goods *in transitu,* or, if he is in possession of the goods, to a lien on them for the price. I, however, cannot find that there is any foundation for such a right at common law.

There is certainly no such right under the Sale of Goods Act . . ., unless I am prepared to hold, and I am not going to make new law, that a person in the same position as the defendants comes within s. 38 of the Sale of Goods Act . . ., which, after defining an unpaid seller, includes within the term "seller" "any person who is in the position of a seller, as, for instance, an agent of the seller".

I am unable to say that a person who has bought and paid for, and afterwards rejected goods, is a person like an unpaid seller. Neither am I impressed by what I consider the entirely false analogy with regard to the lien of a purchaser for the deposit on the sale of real property, because a deposit paid on the sale of real property is a thing *sui generis*.

(2) Effect of Sub-Sale or Pledge by Buyer

D. F. Mount Ltd. *v.* Jay & Jay (Provisions) Co. Ltd.

[1959] 3 All E.R. 307

By s. 47(1): ". . . The unpaid seller's right of lien . . . is not affected by any sale or other disposition of the goods which the buyer may have made, unless the seller has assented to it". Such an "assent" must show that the seller intends to renounce his rights against the goods.

The buyers purchased 500 cartons of tinned peaches and left them at the wharf of a storage company. They sold 250 of them to Merrick for resale to one of his customers. Merrick told the buyers that they would be paid with the money which he received from the sub-purchasers. The buyers then sent him delivery orders which he forwarded to the storage company. They sold 250 of them to Merrick for resale to one of his customers. delivery order. The buyers were never paid, so they claimed that they had a lien over the goods.

Held, by the Queen's Bench Division, that the buyers had "assented" to the sale of the cartons by Merrick, within the meaning of s. 47(1), and so were not entitled to a lien.

Salmon, J. (at page 310)

The plaintiffs first rely on s. 47(1) of the Sale of Goods Act . . . , which reads as follows:

"Subject to this Act, the unpaid seller's right of lien or retention or stoppage *in transitu* is not affected by any sale, or other disposition of the goods which the buyer may have made, unless the seller has assented [to it]".

There is a proviso to the section, with which I shall deal in a moment. The plaintiffs contend that the defendants assented to the sale or disposition of the 250 cartons by Mr Merrick to the plaintiffs, and thereby lost their right as unpaid sellers to the lien which they would otherwise have had on the cartons. The defendants contend that if they assented to the sub-sale by Mr Merrick, their assent was not an assent within the meaning of s. [47(1)], and rely on *Mordaunt Brothers* v. *British Oil & Cake Mills Ltd.*[94] It is clear from the judgment of Pickford, J.,[95] that the assent contemplated by s. 47 means:

---

[94] [1910] 2 K.B. 502.
[95] *Ibid.*, at p. 507.

"an assent given in such circumstances as show that the unpaid seller intends that the sub-contract shall be carried out irrespective of the terms of the original contract"

and must be:

"such an assent as in the circumstances shows that the seller intends to renounce his rights against the goods".

PICKFORD, J., held that there had been no such assent on the part of the sellers. The facts of that case are, however, very different from those of the present case. There the sellers had at no time any reason to doubt the buyer's ability to pay, and were not informed of the sub-sale until after the sale was effected. PICKFORD, J., held that the sellers had assented to the sub-sale merely in the sense that they acknowledged its existence and the right of the sub-buyer to have the goods subject to their own paramount rights under the contract with the original buyer to hold the goods until paid the purchase price.

In the present case the defendants were anxious to get rid of the goods on a falling market. They knew that Mr Merrick could only pay for them out of the money he obtained from his customers, and that he could only obtain the money from his customers against delivery orders in favour of those customers. In my view, the true inference is that the defendants assented to Mr Merrick reselling the goods, in the sense that they intended to renounce their rights against the goods and to take the risk of Mr Merrick's honesty. The defendants are reputable merchants and I am sure that it was not their intention to get rid of their goods on a falling market through Mr Merrick on the basis that if he defaulted, they could hold the goods against the customers from whom he obtained the money out of which they were to be paid.

The sale of the 250 cartons was a sale of unascertained goods. In my judgment, however, there is no reason why s. [47(1)] of the Act . . . should not apply to unascertained goods, although I respectfully agree with PICKFORD, J.,[96] that an inference can in some circumstances more readily be drawn against the seller in the case of a sale of specific goods than in the case of a sale of unascertained goods.

I hold that the defendants assented to the sale of the cartons by Mr Merrick within the meaning of s. [47(1)].

---

[95] *Ibid.,* at p. 506.

Ant. Jurgens Margarinefabrieken *v.* Louis Dreyfus & Co.

(1914), 111 L.T. 248

By s. 47(2): "*Where a document of title to goods has been lawfully transferred to any person as buyer or owner of the goods, and that person transfers the document to a person who takes it in good faith and for valuable consideration, then (a) if such last-mentioned transfer was by way of sale the unpaid seller's right of lien ... is defeated ...*".

The owners of a consignment of 6,400 bags of mowra seed sold 2,640 of them to Finkler & Co. and gave them a delivery order. Finkler & Co. sent them a cheque for the purchase price, and endorsed the delivery order to sub-purchasers. The cheque was dishonoured, and the owners refused to deliver the seed to the sub-purchasers. They claimed that they had an unpaid seller's lien under s. 38, and that it was not defeated in this case by s. 47(2), because here there were not two "transfers" of the delivery order, as required by that section, for the word "transfer" could not be applied to the issue of the delivery order by them to Finkler & Co.

Held, by the King's Bench Division, that the lien was defeated. The meaning of the word "transfer" could not be narrowed in this way.

PICKFORD, J. (at page 249)

It was then argued on behalf of the defendants that the delivery orders were not documents of title within the meaning of the Factors Act 1889 and the Sale of Goods Act ... because they were created by the defendants themselves, and that as the documents did not come to them from someone else, they could not be transferred by the defendants to Finkler & Co. In my opinion, a delivery order is none the less a document of title because it is created by the owner of the goods. It would be a curious result if the document by which the owner gets a title can, if passed on by him, give a title to someone else, but that a document created by himself cannot give a title when passed on because it is not a transfer, but only a delivery or issue. Therefore, I cannot narrow the meaning of the word "transfer" in the way suggested. It seems to me that the delivery orders in this case were documents created by the defendants, the owners of the goods, for the purpose of transferring the title to the goods, and the handing of these to Finkler & Co. was a transfer of the documents just as much as if they had come into existence by the act of someone other than the defendants, and had been handed to the defendants, and by them handed on. If that is so, it concludes the case, because I have no doubt that Finkler & Co. were either the buyers or mercantile agents for the buyers, and they transferred the documents of title to the plaintiffs, who took them in good faith and for valuable consideration.

(3) RESALE BY SELLER

The "Bineta"

[1966] 2 Lloyd's Rep. 419

By s. 48(2): "Where an unpaid seller who has exercised his right of lien . . . resells the goods, the buyer acquires a good title thereto as against the original buyer".

A yacht was sold by a Miss Simmonds to a Mr Garthwaite in June, 1963, and was registered in his name. He defaulted in the payment of the purchase price, and she retained possession of the yacht in exercise of her unpaid seller's lien. In March, 1965, she sold her to a Mr Dalby. Mr Dalby sought a declaration that he was the owner and was entitled to be registered as such in place of Mr Garthwaite under the Merchant Shipping Act 1894 because Miss Simmonds could vest a good title in him under s. 48(2).

Held, by the Probate, Divorce and Admiralty Division, that the declaration would be made accordingly.

BRANDON, J. (at page 420)

I consider that Miss Simmonds had power to resell the ship under the Sale of Goods Act '. . . . The plaintiff acquired a good title from the bill of sale which she gave him. He is, therefore, the owner of the ship and is entitled to be registered as such under the Merchant Shipping Act 1894.

R. V. Ward Ltd. *v.* Bignall

[1967] 2 All E.R. 449

By s. 48(3): "Where the goods are of a perishable nature or where the unpaid seller gives notice to the buyer of his intention to resell, and the buyer does not within a reasonable time pay or tender the price, the unpaid seller may resell the goods and recover from the original buyer damages for any loss occasioned by his breach of contract". If the seller resells under s. 48(3), the contract of sale is rescinded, and he cannot recover the purchase price, but only damages for any loss sustained by the buyer's default.

On 6th May, 1965, the seller sold to the buyer a Vanguard car and a Zodiac for £850. The buyer paid a deposit of £25, but then refused to pay the balance. The seller's solicitors immediately wrote to the buyer stating that if he did not pay the balance by 11th May, the seller would try to resell the cars. The buyer failed to pay, and on 24th May the seller sold the Vanguard for £350, but could not find a purchaser for the Zodiac. The seller now claimed the balance of the total purchase price, i.e., £475 and advertising expenses of £22 10s.

Held, by the Court of Appeal, that the resale of the Vanguard rescinded the contract of sale. The seller could not recover the price of the Zodiac, which in the circumstances was his property, but only the loss sustained by the buyer's default. The value of the Zodiac was £450, so the loss was £25. This could be claimed together with the advertising expenses of £22 10s.

SELLERS, L.J. (at page 452)

Sub-section (1) and sub-s. (2) speak clearly. Sub-section (4) expressly provides "the original contract of sale is thereby rescinded". That was necessary because where the seller "expressly reserves a right of sale in case the buyer should make default", a seller who resells under such a contract would be applying and affirming the contract and his action would be consistent with it. Under sub-s. (3) no such provision of rescission is necessary, for if an unpaid seller resells, he puts it out of his power to perform his contract and his action is inconsistent with a subsisting sale to the original buyer. Once there is a resale in accordance with s. 48 by an unpaid seller in possession of the contractual goods the contract of sale is rescinded, whether the sale be of the whole of the goods or a part, and in this respect sub-s. (3) and sub-s. (4) fall into line. As the property in the goods reverts on such a resale, the seller retains the proceeds of sale whether they be greater or less than the contractual price. The probability in normal trade is that the price would be less and give rise to a claim for damages, as for non-acceptance of the goods. . . . The express reservation in a contract would permit the unpaid seller to sell without acting inconsistently or in conflict with his obligations. His conduct would not evidence a rescission by him on the buyer's breach. Nevertheless sub-s. (4) makes the resale operate as a rescission and leaves the remedy, if any loss ensues, in damages. This brings it into harmony with sub-s. (3), which also gives a claim for damages for any loss occasioned by the original buyer's breach of contract. If the unpaid seller resells the goods, he puts it out of his power to perform his obligation under the original contract, that is, to deliver the contractual goods to the buyer. By the notice to the buyer the seller makes payment of the price "the essence of the contract", as it is sometimes put. It requires the buyer to pay the price or tender it within a reasonable time. If he fails, the seller in possession of the goods may treat the bargain as rescinded and sell the goods. The suit for damages becomes comparable to a claim for damages for non-acceptance of the goods where the property never has passed. The property has reverted on the sale and the second buyer gets a good title. The seller resells as owner. Sub-section (2) expressly gives the buyer a good title thereto as against the original buyer.

On this view of the law the seller cannot recover the price of the Zodiac, which is in the circumstances its property. It can, however, recover any loss which it has sustained by the buyer's default. The parties have sensibly agreed that the value of the Zodiac in May, 1965, was £450. The total contract price was £850, against which the seller had received £25 in cash, £350 for the Vanguard, and has to give credit for £450 for the Zodiac. To the loss of £25 must be added the sum for advertising, which was admittedly reasonably incurred—£22 10s. The seller's loss was therefore £47 10s.

F. ACTIONS FOR BREACH OF THE CONTRACT

(1) DAMAGES FOR NON-ACCEPTANCE

Charter *v.* Sullivan

[1957] 1 All E.R. 809

As regards damages for non-acceptance, s. 50(2) states that: "The measure of damages is the estimated loss directly and naturally resulting, in the ordinary course of events, from the buyer's breach of contract".

When Hillman Minx cars were in short supply, a motor car dealer agreed to sell such a car to the defendant for £773 15s., the retail price fixed by the manufacturers. The defendant did not pay the purchase price, so the dealer resold the car to a third party. The dealer now claimed damages (amounting to £97 15s.), which he stated was the loss of profit which he would have made if he had sold the car to the defendant as well as a similar car to the third party.

Held, by the Court of Appeal, that the dealer was entitled to nominal damages of 40s. only. Section 50(2) stated that the buyer was only responsible for the loss directly and naturally resulting from the breach of contract. The seller had not proved a loss of profit, as he had sold the same number of cars as he would have done if the sale had been completed.

Held (obiter), that there could not be an "available market" for goods within the meaning of s. 50(3) unless their price was fixed with reference to supply and demand. Section 50(3) could therefore not apply.

JENKINS, L.J. (at page 811)

Counsel for the defendant argued that in the present case there was an available market for Hillman Minx de luxe saloon cars within the meaning of s. 50(3) of the Act, and accordingly that the measure of damages ought, in accordance with the *prima facie* rule laid down by that sub-section, to be ascertained by the difference between the contract price and the market or current price at the time of the defendant's refusal to perform his contract. The result of this argument, if accepted, would be that the plaintiff could claim no more than nominal damages, because the market or current price could only be the fixed retail price, which was necessarily likewise the price at which he sold to the defendant and resold to [the third party].

The plaintiff, however, is a motor car dealer whose trade for the present purpose can be described as consisting in the purchase of recurrent supplies of cars of the relevant description from the manufacturers, and selling the cars so obtained, or as many of them as he can, at the fixed retail price. He thus receives, on each sale that he is able to effect, the predetermined profit allowed by the fixed retail price, and it is obviously in his interest to sell as many cars as he can obtain from the manufacturers.

The number of sales that he can effect, and consequently the amount of profit which he makes, will be governed, according to the state of trade, either by the number of cars that he is able to obtain from the manufacturers, or by the number of purchasers whom he is able to find. In the former case demand exceeds supply, so that the default of one purchaser involves him in no loss, for he sells the same number of cars as he would have sold if that purchaser had not defaulted. In the latter case supply exceeds demand, so that the default of one purchaser may be said to have lost him one sale.

Accordingly, it seems to me that, even if there was within the meaning of s. 50(3) an available market for cars of the description in question, and even if the fixed retail price was the market or current price within the meaning of the same sub-section, the *prima facie* rule which it prescribes should be rejected in favour of the general rule laid down by sub-s. (2); for it does not by any means necessarily follow that, because the plaintiff sold at the fixed retail price to [the third party] the car which the defendant had agreed to buy at the self-same fixed retail price, but refused to take, therefore the plaintiff suffered no "loss directly and naturally resulting, in the ordinary course of events" from the defendant's breach of contract.

This makes it strictly unnecessary to decide whether there was in the present case an available market for cars of the description in question within the meaning of s. 50(3). But I would find it difficult to hold that there was. Given default by some purchaser of one of his cars of the relevant description, the plaintiff's only alternative mode of disposal would be to sell it at the fixed retail price to some other purchaser. He could endeavour to find another purchaser by displaying the car in his saleroom, circularising or canvassing old customers or the public at large, and advertising by posters or in newspapers. The car would obviously be of interest to retail customers only (i.e., the car-using public as distinct from the trade) and any purchaser he might succeed in finding would necessarily have to be a purchaser at the fixed retail price. At that price there might be no takers, in which case the plaintiff would be left with the car on his hands. Section 50(3) seems to me to postulate a market in which there is a market or current price, i.e., a price fixed by supply and demand at which (be it more or less than the contract price) a purchaser can be found. If the only price at which a car can be sold is the fixed retail price and no purchaser can be found at that price, I do not think it can reasonably be said that there is a market or current price or that there is an available market. If the state of the trade were such that the plaintiff could sell at the fixed retail price all the cars that he could get, so that the defendant's default did not result in the plaintiff effecting one sale less than he would otherwise have effected, it may well be that the plaintiff could not make out his claim to anything more than nominal damages. I am, however, inclined to think that this would not be on account of the necessary equality of the contract price and the fixed retail price at which alone the car could be sold, taken for the present purpose as the market or current price within the meaning of s. 50(3), but because on an application of the general principle laid down by s. 50(2) the plaintiff would be found to have suffered no damage.

In *W. L. Thompson Ltd.* v. *R. Robinson* (*Gunmakers*) *Ltd.*[97] UPJOHN, J., had before him a claim for damages in a case resembling the present case to the extent that the damages were claimed in respect of the defendants' refusal to perform a contract with the plaintiffs for the purchase from the plaintiffs of a car (in that instance a Standard Vanguard car) which, like the car in the present case, could only be sold by the plaintiffs at a fixed retail price. It is, however, important to note that that case to which I am now referring proceeded on certain admissions, including an admission to the effect that in the relevant district at the date of the contract (which was also the date of the breach):[98]

". . . there was no shortage of Vanguard models to meet all immediate demands, at any rate in the locality",

which I take to mean (in effect) that the supply of such cars exceeded the demand. In these circumstances the plaintiffs by agreement with their suppliers rescinded their contract with them, and returned the car. In the ensuing action the plaintiffs claimed from the defendants damages amounting to the profit the plaintiffs would have made on the sale of the car to the defendants if the defendants had duly completed their purchase of it, and the learned Judge held them entitled to those damages. The defendants raised the same argument as has been raised by the defendant in the present case, viz., that there was an available market for a car of the kind in question, within the meaning of s. 50(3), that there was a market or current price in the shape of the fixed retail price, and that, as the fixed retail price was the same as the contract price, the plaintiffs had suffered no damage. In the course of his judgment, UPJOHN, J., referred to JAMES, L.J.'s definition of a market in *Dunkirk Colliery Co.* v. *Lever*.[99] JAMES, L.J., said:[100]

"Under those circumstances the only thing that we can do is to send it back to the referee with an intimation that we are of opinion upon the facts (agreeing with the Master of the Rolls in that respect), that the facts do not warrant the application of the principle mentioned in the award, namely, that there was what may be properly called a market. What I understand by a market in such a case as this is, that when the defendant refused to take the 300 tons the first week or the first month, the plaintiffs might have sent it in waggons somewhere else, where they could sell it, just as they sell corn on the Exchange,

---

97 [1955] 1 All E.R. 154.
98 *Ibid.*, at p. 156.
99 (1878), 9 Ch. D. 20, at pp. 24 to 25.
100 *Ibid.*, at p. 24.

or cotton at Liverpool: that is to say, that there was a fair market where they could have found a purchaser either by themselves or through some agent at some particular place. That is my notion of the meaning of a market under those circumstances".

UPJOHN, J., also referred to the Scottish case of *Marshall & Co.* v. *Nicoll & Son*,[101] where it was held in the Court of Session that there was an available market within the meaning of s. 51(3) . . . for annealed steel sheets, although they were not kept in stock and were not purchasable in the open market. In the House of Lords the decision was affirmed, but their Lordships would seem to have been equally divided on the question whether there was an available market for the goods. In this state of the authorities, the learned Judge felt himself bound by *Dunkirk Colliery Co.* v. *Lever*,[102] and held (in effect) that JAMES, L.J.'s definition in that case prevented him from holding that in the case then before him there was an available market within the meaning of s. 50(3).

UPJOHN, J., went on to propound a more extended meaning for the phrase "available market" in these terms:[103]

"Had the matter been *res integra*, I think I should have found that an 'available market' merely means that the situation in the particular trade in the particular area was such that the particular goods could freely be sold, and that there was a demand sufficient to absorb readily all the goods that were thrust on it, so that if a purchaser defaulted, the goods in question could readily be disposed of".

He went on to say (in effect) that in the case then before him there was no available market because the supply of Vanguard cars at the material time exceeded the demand.

I doubt if JAMES, L.J.'s observations in *Dunkirk Colliery Co.* v. *Lever*[104] should be literally applied as an exhaustive definition of an available market in all cases. On the other hand, I do not find UPJOHN, J.'s definition entirely satisfactory. I will not, however, attempt to improve on it, but will content myself with the negative proposition that I doubt if there can be an available market for particular goods in any sense relevant to s. 50(3) of the Sale of Goods Act . . . unless those goods are available for sale in the market at the market or current price in the sense of the price, whatever it may be, fixed by reference to supply and demand as the price at which a purchaser for the goods in question can be found, be it greater or less than or equal to the contract price. The language of s. 50(3) seems to me to postulate that in the cases to which it applies there will, or may, be a difference between the contract price and the market or current price, which cannot be so where the goods can only be sold at a

---

[101] 1919 S.C. (H.L.) 129.
[102] *Supra*.
[103] [1955] 1 All E.R. at p. 159.
[104] *Supra*.

fixed retail price. Accordingly, I am of opinion that, whether there was in this case "an available market" within the meaning of s. 50(3) or not, it is a case in which s. 50(2) should be applied to the exclusion of s. 50(3).

Campbell Mostyn (Provisions) Ltd. *v.* Barnett Trading Co.

[1954] 1 Lloyd's Rep. 65

By s. 50(3): "*Where there is an available market for the goods in question the measure of damages is* prima facie *to be ascertained by the difference between the contract price and the market or current price at the time or times when the goods ought to have been accepted or, if no time was fixed for acceptance, then at the time of the refusal to accept*". *It is irrelevant that the market price of the goods has risen since the date of the breach.*

The sellers sold a quantity of tinned ham to the buyers. The buyers wrongfully rejected it, so the sellers claimed damages for non-acceptance under s. 50(3), i.e., the difference between the contract price and the market price at the date of the breach.

Held, by the Court of Appeal, that they were so entitled. It was irrelevant that the market price subsequently rose, and that the sellers by not reselling immediately on the breach, but only later, had in fact made a profit on the resale.

SOMERVELL, L.J. (at page 67)

The goods tendered were not sold on 24th October. The goods were South African tinned ham of a particular brand, which was said to be not a popular brand on the market. Early in that year, 1951 . . . there had been considerable imports of tinned ham; the best varieties, one gathers, coming from Germany and Belgium. The market became somewhat overcharged and prices fell. The fact that the market was inactive affected, apparently, the Dominion ham, particularly the brand in question, more than the German brand. There was undoubtedly a fall in price. Subsequently, after the breach, within a fortnight, the Government, which had been then recently elected and had taken office, made an announcement with regard to imposing an extra measure of control on imports from Continental countries. That, with Christmas not very far off, improved the market for ham and with it the less popular Dominion brands, with one of which we are concerned. In fact, the sellers sold these 18 oz. tins after 7th November, at a sum in excess of the market price, and therefore, on the face of it, suffered no damage. One can understand, in those circumstances, the buyers thinking that that was the end of it and feeling aggrieved if the provisions of the law held them liable to pay a sum in damages.

The learned Master and the Divisional Court have held that the defendants are liable to pay damages, notwithstanding the events which I have recounted, on the principle which is stated concisely in the Privy Council opinion in *A.K.A.S. Jamal* v. *Moola Dawood, Sons & Co.*[105] That dealt, as will be seen, with negotiable securities, but in my opinion the principle is equally applicable to the sale of goods:

"The question therefore is the general question and may be stated thus: In a contract for sale of negotiable securities, is the measure of damages for breach the difference between the contract price and the market price at the date of the breach—with an obligation on the part of the seller to mitigate the damages by getting the best price he can at the date of the breach—or is the seller bound to reduce the damages, if he can, by subsequent sales at better prices? If he is, and if the purchaser is entitled to the benefit of subsequent sales, it must also be true that he must bear the burden of subsequent losses. The latter proposition is in their Lordships' opinion impossible, and the former is equally unsound. If the seller retains the shares after the breach, the speculation as to the way the market will subsequently go is the speculation of the seller, not of the buyer; the seller cannot recover from the buyer the loss below the market price at the date of the breach if the market falls, nor is he liable to the purchaser for the profit if the market rises".

No doubt it is small comfort to the defendants in this case to know that if the market had gone even worse than it was on 24th October, they would not have been liable to pay more than whatever sum was fixed, assuming there was a market, for the market price on that day.

(2) DAMAGES FOR NON-DELIVERY

Re R. & H. Hall Ltd. and W. H. Pim (Junior) & Co.'s Arbitration
[1928] All E.R. Rep. 763

As regards damages for non-delivery, s. 51(2) states that: "The measure of damages is the estimated loss directly and naturally resulting, in the ordinary course of events, from the seller's breach of contract".

On 3rd November, 1925, the sellers sold a quantity of unascertained cargo of wheat at a fixed price. The contract of sale contained a number of provisions as to what was to happen if the buyers resold the wheat. Both parties, however, knew that there was an even chance that the buyers might either resell or keep the goods themselves. On 21st November the market price rose, and the buyers resold the wheat to sub-buyers. On 10th February, 1926, the sellers appropriated the wheat to the contract. Later there was a fall in the market price, and on 22nd March the sellers failed to deliver the wheat. The sellers contended that they were only liable for damages calculated on the difference between the price at 3rd November, 1925, and that on 22nd March, 1926.

Held, by the House of Lords, that this contention failed. The buyers were entitled to their own loss of profit on the resale and damages which they had had to pay to their sub-buyers, because such damages must be supposed to have been contemplated by the parties, since the possibility of sub-sales was expressly mentioned in the contract, and it was not unlikely that they would take place.

---

[105] [1916] 1 A.C. 175, at p. 179.

VISCOUNT HALDANE (at page 765)

I think further that the contract and the conditions which it incorporates show that it was contemplated that the cargo might be passed on by way of sub-sale if the buyer did not choose to keep it for himself, and that the seller in such a case contracted to put the buyer in a position to fulfil his sub-contracts if he entered into them. They were regarded by the terms of the original contract as sub-contracts which the original buyer was to be in a position to enter into, with stipulations which bound the original seller to enable the original buyer to fulfil them. Whether the latter was likely to enter into such sub-contracts and pass the cargo down a chain of resales is not material. It is enough that the contract contemplated by its terms that he should have the right to do so if he chose. This being the case, there has been an admitted breach. The original seller has failed to deliver at the due date, and the buyer has been left open to claims from his sub-buyers based on the contracts made with them in reliance on the clauses in the document of 3rd November.

In these circumstances I am of opinion that the measure of damages is clear. It is not merely the amount of damage, measured by loss in the market, which arises in the usual course of business from the breach. It extends, whenever the special circumstances require this, to such possible damages as may reasonably be supposed to have been in the contemplation of both parties at the time they made the contract, as the probable result of the breach of it. This is in accordance with what is called the second branch of the rule in *Hadley* v. *Baxendale*,[106] a rule which is fully explained by Lord ESHER, M.R., in *Hammond & Co.* v. *Bussey*.[107] He points out that the principle is not to be confined to a sub-contract already actually made at the date of the original contract, but applies also to the case of a sub-contract which will probably be made. There is no doubt that the law is correctly explained in *Hammond & Co.* v. *Bussey*, and I am of opinion that the case before me depends on a question of construction which comes directly within it and must be answered in accordance with the buyers' contention.

VISCOUNT DUNEDIN (at page 766)

There is, I believe, a general agreement that the law as to the calculation of damages due for breach of a contract is settled by *Hadley* v. *Baxendale*, as explained in *Hammond & Co.* v. *Bussey*. The difficulty lies in the application to the facts of each case.

I take, in their order, the three points which FRY, L.J., in *Hammond's Case*, said must be determined before the final question is put. First, what are the damages which actually resulted from the breach? Undoubtedly, loss of profit and also—

---

[106] (1854), 9 Exch. 341.
[107] (1887), 20 Q.B.D. 79, C.A.

though I shall revert to this—damages which the buyer would have to pay to his sub-buyer Williams. Secondly, was the contract made under any special circumstances, and, if so, what? And thirdly, what, at the time of the making of the contract, was the common knowledge of the parties?

I take these two together. This was the sale not of wheat, but of a cargo of wheat, and the particular cargo was, according to the terms of the bargain, to be identified by nomination before a certain date. It was well known to both parties that it was a common practice in the trade to resell cargo whilst still afloat, and the contract itself, apart from common knowledge, shows this distinctly by the provisions of condition 1, which were quoted by [Viscount HALDANE]. Then there is the correspondence as to the actual appropriation of the *Indianic*. I do not use this correspondence as explaining the contract itself, which was of date in November previous, but I do use it as an additional proof, if proof were needed, of the perfect familiarity of the seller with the practice of successive resales of cargo afloat, or, as it is termed, of a "string of contracts". The seller necessarily knew that as soon as he nominated a cargo, the delivery of that cargo, and of no other, could alone satisfy the contract.

In the light of these facts, I put to myself the crucial question as expressed by FRY, L.J., who is therein repeating what had already been said by Lord ESHER, M.R.:

"What may the Court reasonably suppose to have been in the contemplation of the parties as the probable result of breach of the contract, assuming the parties to have applied their minds to the contingency of there being such a breach?"

Be it observed that it is for the Court to decide the question; not for the jury or, as in a case like the present, for the arbitrator, although it is in the province of the jury, or arbitrator, to find any actual fact which will help the Court to arrive at the supposition. In following FRY, L.J., as to the matter to be considered before the final question is put, I do exactly what the learned Chief Justice did in this case. He, however, proceeds as follows. He quotes the finding of the arbitrators:

"The arbitrators are unable to find that it was in the contemplation of the parties or ought to have been in the contemplation of [the seller] at that time that the cargo would be resold or was likely to be resold before delivery; in fact, the chances of its being resold as a cargo and of its being taken delivery of by (the buyer) were about equal".

And then continues:

"In other words, as I understand the meaning of that finding of fact, not only do the arbitrators say that on the materials before them they could not find that a resale was within contemplation of the parties, and, therefore, possibly damages from breach of subsequent contracts within the scope of the measure of damage, but they actually state as a fact that the chances of this cargo being resold or of its not being resold were equal, and, therefore, that it is idle to speak of a likelihood or of a probability of resale".

On this I have two observations to make. The arbitrators' findings that they are unable to find, etc., must be read in the light of what was just said before the passage quoted, namely:

> "It was not suggested on behalf of the buyers that they had at the time of the transaction of 3rd November, 1925, expressly notified the sellers of any intention on their part to resell the cargo and in the circumstances . . .".

If more were meant, it was usurping the province of the Court. And further—and here, I think, is the key to the learned Judge's decision—after setting out that they state as a fact that the chances of the cargo being resold, or not being resold, were about equal, he adds words which they do not use, "and therefore that it is idle to speak of the likelihood or the probability of a resale". With deference to the learned Judge, it is here that I part company with him. I do not think that "probability", as it is used in *Hammond & Co.* v. *Bussey*,[108] means that the chances are all in favour of the event whatever its happening. To make a thing probable, it is enough, in my view, that there is an even chance of its happening. That is the criterion I apply, and in view of the fact, which I have said above, I think there was here in the contemplation of parties the probability of a resale. And if that was so, the results of a breach on the part of the first seller, as the sale was of a named cargo, meant inevitably default on the part of the first buyer.

(3) SPECIFIC PERFORMANCE

Re Wait

[1926] All E.R. Rep. 433

Specific performance of a contract cannot be ordered under s. 52 unless the goods are "specific" or "ascertained" goods.

The buyers bought 500 tons of wheat to be shipped on board the *Challenger* between 16th and 31st December, 1925, c.i.f. Avonmouth. The goods formed part of a consignment of 1,000 tons which already belonged to the seller. The buyers paid for the wheat on 6th February, 1926, and shortly afterwards the sellers were adjudicated bankrupt. When the vessel arrived at Avonmouth, the 500 tons had not been appropriated to the contract and the sellers' trustee in bankruptcy refused to deliver the wheat, so the buyers claimed specific performance of the contract.

Held, by the Court of Appeal, that a decree of specific performance would not be granted, for the goods were not "specific" or "ascertained" as required by s. 52 of the Sale of Goods Act.

---

[108] *Supra.*

LORD HANWORTH, M.R. (at page 436)

It is necessary, therefore, to examine the meaning and effect of s. 52 in relation to the facts of the present case. Section 52 remains a section which is to be put in force upon the application of the plaintiff. It provides one of the remedies of the buyer, and it does not give correlative rights to the seller. Its operation remains limited. It is not possible to overlook the original purpose and scope of its predecessors, which was to meet a difficulty and hardship suffered by a buyer in respect of specific goods, and the section reproduces the old law in a codifying statute. It has not changed the law. The section applies to all cases where the goods are specific or ascertained, whether the property has passed to the buyer or not: see *James Jones & Sons Ltd.* v. *Earl of Tankerville* . . . [109]

The problem to be solved comes back to the question: Were the 500 tons specific goods? They were never appropriated, and it is admitted that the legal property has not passed, for these were "future goods" within s. 5 of the Act in respect of which no property passed to the purchaser: see ss. 16, 17, and 18, r. 5. There was no ascertainment or identification of the 500 tons out of the cargo in bulk of the motor vessel *Challenger*. The bankruptcy of the vendors does not, in my judgment, affect the question, though it may emphasise the hardship to the purchasers, for the question must be determined upon the rights of the parties under the contract upon the arrival of the wheat. . . .

Considering the facts of the present case in the light of the authorities to which I have called attention, it is, in my judgment, not possible to hold that the 500 tons of wheat, ex motor vessel *Challenger*, were specific or ascertained goods, and thus specific performance would not be ordered as the remedy of the buyer under s. 52 of the Act.

Behnke *v.* Bede Shipping Co. Ltd.

[1927] All E.R. Rep. 689

The Court will not exercise its power under s. 52 to order a decree of specific performance if damages are an adequate remedy.

The seller had agreed to sell the *City*, which was a vessel of peculiar and practically unique value to the buyer. The seller refused to deliver her, so the buyer applied to the Court for a decree of specific performance of the contract.

Held, by the King's Bench Division, that damages were an inadequate remedy, and a decree of specific performance would be ordered.

---

[109] [1909] 2 Ch. 440.

WRIGHT, J. (at page 690)

It is curious how little guidance there is on the question whether specific performance should be granted of a contract for the sale of a ship. Section 52 of the Sale of Goods Act gives the Court a discretion, if it thinks fit, in any action for breach of contract to deliver specific or ascertained goods, to direct that the contract shall be performed specifically. I think a ship is a specific chattel within the Act. . . . In the present case there is evidence that the *City* was of peculiar and practically unique value to the plaintiff. She was a cheap vessel, being old, built in 1892, but her engines and boilers were practically new, and such as to satisfy the German regulation, and hence the plaintiff could, as a German shipowner, have her at once put on the German register. A very experienced ship valuer has said that he knew of only one other comparable ship, but that may now be sold. The plaintiff wants the ship for immediate use, and I do not think damages would be an adequate compensation. I think he is entitled to the ship and a decree of specific performance in order that justice may be done. What is the position between the defendants and the other buyers, whose contract was later in time than that of the plaintiff, is irrelevant in this action.

(4) DAMAGES FOR BREACH OF WARRANTY

Mason *v.* Burningham

[1949] 2 All E.R. 134

By s. 53(2): "The measure of damages for breach of warranty is the estimated loss directly and naturally resulting, in the ordinary course of events, from the breach of warranty".

The buyer of a typewriter spent £11 19s. in getting it overhauled, and then found that it had been stolen. So she claimed this sum damages for breach of the warranty of quiet possession of the goods implied under s. 12(2).[110]

Held, by the Court of Appeal, that the claim succeeded, since she had done the natural thing in having the typewriter overhauled, for the sum she had spent was a loss directly and naturally resulting from the breach of warranty within the meaning of s. 53(2).

SINGLETON, L.J. (at page 141)

The question to be considered was whether or not it was the natural and ordinary thing that the purchaser of a second-hand typewriter of this kind should have it overhauled, and the learned Judge had already said that that was the fact, for he said: "She did the ordinary and natural thing". He went on to say:

---

[110] For another illustration of the implied warranty as to quiet possession, see *Niblett Ltd.* v. *Confectioners' Materials Co. Ltd.*, [1921] All E.R. Rep. 459, C.A., p. 9, *ante.*

"I hold that the extra amount spent on the article by the plaintiff quite naturally is not a loss due to the fact that the defendant sold an article which he should not have sold. Although what the plaintiff did was right and proper, I must decide against her".

Counsel for the plaintiff submitted to this Court that that judgment was wrong. His argument was based almost wholly on two or three sections of the Sale of Goods Act . . . . He referred the Court to two cases further back in date which are of interest. They are *Bunny* v. *Hopkinson*[111] and *Rolph* v. *Crouch*,[112] both of which have to do with land. In *Bunny* v. *Hopkinson*:

"A. sold some building land to B., and he covenanted for title. After some houses had been built on the land, the purchaser was evicted.

Held, that the purchaser was entitled to recover upon the covenants, not only the value of the land, but also that of the houses subsequently built thereon".

Sir John ROMILLY, M.R., in the course of a very short judgment, said:[113]

"I am of opinion that the measure of the damages upon these covenants include the amount expended in converting the land into the purposes for which it was sold".

In *Rolph* v. *Crouch*:[114]

"The defendant demised premises for a term of years to the plaintiff, and covenanted that the plaintiff should occupy the same during the term 'without any interruption whatsoever from or by the said defendant, his executors, etc., or any other person or persons lawfully claiming by, from, or under him or them'. An action of trespass was afterwards brought by a person claiming under the defendant against the plaintiff, who gave notice of it to the defendant. The defendant paid no attention to the notice, and the plaintiff, acting on his own judgment and without express authority, defended the action. A verdict was eventually found against him, and he was obliged to pay damages and costs. In an action against the defendant, his landlord, for breach of the covenant for quiet enjoyment contained in the demise: *Held*, that the plaintiff was entitled to recover from the defendant the costs and damages he had paid, and also the expenses he had himself incurred in defending the action of trespass".

It appeared that there was a further claim to damages because the lessee had expended money in erecting a greenhouse on the land demised in reliance on the defendant's covenant and had lost the profits he would have acquired from the sale. Sir Fitzroy KELLY, C.B., said:[115]

"Under these circumstances, I am of opinion that the plaintiff was justified in the course which he took, and therefore that the damages, costs and expenses which he incurred in the action brought against him by Cook, are the natural and immediate consequence of

---

111 (1859), 27 Beav. 565.
112 (1867), L.R. 3 Exch. 44.
113 27 Beav., at p. 567.
114 *Supra*.
115 (1867), L.R. 3 Exch. 44, at p. 49.

the defendant's breach of covenant. . . . Then, lastly, as to the conservatory. The plaintiff, relying on the performance by the defendant of his covenant, erected it for the better and more conveniently carrying on of his trade as a florist. He has lost the use of it, and I think that he is entitled to the sum given him by the jury for that loss".

Those cases, though on different subject-matter, are in point, but really, to come to a decision, one has to look first at s. 12 and then at s. 53 of the Sale of Goods Act. . . . Counsel for the defendant submitted that it was not shown that the defendant had any foreknowledge that this kind of damage might flow in case there was a breach. He further submitted that there was no evidence to show that the overhaul of the typewriter took place at once or soon after the purchase, and, unless that was shown, the damage would not flow and did not flow naturally from the breach. No such point as the second was raised at the hearing in the Court below, and no suggestion whatever was made to the plaintiff that she did not send the typewriter to be overhauled soon after she purchased it. It was accepted, as far as one can see, that she had, in fact, done so.

On the submission that the defendant had no foreknowledge that this kind of damage might flow, we were referred to the judgment of this Court, delivered by ASQUITH, L.J., in *Victoria Laundry (Windsor) Ltd.* v. *Newman Industries Ltd.*,[116] and in particular to a passage in the judgment where the Lord Justice said:[117]

"What was at that time reasonably foreseeable depends on the knowledge then possessed by the parties, or, at all events, by the party who later commits the breach. For this purpose, knowledge 'possessed' is of two kinds—one imputed, the other actual. Everyone, as a reasonable person, is taken to know the 'ordinary course of things' and consequently what loss is liable to result from a breach of that ordinary course".

In the present case the learned County Court Judge found that the plaintiff "behaved in a common-sense way", that she did "the ordinary and natural thing", that what she did was "quite naturally" done, and that it was "right and proper". In those circumstances that which followed flowed directly and naturally from the breach. It resulted "in the ordinary course of events". Damages have to be assessed under s. 53(2) of the Sale of Goods Act . . . and those damages, resulting from the breach of warranty on the part of the seller, would have been, if there had been no payment on account, the total amount of £20 which the plaintiff paid for the typewriter and the amount which she "rightly" and "properly" and "naturally" expended to have it overhauled and put in proper order. The learned County Court Judge, in my view, approached this matter from the wrong angle. He ought to have held that the plaintiff was entitled to the sum of £11 10s., which was the balance remaining due.

---

116 [1949] 1 All E.R. 997, C.A.
117 *Ibid.*, at p. 1002.

(5) MITIGATION OF DAMAGES

James Finlay & Co. Ltd. *v.* N.V. Kwik Hoo Tong, Handel Maatschappij[118]

[1928] All E.R. Rep. 110

The buyer is under no duty to mitigate the damages which he has suffered if to do so he might endanger his commercial reputation.

The buyers bought from the sellers a quantity of sugar c.i.f. Bombay to be shipped in September, 1920, and entered into a sub-contract to sub-sell the same goods to sub-buyers. The sub-contract with the sub-buyers contained a clause that "the bills of lading shall be conclusive evidence of the date of shipment". In fact, the sugar was shipped in October, 1920. The buyers sued the sellers for breach of contract, but the sellers contended that the buyers should have minimised their damages by enforcing the sub-contract against the sub-buyers and insisting on the clause concerning the date of shipment.

Held, by the Court of Appeal, that the buyers were under no duty to do so, for, if they had done so, they might well have damaged their commercial reputation.

GREER, L.J. (at page 117)

But there is another point upon which it is necessary to say something. I agree with my Lord that once you get the position of the buyers as I have stated it, it does not seem necessary to go any farther and consider the sub-contracts at all, because, if the term of the contract which requires a true bill of lading had been duly performed, there never would have been any question of having any goods to use for the purposes of the sub-contract. But counsel for the sellers say: "At any rate you have to consider it from the point of view of minimising damages, and, assuming that the measure would be otherwise correct, still, the plaintiffs, having taken the goods, must do their best to minimise the damages, and they ought, therefore, to have forced their sub-purchasers to take these goods and pay for them, or if they would not do that, then the plaintiffs ought to have brought the sub-purchasers into Court and made them pay the damages which necessarily resulted from their refusal". For myself, I have come to the conclusion that the sub-contractors would have had no answer to the claim if it had been made, but I do not say that the claim is necessarily one that ought to be regarded by everybody as a claim which could not receive any answer, and Messrs Finlay were faced with the position that in order to recover these damages and so minimise the damages recoverable from the defendants, they would have had to embark upon litigation in India. I see nothing immoral or unconscientious in an endeavour, if it had been made, to hold the Indian purchasers to their bargain. They had, in my judgment, bought goods on different terms from the terms under which

---

118 Another aspect of this case is considered under "C.I.F. Contracts", p. 135, *post*.

Messrs Finlay had bought them; they had bought them as goods certified by a bill of lading to be delivered in September; and they would have been perfectly entitled, as a matter of business morals, to have said: "You made that bargain, and you must stick to it, and if you do not you must pay damages". But I think at the same time it is a wholly unreasonable thing to say that that would be the ordinary course of business, which they ought to pursue in order to diminish the damages. People have not got to consider merely what is right in a strict court of conscience, but they have got to consider what is the effect of their conduct upon their business relations with other people, and I can have very little doubt that it would not have suited their business to have taken the extreme course which is suggested; and, in my judgment, it is not in the reasonable course of business to require them to do what is suggested in order to diminish damages, if *prima facie* they are entitled to recover damages from the defendants.

Lesters Leather & Skin Co. Ltd. *v.* Home & Overseas Brokers Ltd.

(1948), 82 Ll.L.Rep. 202

Where the seller has failed to deliver the goods, the buyer is under no duty to attempt to mitigate the damages, which he has suffered, by hunting the globe to find out where he can obtain similar goods.

The buyers bought a quantity of Indian snakeskins from the sellers c.i.f. a United Kingdom port. The goods were not delivered, and it was impossible to buy similar goods in England. But they might have been obtained in India, though they would not have arrived here for many months after the date fixed for delivery. In an action by the buyers for breach of contract

Held, by the Court of Appeal, that they were under no duty to minimise their damages by entering into a contract with an unknown seller in India to see whether they could get the goods delivered in England many months later.

LORD GODDARD, C.J. (at page 204)

On 19th September, 1946, the defendants sold to the plaintiffs "10,000 bark-tanned Whipsnakes, Madras tanning, eighty per cent. firsts, twenty per cent. seconds, size 4 in. and up, average size $4\frac{1}{2}$ in.", at a price of 58 pence per piece, and the sale was c.i.f. a United Kingdom port. "Net cash against documents on first presentation. Shipment: October-November". There seems to have been some delay in shipment, but at any rate, whether there was or whether there was not, the plaintiffs were willing to accept the goods when they arrived in February. But when the goods arrived in February, they rejected them, and it was not disputed that they were entitled to reject them, because they were a lot of rubbish and were not merchantable. Therefore there was a failure to deliver on the part of the defendants.

Now, the learned Judge had before him evidence that it would have been possible at this time for the plaintiffs to have bought goods in India to replace these goods.

Was there an available market for the goods? So far as that goes, the first thing to see is, What was the contract? The contract was not to deliver goods in India; the contract was to deliver goods in London, and there was (as was found by the learned Judge and is not really in dispute) no available market for such goods in London at that time; nor indeed is there any suggestion that there was an available market for such goods in India. I am far from saying that, if for instance, it could be shown that at the port of Liverpool or at the port of Glasgow, or somewhere of that sort, such goods were available, it would not have been the duty of the plaintiffs to buy there.

I said that the place of delivery was London. That was a mistake on my part, because the contract is not London; it is any United Kingdom port; and if at any port in the United Kingdom it could have been shown that there were snakeskins available at that time, it would obviously have been the duty of the plaintiffs to have bought there to mitigate their damages, but no such thing is proved. It is shown here that the plaintiffs did what they could, which was to buy a small quantity of available dressed skins. But it is said, and no doubt truly said, that if they had sent out to India, they might have been able to buy or would have been able to buy out there. I do not think they were under any duty to do that.

The principle under which damages, in the case of non-delivery, are *prima facie* limited to the difference between the contract price and the market price at the time of the breach where there is an available market, is well known. The fact that the buyer had actually paid under this contract does not make any difference. Presumably having the money in hand, he can take that and go and get his goods elsewhere directly there is a failure on the part of the seller to deliver. After all, these matters always come down to whether the party aggrieved has acted reasonably in mitigating or not mitigating the damages. I cannot say that the buyer is bound to go hunting the globe to find out where he can get skins and then have them shipped, months after the contract time, so that they will arrive here many months after the date at which, had they been shipped in accordance with the contract, they would have arrived.

(6) DAMAGES FOR BREACH OF STRING CONTRACTS

Kasler & Cohen *v*. G. & A. Slavouski

(1927), 137 L.T. 641

Where the terms of string contracts are the same, the original buyer can claim against the original seller the damages and costs which he has had to pay to the other parties in the chain.

The original buyers bought from the original sellers a quantity of skins. They were resold under a series of string contracts, and the ultimate purchaser recovered damages and costs from the immediate seller, and a series of intermediate actions along the chain of sellers resulted. In an action by the original buyers against the original sellers

Held, by the King's Bench Division, that the original buyers were entitled to include in their claim the damages suffered by the ultimate purchaser and the costs of both sides in that action, and the costs of all the intermediate actions.

BRANSON, J. (at page 643)

The plaintiffs say that they are entitled to claim both the original damages which they had to pay, namely the £674 10s., and also in addition by way of damages the costs which they had to pay to the parties to whom they sold, and to whom their vendee sold, and to whom the vendee of that vendee sold these goods, with the same warranties and in the same circumstances. The question is whether they can recover or not. It was said in the argument before me that it is admitted for the purpose of this case that the £674 10s. damages can be so recovered, but counsel for the defendants contends that, in regard to costs, different considerations apply, and that those damages are too remote. . . . What the plaintiffs say is that where there is a case in which the purchaser in buying goods has expressly or impliedly made known to the vendor the purposes for which the goods are supplied, and the purchaser, relying on the goods being fit for that purpose, has resold and his vendee has recovered damages against him, then the purchaser may go back on his vendor and claim not only the damages he has had to pay, but also the costs reasonably incurred in defending the claim of the sub-vendee against himself. That seems to be the state of the law as laid down by those two cases. If a man has sold goods to another in such circumstances as to fix him with special knowledge of the purpose for which the goods are required, and that other sells on the same terms and conditions and is then subject to an action, because the goods do not come up to the contract quality, or for any reason giving rise to a claim for damages on such a contract, the intermediate purchaser—that is to say, the first purchaser—is entitled, if he has acted reasonably in defending the action and yet has been cast in damages and costs, to claim from his seller not only the damages but also the costs which he has had to pay.

It is said that that rule extends so as to enable the first purchaser to recover from the original seller what he may have had to pay to his sub-vendee, and that it may entitle the sub-vendee, if he has sold again, to recover from the first purchaser; but it is said that one can never go back more than two steps—that is to say, that there can only be three people involved in any such case, and that to allow a purchaser from a sub-vendee to recover against the first purchaser involves the introduction of some theory of remoteness of damage which would be a violation of the law in regard to remoteness of damage. With the greatest respect for the judgment of SHEARMAN, J., I cannot follow that proposition. It seems to me that so long as there is the same contract passing the same article from hand to hand with the same warranty, and particularly in a case such as this, where the breach of contract giving rise to damages consists in there being something in the article which the maker of it and which each vendor knows can be discovered only when it comes into the hands of the person who is ultimately going to put it into use, there can be no logical reason and no reason in justice for drawing such a distinction as is suggested. . . .

It seems to me that in this case it must have been in the contemplation of the parties that damages would be claimed if there were a breach of this contract of the nature of that which has occurred by parties separated by several contractual steps from each of the immediate parties to each of the contracts along the line. Slavouski, when he sold these skins to Cohen, did not expect Cohen to wear them round his own neck; he knew that Cohen was going to make them into collars which he, not being a retail trader, would sell to someone else, who would use them in some other way, but each party contemplated that at long last the collar was going to be worn by somebody, and that, if it was faulty in the way in which this collar was faulty, somebody at the end of the line would suffer, and, therefore, there might be a claim removed not one step, but many steps, from the original seller. In my opinion, therefore, it is correct to say that the £674 10s. damages which Miss White recovered from Macmillan are properly recoverable by the plaintiffs in this action, and I can formulate no distinction between damages and costs reasonably and properly incurred in defending an action for damages, whether they succeed in reducing the damages or not. If the claim is reasonably and properly resisted, as it seems to me, the amount the person sued has to pay in costs is just as much his damage as that which he has to pay in actual damages.

Dexters Ltd. *v.* Hillcrest Oil Co. (Bradford) Ltd

[1925] All E.R. Rep. 273

Where the terms of string contracts are not the same, the original buyer cannot claim against the original seller the damages and costs which he has had to pay to the other parties in the chain.

A quantity of cotton seed grease was sold under a series of string contracts, and was rejected by the ultimate purchasers on the ground that it was not of merchantable quality. The terms of the various sub-contracts were not the same. In an action by the original buyers against the original sellers for damages for breach of contract.

Held (*obiter*), by the Court of Appeal, that the original buyers could not claim damages based on the amount which they had had to pay to their sub-buyers, because the terms of the sub-contract were not the same as the original contract.

SCRUTTON, L.J. (at page 278)

While I am not expressing a final opinion, it would seem that the buyers were not entitled to damages based on the amount which they had had to pay to their sub-buyers. I have always considered it as essential to running damages along a chain of contracts that the contracts should be the same. Where, as in this case, the first contract contains one description—a description difficult to interpret because it is not an ordinary trade description—and at some stage in the chain the contract shifts and becomes a contract under a well-known trade description, different from the one in any previous contract, I find it difficult to hold that one can base any claim for damages on sums which are paid under contracts, or in respect of contracts which are different from the one being investigated, and on which the damages are claimed.

PART II

THE SALE OF GOODS ACT 1893

Lloyds and Scottish Finance Ltd. *v.* Modern Cars and Caravans (Kingston) Ltd.

[1964] 2 All E.R. 732

The proviso to s. 26(1) of the Sale of Goods Act 1893[1] (which states that "a writ of fieri facias . . . shall bind the property in the goods of the execution debtor . . . Provided that no such writ shall prejudice the title to such goods acquired by any person in good faith and for valuable consideration unless [he] had at the time when he acquired his title notice that such writ . . . had been delivered to and remained unexecuted in the hands of the sheriff") does not apply when an actual seizure has been effected.

On 14th April, 1961, a sheriff's officer entered a caravan, which was owned by Mr Wood, in order to execute a writ of *fieri facias* on his property to satisfy a judgment debt, and left a card stating that the sheriff held an execution against him. From 18th April to 15th May the sheriff's officer went to the site on a number of occasions to see whether the caravan was still there. On 8th May Wood sold the caravan to the defendants, who knew of the writ. They then sold the caravan to the plaintiffs. A question arose as to whether the plaintiffs had obtained an unencumbered title under the proviso to s. 26(1) of the Sale of Goods Act 1893.

Held, by the Queen's Bench Division, that the plaintiffs had not obtained an unencumbered title, for the caravan had been effectively seized by the sheriff's officer and the proviso to s. 26(1) did not apply in these circumstances.

EDMUND DAVIES, J. (at page 737)

I hold that on 14th April there was a seizure by the sheriff's officer of the caravan and its contents as against the judgment debtor. He did not merely demand payment of the debt (as was done in *Nash* v. *Dickenson*[2]) but, having entered and told the debtor that he had come to levy execution and read out his warrant, he handed him the written intimation already referred to. Furthermore, he proffered for signature a "walking possession" agreement, and he warned Wood and his wife that the caravan must not be moved. It is said that he should have done more: that he should have asked the Wood family to leave the caravan, and then locked it up or towed it away.

---

[1] Section 26 of the Sale of Goods Act 1893 is the only one which still remains in force. The rest of the Act is repealed by the Sale of Goods Act 1979, s. 63(2) and Sched. 3.
[2] (1867), L.R. 2 C.P. 252.

Such a submission is unrealistic, for their refusal to sign the agreement indicated clearly that they would not have consented to the much more drastic course of leaving. Had the officer proceeded to move the caravan with the Wood family still inside, and this after Mrs Wood had laid claim to its ownership, he would have run a grave risk of involving the sheriff in liability to pay damages for wrongful execution, wrongful imprisonment and trespass against the person, as occurred in *Cave* v. *Capel*.[3] It would have been highly inconvenient (though, it seems, physically possible) for him to have remained in the caravan with its four occupants, and he had no legal right to camp outside on the caravan site. Having done what he did, he went away. In my judgment, he departed after having effectively seized the caravan and its contents. It has been submitted that to do so after he had been refused consent to "walking possession" indicates that he never seized at all. I interpret this incident in quite a different way, for in my view the fact that he requested such a consent supports the view that he was then levying execution. . . .

Notwithstanding these findings as to seizure on 14th April and non-abandonment thereof, defence counsel submits that in May his clients acquired from Wood a good title unencumbered by the judgment debt due from his vendor or by any rights possessed by the sheriff under the writ, and this title they in due course passed on to the plaintiffs. The submission is a startling one, for, baldly stated, it amounts to an assertion that, even although the sheriff had already seized the caravan, the defendants acquired title free from any liability to have their property seized. The corollary to this submission would appear to be that they could have demanded its unconditional surrender by the sheriff. Insofar as I was able to follow it, the basis for the submission appears to be this: (A) Under the proviso to s. 26 of the Sale of Goods Act 1893, a purchaser in good faith and for valuable consideration gets a good title unfettered by any right of seizure in the sheriff provided that when he purchased, he had no notice that a writ of *fieri facias* "by virtue of which the goods of the execution debtor might be seized . . . had been delivered to and remain unexecuted in the hands of the sheriff". (B) Where an execution is issued, the transaction involves four stages: (1) delivery of the writ to the sheriff; (2) seizure; (3) the possible payment of the money after the seizure; and (4), if no payment, sale (see *Mortimore* v. *Cragg*[4] and *Watson* v. *Murray & Co.*[5]). (C) Until either payment or sale, the writ remains "unexecuted". (D) The defendants having bought the caravan from Wood in May and the sheriff's sale not taking place until August, the writ (of which they had no notice) "remained unexecuted" when they bought. (E) As against the sheriff, they

---

[3] [1954] 1 All E.R. 428.
[4] (1878), 3 C.P.D. 216.
[5] [1955] 2 Q.B. 1; [1955] 1 All E.R. 350.

were accordingly protected by the proviso to s. 26, and this protection enured to the plaintiffs when they in due course purchased the caravan from the defendants.

I propose to deal with this submission briefly. The proviso must of necessity be limited in its operation to the ambit of the section which it qualifies. When by the opening words of the section it is provided that, "A writ of *fieri facias* . . . shall *bind* the property in the goods of the execution debtor . . .", this simply means that on delivery of the writ the sheriff acquires a legal right to seize sufficient of the debtor's goods to satisfy the amount specified in the writ (*Samuel* v. *Duke*[6]). The proviso, accordingly, does no more than protect a purchaser of the goods against that right of seizure if the stated conditions are fulfilled. It has no scope for operation where an actual seizure of the debtor's goods has already been effected; and where this has occurred, it is immaterial whether or not the purchaser from the debtor had notice of the seizure, or even of the writ. Furthermore, by its wording the proviso relates only to a writ "by virtue of which the goods of the execution debtor might be seized", and where such an essential step in execution as actual seizure has already been effected, it is, I hold, impossible to regard the writ as one which still "remained *unexecuted* in the hands of the sheriff". In my judgment, accordingly, the defendants are not saved by the proviso.

The result of these findings is that, although the defendants transferred a good title in the caravan to the plaintiffs, they did so in breach of the express warranty in their dealers' invoice that it was unencumbered, and also in breach of the warranties as to quiet possession and freedom from encumbrance implied by s. 12 of the Sale of Goods Act . . .

---

[6] (1838), 3 M. & W. 622.

PART III

THE FACTORS ACT 1889

Lowther *v*. Harris

[1926] All E.R. Rep. 352

By s. 1(1) of the Factors Act 1889: ". . . The expression 'mercantile agent' shall mean a mercantile agent having in the customary course of his business as such agent either authority to sell goods, or to consign goods for the purpose of sale, or to buy goods, or to raise money on the security of goods". A person can be a "mercantile agent" even though he acts for one principal only.

Lowther, the owner of some tapestry, left it with Prior to dispose of for him. Prior had his own shop, and gave receipts and took cheques in his own registered business name. He had no general occupation as an agent, and acted only for one principal, i.e., Lowther. Although he had no authority to complete a sale without Lowther's authority, he sold the tapestry to Harris. Lowther then claimed damages for conversion from Harris.

Held, by the King's Bench Division, that the claim failed. Harris had obtained a good title under the Factors Act 1889, for Prior was a mercantile agent within the meaning of s. 1(1), and the other conditions necessary under the Act in order to pass a good title had all been fulfilled.

WRIGHT, J. (at page 354)

The first question is whether Prior was a mercantile agent—that is, an agent doing a business in buying or selling, or both, having in the customary course of his business as such authority to sell goods. I hold that he was. Various objections have been raised. It was contended that Prior was a mere servant or shopman and had no independent status such as is essential to constitute a mercantile agent. It was held under the earlier Acts that the agent must not be a mere servant or shopman: *Cole* v. *North Western Bank*,[1] *Lamb* v. *Attenborough*,[2] *Hayman* v. *Flewker*.[3] I think this is still law under the present Act. In my opinion, Prior, who had his own shops and who gave receipts and took cheques in his own registered business name and earned commissions, was not a mere servant, but an agent, even though his discretionary authority was limited. It is also contended that even if he were an agent, he was acting

---

1 (1875), L.R. 10 C.P. 354.
2 (1862), 31 L.J.Q.B. 41.
3 (1863), 32 L.J.C.P. 132.

as such for one principal only, the plaintiff, and that the Factors Act requires a general occupation as agent. This, I think, is erroneous. The contrary was decided under the old Acts in *Hayman* v. *Flewker*,[4] and I think the same is the law under the present Act. In *Weiner* v. *Harris*[5] it appears the agent was not acting for any other principal than the plaintiff, and this was the case also in *Hastings Ltd.* v. *Pearson*,[6] in respect of which case the Court of Appeal in *Weiner* v. *Harris*[7] held that the agent was a mercantile agent.

Budberg *v.* Jerwood and Ward

(1934), 51 T.L.R. 99

Even though a person takes goods under a disposition by a "mercantile agent", he will not get a good title to them where the agent was not in possession of them in his capacity of "mercantile agent". Possession in any other capacty, e.g., that of a friend, is not enough.

The plaintiff entrusted a necklace to Dr de Wittchinsky, a Russian lawyer, to obtain offers for it, but instead he sold it to the defendants. The plaintiff claimed its return, but the defendants contended that they had a good title to it under the Factors Act 1889, s. 2(1), for Dr de Wittchinsky was a mercantile agent acting in the ordinary course of his business, and the other requirements of s. 2(1) had been fulfilled.

Held, by the King's Bench Division, that the action succeeded, for, on the evidence, the plaintiff had entrusted the necklace to Dr de Wittchinsky in his capacity of a friend and not that of a mercantile agent, and that consequently the Factors Act 1889 did not apply.

MacNaghten, J. (at page 100)

With regard to the third point, a mercantile agent was a person who in the ordinary course of his business as such agent had authority to sell goods. Now, Dr de Wittchinsky was a doctor of laws, who, towards the end of his life, had a permanent residence in London and there carried on business as a lawyer advising Russians living in this country. None of the witnesses had treated him as having any other business than that of a lawyer. But it was suggested that he acted as a mercantile agent in this transaction. It was said that it was possible that a man could be a mercantile agent although he had only one customer. In support of that proposition the defendants cited *Lowther* v. *Harris*.[8] He accepted that proposition, but it was qualified to this extent, that the alleged agent must be acting in the particular transaction in a business capacity. Here it was clear that the relationship between the plaintiff and Dr de Wittchinsky

---

[4] *Supra.*
[5] [1910] 1 K.B. 285.
[6] [1893] 1 Q.B. 62.
[7] *Supra.*
[8] [1926] All E.R. Rep. 352. See p. 115, *ante.*

was not a business relationship. There was no suggestion of remuneration, and he was acting merely as a friend. In those circumstances the Factors Act did not apply, and that defence also failed.

Pearson *v.* Rose & Young Ltd.

[1950] 2 All E.R. 1027

For the purposes of s. 2(1) *of the Factors Act* 1889 *a mercantile agent is in possession of the goods "with the consent of the owner" even though he may have obtained possession of them by a trick.*[9]

Pearson left his car with Hunt, a mercantile agent, to see what offers for it were made. He had not authorised Hunt to conclude a sale, nor did he intend to pass the property in the car. Hunt had the *animus furandi* when he obtained it. Shortly after obtaining the car he sold it to a third party. One of the contentions in the case was that a good title could not be passed under the Factors Act 1889 because Pearson had not "consented" to Hunt having possession of the car.

Held, by the Court of Appeal, that even though possession of the car had been obtained by a trick, this was sufficient "consent" for the purpose of the Act.

DENNING, L.J. (at page 1031)

If the goods are stolen from the true owner by the mercantile agent, does that mean that the owner does not consent to the mercantile agent having possession of them? At first sight the answer seems to be obvious. No man ever consents to the theft of his goods, but therein lurks a fallacy. There are many cases of larceny where the true owner consents to the thief having possession of the goods, but not to his stealing them. For instance, if the true owner allows the agent to have the goods on hire or for repair, and the agent later on makes up his mind to steal them and does so, either by breaking bulk . . . or by converting them to his own use . . . the true owner undoubtedly consented to his having possession of them. Take the same instance where the owner lets the agent have the goods on hire or for repair, but, with this difference, that the agent from the very beginning intended to steal the goods, . . . the owner undoubtedly consented to his having possession of them. His state of mind is the same in both instances. He consented to possession, but not to the theft of the goods. . . .

---

[9] A considerable part of the case was concerned with the difference between obtaining by false pretences and larceny by a trick. These offences have been abolished by the Theft Act 1968, s. 33(3). Section 15(1) of that Act creates the new offence of obtaining property by deception, and this covers both obtaining by false pretences and larceny by a trick. Accordingly, those parts of the extract of the judgment concerning obtaining by false pretences and larceny by a trick are omitted as they are no longer relevant.

If the true owner was induced to part with the goods by some fraud on the part of the mercantile agent, does that mean that he did not consent to the mercantile agent having possession of them? Again the answer at first sight seems obvious. A consent obtained by fraud is no consent at all, because fraud negatives consent. The effect of fraud, however, in this, as in other parts of the law, is as a rule only to make the transaction voidable and not void, and if, therefore, an innocent purchaser has bought the goods before the transaction is avoided, the true owner cannot claim them back. For instance, if a mercantile agent should induce the owner to pass the property to him by some false pretence, as by giving him for display purposes, by falsely pretending that he was in a large way of business when he was not, then the owner cannot claim the goods back from an innocent purchaser who has bought them in good faith from the mercantile agent. . . . Whether the owner intended to pass the property or not, at any rate he consented to the agent having possession. The consent may have been obtained by fraud but, until avoided, it is a consent which enables the Factors Act to operate: see *per* SCRUTTON, L.J., in *Folkes* v. *King*.[10]

Oppenheimer *v.* Attenborough & Son

[1904-7] All E.R. Rep. 1016

A buyer of goods from a "mercantile agent" will not get a good title to them under s. 2(1) of the Factors Act 1889 unless the sale takes place when the agent is "acting in the ordinary course of business of a mercantile agent".

Oppenheimer, a diamond merchant, was induced by Schwabacher, a diamond broker, to let him have some diamonds so that he could show them to potential purchasers. Instead of selling them, Schwabacher pledged them with Attenborough & Son (a firm of pawnbrokers), as security for an advance to himself. The pawnbrokers did not know of a custom in the diamond trade that a broker had no authority to pledge diamonds, and they took the diamonds in good faith.

Held, by the Court of Appeal, that the pledge was valid under the Factors Act 1889, s. 2(1), for the disposition had been made by a mercantile agent acting in the ordinary course of business, even though he had no authority to pledge by the custom of the trade.

LORD ALVERSTONE, C.J. (at page 1017)

It has been strenuously contended before us that the insertion of the words "when acting in the ordinary course of business as a mercantile agent" in sub-s. (1) of s. 2 was intended to impose some limit upon the generality of the previous Act. I think, after carefully considering the argument of counsel for the defendants, who pointed out the change from the expression in sub-s. (1) of s. 1, "course of his business" to

---

10 [1923] 1 K.B. 282, at pp. 301-302, C.A.

the expression in sub-s. (1) of s. 2, "course of business of a mercantile agent", that there is a good deal to be said in favour of the view which he presented, that we ought not, at any rate unless we see clearly the argument in favour of such a view, to hold that the words "the ordinary course of business of a mercantile agent" were meant to deprive the pledgee of the protection given by former legislation, solely on the ground that the mercantile agent has acted in a way contrary to the custom of the particular trade and contrary to the way in which his principal in the particular case intended he should act.

In this case evidence was tendered before CHANNELL, J.,[11] and, I understand, not seriously disputed, that it was very unusual indeed, if not without exception, for diamond merchants ever to get advances on diamonds through agents. It was said that they always did this business themselves. For the purpose of this case therefore I will assume that counsel for the plaintiff has satisfied us, on evidence that was practically uncontradicted, that diamond merchants, as a matter of the custom of the trade, did not employ agents to obtain advances on diamonds. It seems to be conceded by the plaintiff's argument that an express prohibition by a principal to his agent would not be sufficient to prevent a pledge made by the agent in the course of business being protected in favour of the pledgee. I think that my brother CHANNELL has taken a right view in this case, and that the protection given by the Act to a pledgee cannot be cut down by evidence of a custom of a particular trade, that merchants in that trade always themselves conduct their business of obtaining advances on goods which were the subject of that trade. However, I think my brother CHANNELL has taken the right view, that evidence of this custom was not admissible for the purpose of defeating the protection which otherwise would be given to the pledgee.

It is quite plain when you are dealing with a person who is a mercantile agent, you have got to find out whether in the ordinary and customary course of his business as such agent he has authority to sell goods or consign them for sale or buy or raise money on them. I think one can clearly see, therefore, why the words "the customary course of his business as such agent" were inserted in sub-s. (1) of s. 1. There are many agents, such as carriers of goods, who receive goods, and yet it is not part of the customary course of the business of such agents to sell or consign them for the purpose of sale or to buy or raise money on them. Therefore, when you are dealing with an agent in possession of goods, you have, no doubt, to consider what the condition of the agent is, and what his habits and customs would be when he is acting in the capacity of agent. Undoubtedly the case of an auctioneer entrusted with goods for sale, which counsel for the plaintiff pressed us with, is one of difficulty. He suggested

---

[11] In the Court below.

that under sub-s. (1) of s. 2, if that sub-section is not construed in the way he maintains it should be, an auctioneer would have power to pledge. But it seems to me that there may be particular agents, such for instance as auctioneers, by whom a pledge would be such a departure from the ordinary course of their business as to put the pledgee upon notice. No question of that kind arises here. Having therefore got the class of mercantile agent whose transactinos are to be protected in the interest of the pledgee, you now get to sub-s. (1) of s. 2 as to the circumstances under which the transaction must be carried out. [HIS LORDSHIP read the sub-section.] I think the expression in question means "acting in the transaction as a mercantile agent". There is no doubt that includes the limits suggested, such as that the sale must not take place outside business hours, or under circumstances under which no agent in the trade would transact business.

In my opinion, these words "acting in the ordinary course of business of a mercantile agent" mean that he shall be acting in the transaction as a mercantile agent would act who was carrying out a transaction which his master authorised him to carry out.

BUCKLEY, L.J. (at page 1020)

There is a difference between the expression in s. 1(1) and that used in s. 2(1), one being "in the course of his business", and the other "course of business of a mercantile agent", and I think I see the reason. Section 1(1) says:

"A mercantile agent having, in the customary course of his business as such agent, authority either to sell",

and so on. That is speaking of the arrangement made between the true owner of the goods and the mercantile agent. It contemplates that the principal has given possession of the goods to the agent in the customary course of the business which the principal knows, or believes, the mercantile agent carries on as such. That has to do with the circumstances under which the agent gets possession of the goods, and to satisfy the definition he must get them in the customary course of his business as a mercantile agent. Section 2(1) deals with another matter. It deals with the stage at which the agent is going to deal with the goods in his possession with reference to some other person, and then the form of expression is altered thus: "when acting in the ordinary course of business of a mercantile agent".

The plaintiff's argument involves that we should read that as "of such mercantile agent", or, "of a mercantile agent in such trade as that in which he carries on business". I do not think it means that. I think it means "acting in such a way as a mercantile agent in the ordinary course of business as a mercantile agent would act"; that is to say, within business hours, at a proper place of business, and in other respects in the ordinary way in which a mercantile agent would act, so that there is nothing to lead the pledgee to suppose that anything is being done wrong, or to give him notice that the disposition is one which the mercantile agent had not authority for. Dealing with it in that way, it seems to me there is no great difficulty in the Act of Parliament.

KENNEDY, L.J. (at page 1021)

I do not feel quite sure as to the exact effect of the words in s. 2(1) "when acting in the ordinary course of business of a mercantile agent", and I reserve to myself the right to consider further what these words mean. But I am sure of this, that CHANNELL, J., was right in saying that they ought not to be taken to exclude a case in which a mercantile agent would not, as agent, have authority according to the custom of a particular trade to pledge goods which are the subject of that trade, on the ground that the pledging of such goods is a transaction which, in accordance with the custom of the particular trade, merchants prefer to do for themselves. I think that what has been already said by my Lord and by BUCKLEY, L.J., affords admirable reasons for that view, and the learned Judge himself has pointed out that it would be a very strange thing if the members of any particular trade could take themselves out of the operation of the Factors Act by saying that they only authorised their agents to sell, and never gave them authority to pledge. If, as it has been said, it is notorious in any business that the person who is in the position of an agent does not have authority in the ordinary course of business to pledge, then the proviso at the conclusion of the sub-section protects the real owner of the goods whose property has been improperly dealt with by the agent. What is exactly meant by the words, "made by him when acting in the ordinary course of business of a mercantile agent", I am not quite sure. I am inclined to think that it is meant to apply to a person who, being a mercantile agent, is acting in time, and manner, and other circumstances when he pledges as a mercantile agent, as if he had authority to do it, and might reasonably do it.

Newtons of Wembley Ltd. *v.* Williams

[1964] 3 All E.R. 532

By s. 9 of the Factors Act 1889: "*Where a person having bought or agreed to buy goods, obtains with the consent of the seller possession of the goods . . . the delivery . . . of the goods . . . under any sale . . . to any person receiving the same in good faith and without notice of any lien or other right of the original seller in respect of the goods shall have the same effect as if the person making the delivery were a mercantile agent in possession of the goods . . .*".

On 15th June, 1962, the plaintiffs sold a car to a Mr Andrew, who gave them a cheque in payment. On 18th June they learnt that the cheque would not be met and disaffirmed the contract, but could not find the car. In July, 1962, Andrew sold the car to a Mr Biss in Warren Street, London, which was an established street market for selling used cars. Biss bought in good faith and sold the car to the defendant. The plaintiffs claimed the car from him. The defendant claimed that he had a good title because Biss had a good title under s. 9 of the Factors Act 1889, for Andrew had acted in the way in which he would have been expected to act if he had been a mercantile agent, and must be regarded as having done so in view of the fact that the sale had taken place in a recognised street market.

Held, by the Court of Appeal, that this contention succeeded, and that the action failed.[12]

SELLERS, L.J. (at page 535)

Andrew had bought the goods and obtained them with the consent of the plaintiffs. He had subsequently delivered them on a sale to Biss and, if Biss was a person receiving them in good faith and without notice of any lien or other right of the original seller, then this section provides that the transaction shall have the same effect as if the person making the delivery (that is Andrew) were a mercantile agent in possession of the goods or documents of title with the consent of the owner. So the first part of s. 9 is complied with on the facts of this case and the question arises whether the second part, the receiving of the goods in good faith (and it was not suggested that Biss had notice of any lien or other right of the original seller), had been complied with, and whether, in treating Andrew as a mercantile agent, the requirements had been complied with.

That requires a consideration in the first place of the question what is a mercantile agent. In s. 1(1) of the Factors Act 1889;

"The expression 'mercantile agent' shall mean a mercantile agent having in the customary course of his business as such agent authority either to sell goods, or to consign goods for the purpose of sale, or to buy goods, or to raise money on the security of goods".

That description is to be applied to Andrew on the facts of this case. Section 2(1) deals with the powers of a mercantile agent with respect to the disposition of goods; it provides:

"Where a mercantile agent is, with the consent of the owner, in possession of goods . . . any sale . . . made by him when acting in the ordinary course of business of a mercantile agent, shall, subject to the provisions of this Act, be as valid as if he were expressly authorised by the owner of the goods to make the same: provided that the person taking under the disposition acts in good faith, and has not at the time of the disposition notice that the person making the disposition has not authority to make the same".

---

[12] In April, 1966, the Law Reform Committee in their 12th Report (Transfer of Title to Chattels) (Cmnd. 2958), in commenting on the decision in the above case, said in par. 33: "We do not think it is satisfactory that a person who obtains goods under a voidable contract which is avoided should nevertheless be treated for the purposes of s. [25(1)] of the Sale of Goods Act as a person 'who having bought or agreed to buy goods obtains, with the consent of the seller, possession of the goods' and thus enabled to pass a good title to a third party. This is the result of the reference in s. [25(1)] to a mercantile agent. . . . We accordingly think that where a contract of sale has been effectively rescinded by the owner notifying the person in possession of the goods it should not be possible for the latter to pass a good title, and it should be made clear that for this purpose s. 23 of the Sale of Goods Act prevails over s. [25(1)]".

One of the points taken on behalf of the plaintiffs was that although at the outset Andrew was a person who obtained, with the consent of the seller, possession of the goods, at the time when this transaction took place that consent no longer operated: it had been withdrawn by the rescission of the contract; but Andrew was in possession of the goods of the plaintiffs, a possession which he had obtained at the outset with their consent. Sub-section (2) of s. 2 provides that

> "Where a mercantile agent has, with the consent of the owner, been in the possession of goods . . . any sale . . . which would have been valid if the consent had continued, shall be valid notwithstanding the determination of the consent . . .".

That is an express provision which altered the law as it had been laid down in an earlier case[13] some time in 1868. Notwithstanding that which the plaintiffs had done to terminate their contract and withdraw their consent, they had in fact—true, through inability to do otherwise—left the possession of their car with Andrew.

The only other question which arises is how far, on the construction of this section, that takes the buyer (the defendant in this case), relying on what happened between Andrew and Biss. It had been treated by the learned Judge[14] applying s. 9, as placing Andrew in the position of a mercantile agent but with the obligation on the defendant of establishing not only that Biss took in good faith (I leave out the other position: nothing arose on that) but also that the transaction between Andrew and Biss (Andrew being treated as a mercantile agent in accordance with s. 9) was an "acting in the ordinary course of business of a mercantile agent". There is a possible construction which was urged on us that he would be so acting under s. 9 as a mercantile agent— that it would be assumed or deemed that he was acting in the ordinary course of business; and investigations were made in other parts of the Act of 1889, and in particular s. 8, to see whether any support could be got for that view. . . .

Before one takes too favourable a view for the buyer and too harsh a view against the true owner of the goods where s. 9 can be invoked, one must remember that it is taking away the right which would have existed at common law, and for myself I should not be prepared to enlarge it more than the words clearly permitted and required. It seems to me that all that s. 9 can be said clearly to do is to place the seller on this second sale, the sub-sale to the buyer, in the position of a mercantile agent when he has in fact in his possession the goods of somebody else and does no more than clothe him with that fictitious or notional position in this transaction. Then when one comes to look at s. 2(1), a mercantile agent to whom that section applies has, in order that the buyer may get the full advantage of this section, to estab-

---

[13] *Fuentes* v. *Montis* (1868), L.R. 3 C.P. 268, *affd.* Ex. Ch., L.R. 4 C.P. 93.
[14] [1964] 2 All E.R. 135, at p. 139.

lish that he, the mercantile agent, was acting in the ordinary course of business. It is
said that that is a somewhat vague phrase, and we have referred to some authorities
with regard to that. It may be that in some cases precisely what is in "the ordinary
course of business" of a mercantile agent may call for some special investigation, but
on the face of it it seems to me that it envisages a transaction by a mercantile agent
and is to be derived from such evidence as is either known to the Court or established
by evidence as to what would be the ordinary course of business.

The question arises here on the evidence whether this transaction is to be said to
have been in the ordinary course of business of a mercantile agent. Counsel for the
plaintiffs sought to establish that a transaction taking place in this somewhat unusual
market, the street kerb in Warren Street, was on the face of it something which was
not an ordinary business transaction in any way, by a mercantile agent or anybody
else, but was to some extent suspect; but the learned Judge had evidence about this
and he said[15] (and I think it is within the knowledge of the Court) that there had
been an established market in secondhand cars in this area on this very site for a long
time. Although the learned Judge said[16] that he had some doubt at one time about
this being in the ordinary course of business—as he pointed out, there were no business
premises, the sale was in the street, and the sale was for cash—on the other hand, he
comes to the conclusion, which I think cannot be challenged, that there was in Warren
Street and its neighbourhood an established street market for cash dealing in cars.
When one looks at what took place and finds the prospective buyer coming up and
getting into contact with the prospective seller in regard to a car in that area, with
an offer and an acceptance, with the trial of the car and a looking over it and some
questions asked and a delivery—I do not find anything to indicate that it was not in
the ordinary course of business of a mercantile agent. It seems to me that the defendant
has established that essential fact.

That leaves only the other matter which has to be proved, likewise by the defendant,
whether Biss acted in good faith. If he did, then the requirements of s. 9 are complete,
and the result follows that he got a good title, as if the goods had been sold to him
with the consent of the owner.

Now on good faith we had a submission made to us stressing very largely the price
that was paid. I do not propose to go into all the evidence about that. This was
apparently a secondhand car. It may have been in fact a 1960 model. It had not the
advantage of being licensed in 1960. It was in fact licensed in November, 1959.
Neither had it an overdrive. When all the evidence is gone into, it does reveal that
Andrew gave a cheque for £745 for the car, but that in no way is an indication of its

---

15 *Ibid.*, at p. 139.
16 *Ibid.*, at p. 139.

value or the price that any honest buyer would have paid for it. Andrew never intended to pay a penny for it. The evidence goes further and makes reference to figures £600 or more appearing in Glass's Guide, which is some indication of its value but it is by no means conclusive, and one has in fact at the other end a sale which has not been attacked as not being a *bona fide* one, no later than 12th July, 1962, when all that the buyer, Mr Biss, could get for it from the defendant was £505. Those matters have all to be looked at in the light of the Judge's finding on the evidence. He appreciated the point that was being made of a low price, of a receipt held by Andrew and not, as would have been appropriate, by Biss, and the whole of the circumstances in which the transaction took place—and the fact that there was a £45 loss on the sale. On the matter of good faith he said:[17]

"One can follow these and other criticisms of the Andrew/Biss deal, but the fundamental answer to counsel for the plaintiffs' submission is that I saw and heard Mr Biss and I entirely accept his evidence. I am completely satisfied, and find, that he acted throughout in complete good faith and without the slightest idea of any defect in Andrew's title".

In those circumstances I find nothing to complain about in the learned Judge's judgment. He applied the facts to s. 9. He interpreted the section in the way in which the plaintiffs submitted it ought to be interpreted. The learned Lord Justice said:[18]

"It follows, therefore, that the sale by Andrew to Biss was covered by s. 9 and s. 2 of the Factors Act, 1889. It had the same effect as though Andrew were a mercantile agent in possession of the car with the consent of the plaintiffs; that is to say, that, if the sale was in the ordinary course of business of a mercantile agent, it was effective to transfer title provided that Biss acted in good faith without notice of any rights of the plaintiffs in respect of the car and without notice that Andrew had no authority to sell".

I think that that was established.

---

[17] [1964] 2 All E.R. 135, at p. 139.
[18] *Ibid.*, at p. 139.

PART IV

THE HIRE-PURCHASE ACT 1964

Barker *v*. Bell (Ness, Third Party)

[1971] 2 All E.R. 867

A private purchaser of a motor vehicle obtains a good title to it under s. 27(2) and s. 29(3) of the Hire-Purchase Act 1964 if he has "no actual notice that the vehicle is or was the subject of any hire-purchase agreement". The word "any" means "any relevant agreement", i.e, one under which the owner claims recovery of the vehicle from him.

A hire-purchaser of a car falsely informed Ness, a private individual, that it was clear of any hire-purchase agreement, and showed him a hire-purchase agreement purporting to relate to the car stating that all sums due under it had been paid. Ness bought it and sold it to Bell, who sold it to Barker. The finance company which had let out the car to the hire-purchaser retook possession of it. Barker brought an action against Bell for breach of the implied condition of title, and Bell brought in Ness as a third party. Barker contended that Ness had no title as he had notice that the car "is or was" the subject of "any hire-purchase agreement" within the meaning of s. 29(3) of the Hire-Purchase Act 1964, and that it was immaterial that he had no notice of the hire-purchase agreement existing between the finance company and the hire-purchaser.

Held, by the Court of Appeal, that the action failed, for Ness had a good title and therefore Barker had one also. The word "any hire-purchase agreement" in s. 29(3) of the Act meant any *relevant* hire-purchase agreement, i.e., the agreement under which the finance company claimed the car.

LORD DENNING, M.R. (at page 868)

At common law, apart from the recent Hire-Purchase Act of 1964, there is no doubt that Mr Ness would be liable for breach of the implied condition as to title. But s. 27(2) of the Hire-Purchase Act 1964 provides that where there is a private purchaser—

"... and he is a purchaser of the motor vehicle in good faith and without notice of the hire-purchase agreement or conditional sale agreement, that disposition shall have effect as if the title of the owner or seller to the vehicle had been vested in the hirer or buyer immediately before that disposition".

So that protects a private purchaser if he takes in good faith and without notice of the hire-purchase agreement. On the facts I have stated, it would appear that Mr Ness did take in good faith and without notice. But the difficulty arises because of a definition in s. 29(3) of the Act, which provides:

"... a person shall be taken to be a purchaser of a motor vehicle without notice of a hire-purchase agreement or conditional sale agreement if, at the time of the disposition made to him, he has no actual notice that the vehicle is or was the subject of any hire-purchase agreement or conditional sale agreement".

After reading the section, the Judge[1] said:

"I am satisfied that [Mr Ness] acted in good faith ... but I am troubled in law as to whether or not he had notice of the ... agreement. Commonsense, and Hudson's assurances, verbal and written, indicate that [Mr Ness] had no such notice".

But the Judge felt compelled by s. 29(3) to find that Mr Ness had notice. The Judge was impressed by the words "or was" and the word "any" in s. 29(3) to hold that Mr Ness was not protected. He so held because Mr Hudson[2] had told Mr Ness that the car had been on hire-purchase, which had been paid off, and had produced a receipt from Bowmaker.

The Judge pointed out that Professor Diamond in his book[3] had so interpreted s. 29(3). But I see that Mr Goode in his book[4] has raised a query whether the use of the word "any" in s. 29(3), in contrast to the word "the" in s. 27(2), makes any difference. I think that the Act is ambiguous on this point. Section 27(2) uses the definite article "*the*". The purchaser must take in good faith and without notice of the hire-purchase agreement, that is, of *the* relevant agreement under which the owner reclaims the goods. That definite article "the" appears repeatedly in this group of sections. But s. 29(3) uses the indefinite article "a" and "any"; and, if taken by itself, would mean that notice of any hire-purchase agreement, however irrelevant, would deprive the purchaser of the protection. Faced with this ambiguity, I think we should give priority to the word "the" in s. 27(2), and that we should confine s. 29(3) to any *relevant* hire-purchase agreement. If a car was originally let on hire-purchase terms, but the instalments have all been paid, or the settlement figure has been paid, that hire-purchase agreement is entirely irrelevant; and I see no reason why notice of it should affect the purchaser's title. So far as the words "or was" are concerned, they should not be construed so as to apply to a past agreement which is entirely irrelevant. They can be given a sensible meaning by restricting them to a case where there is a present hire-purchase agreement (under which the owner now claims the car) which provides that, on an attempted sale or disposition of the car by the hirer, the agreement is automatically terminated. The words "or was" do not apply to a past hire-purchase agreement which has been paid off. In short, a purchaser is only affected by notice if he has actual notice that the car is on hire-purchase. He is not affected merely by being told that it was previously on hire-purchase which has now been paid off.

---

[1] Nevin, J., sitting at Kingston-upon-Hull County Court.
[2] I.e., the hire-purchaser.
[3] *Introduction to Hire-Purchase Law* (1967), p. 17. See now 2nd Edn. (1971), p. 18.
[4] *Hire-Purchase Law and Practice*, 2nd Edn., p. 624.

In this case Mr Ness, as the Judge held, had no notice that this car was on hire-purchase. He only had notice that it had been on hire-purchase but had been paid off. That is not sufficient to defeat him. He is protected by s. 27(2). He got a good title for the car. This means that Mr Bell and Mr Barker each got a good title, although they were trade purchasers: see s. 27(3). So Mr Barker need not have delivered up the car to the Auto Finance Services (Hallamshire) Ltd. But that does not concern us now.

It is a difficult point. The Judge was very reluctant to have to give judgment against Mr Ness but he felt that the Act compelled him. I think that the Act can be so construed as to remove that compulsion.

Stevenson *v*. Beverley Bentinck Ltd.

[1976] 2 All E.R. 606

Only a "private purchaser" can obtain a good title to a motor vehicle under the Hire-Purchase Act 1964, s. 27.

The defendants let out a car to Roberts under a hire-purchase agreement. During the currency of the agreement Roberts sold the car to the plaintiff, a tool inspector, who carried on most evenings and at week-ends the business of purchasing motor vehicles for the purpose of offering them for sale. In the previous 18 months he had engaged in 37 transactions. In the present case he bought the car for his own use or for that of his son. The defendants sought to recover the car, but the plaintiff brought an action claiming that he had a good title under the Hire-Purchase Act 1964, s. 27, for he was a "private purchaser" and had bought the car in good faith without notice of the hire-purchase agreement.

Held, by the Court of Appeal, that the plaintiff had not acquired a good title. He was carrying on business partly as a "trade purchaser", and so was not within the protection given to "private purchasers".

LORD DENNING, M.R. (at page 608)

He was getting rid of his own private Sunbeam and he wanted a Jaguar. He was on the look-out for a good secondhand Jaguar. So he purchased it for his own use, intending to run the Jaguar as his own car. The question is whether he can, in these circumstances, claim the protection of the Act as a private purchaser.

He has in his favour a statement by Professor Goode in his book on Hire-Purchase Law and Practice:[5]

". . . even a person carrying on business as a dealer or financier qualifies as a private purchaser if, in relation to the transaction in question, he purchases in his private capacity and not in the course of his business".

---

[5] 2nd Edn. (1970), p. 622.

The Judge[6] did not agree with the professor. Nor do I. This Act does not contain any words such as "in the course of his business". It simply says that, if the purchaser is a trade or finance purchaser and is carrying on that business at the time of the disposition, he has not got the protection of the Act.

Counsel for the plaintiff placed stress on the words "at the time of the disposition". He submitted that they meant that, at the very moment of the disposition, Mr Stevenson must have been carrying on the business of a trade or finance purchaser; and that at the moment when he entered into a private transaction, he was not carrying it on. But I do not feel able to accept that submission. If he was, over the same space of time, be it a week or a month, carrying on the business of purchasing and offering vehicles for sale, he cannot claim the protection of the Act.

It may be asked: why was no protection given to trade or finance purchasers? No doubt because Parliament thought they were well able to take care of themselves. There is available to them the Hire-Purchase Information Service. Whenever a car is offered to a trade purchaser or motor dealer for sale, he at once wants to know whether it is on hire-purchase or not. If it is on hire-purchase, then he is not going to buy it until the title is clear. So it is a regular practice in the trade to telephone H.P.I. and ask: "Is this vehicle on hire purchase or not?" He then gets an answer on which he can safely act: see *Moorgate Mercantile Co. Ltd.* v. *Twitchings.*[7]

It is unfortunate that Mr Stevenson does not seem to have been aware of the service which is provided by H.P.I. Seeing that he had done 37 transactions, he ought to have been aware of it. He ought to have protected himself by telephoning H.P.I. He did not do so, and must take the consequences. He was carrying on business partly as a trade purchaser, and therefore he is not within the protection given to private purchasers.

---

6 BRIDGE, J.
7 [1975] 3 All E.R. 314. But the decision was reversed by the House of Lords: [1976] 2 All E.R. 641.

PART V

INTERNATIONAL SALES

A. C.I.F. CONTRACTS

Ross T. Smyth & Co. v. T. D. Bailey & Co. Ltd.

[1940] 3 All E.R. 60

In a c.i.f. contract property in the goods only passes when it is intended to pass.[1]

The sellers sold to the buyers a quantity of American corn within the range of 14,250 and 15,750 units of 480 lb. each at their option, c.i.f. London, the goods being unascertained and sold by description. Notice of appropriation was given by the sellers in accordance with the terms of the contract by which they stated that about 15,444 units shipped on a certain vessel had been appropriated to the contract. This notice was assented to by the buyers.

Held, by the House of Lords, that notice of appropriation in the case of a c.i.f. contract did *not* pass the property in the goods. Property passed only when the sellers transferred the bills of lading with the intention that it should pass to the buyers.

LORD WRIGHT (at page 65)

I shall begin with the notice of appropriation, which is the document earliest in date after the contract and the bills of lading. I have already quoted the opinion of the Court of Appeal that the result of the appropriation was that the property in the 15,444 quarters passed to the buyers under the Sale of Goods Act 1893.[2] I think, with respect, that the Court of Appeal, presumably because they had not the bills of lading before them, have by inadvertence fallen into an error, which, if not explicitly and fully controverted by this House, might be taken to lay down a general principle, and so have serious consequences in unsettling the course of business generally in c.i.f. contracts. The notice of appropriation under an ordinary c.i.f. contract is not intended to pass, and does not pass, the property. Where, as here, the sale is of unascertained goods by description, there are, at that stage, no goods to which the contract can attach. The seller is free to appropriate to the contract any goods which answer the contract description. This he does by the notice of appropriation which specifies and defines the goods to which the contract attaches. These thereupon he is bound to

---

[1] For the passing of property between seller and buyer, see pp. 21 to 50, *ante*.
[2] Now Sale of Goods Act 1979.

deliver and the buyer is bound to accept, subject to the terms of the contract. That, however, does not involve the passing of the property. The property cannot pass under a contract of sale until the goods are ascertained (the Sale of Goods Act 1893,[3] s. 16), but, once they are ascertained, the property passes at the time when the parties intend it shall (s. 17(1)). As the parties seldom express any such intention, or perhaps even think of it, the intention will generally be a matter of inference from the terms of the contract, the conduct of the parties, and the circumstances of the case (s. 17(2)). Then s. 18 gives some general rules which are to apply "unless a different intention appears". Of these rules, the Court of Appeal rely on r. 5(1), which provides as follows:

> "Where there is a contract for the sale of unascertained or future goods by description, and goods of that description and in a deliverable state are unconditionally appropriated to the contract, either by the seller with the assent of the buyer, or by the buyer with the assent of the seller, the property in the goods [then] passes to the buyer . . .".

The assent is generally inferred from the terms of the contract or the practices of the trade. Sub-rule (2) deals with the delivery of the goods to the carrier for transmission to the buyer without reserving the right of disposal, and provides that in such a case there is deemed to be an unconditional appropriation. This latter sub-rule, which only deals with delivery to the carrier and not with actual notice of appropriation, is disregarded by the Court of Appeal. In such event, the carrier receives and holds the goods for the buyer, so that in law they are delivered to the buyer. Compare also s. 32(1). However, the Court, I venture to think, should not have disregarded the word "unconditionally" in sub-rule (1). I do not construe sub-rule (1) as limited to a case where there is an express term that the notice of appropriation is unconditional, or, on the other hand, to a case where the notice of appropriation is in terms conditional, though the words contained in the notice of appropriation—namely, "under the usual reserves as per contract"—would, I think, necessarily import that the contract conditions were to be borne in mind. In this case, the facts known to both parties would import that the appropriation was conditional. The bills of lading were held by the appellants. The contract provided for cash or (at sellers' option) an acceptance of sellers' draft against documents. That condition for the transfer of the documents had not been fulfilled. The bills of lading were the symbols of the goods, and the appellants, by retaining them, retained as against the respondents' title and control over the goods. All the respondents had at that stage was a contractual right to obtain control, and thereby become owners upon taking up the documents. It is impossible, in my opinion, to hold that the notice of appropriation was, even apart from the express reservation, unconditional. It is unfortunate that the attention of the Court of Appeal

---

[3] Now Sale of Goods Act 1979.

does not appear to have been drawn to this aspect of the case, or to the form of the bills of lading, which were to shipper's order, and were indorsed in blank and transferred to, and retained by, the appellants. In such circumstances the appellants thus held the *jus disponendi*, whether the goods were shipped by the shippers as their agents or were transferred to them after shipment, at least from the time when they received the bills of lading.

However, there is a more serious objection to the view taken by the Court of Appeal. This objection rests on the Sale of Goods Act 1893,[4] s. 19(1), which expressly deals both with the case of the sale of specific goods and with the case of the appropriation of goods to the contract subsequent to the contract. It provides that the seller may, by the terms of the contract or appropriation, reserve the right of disposal until certain conditions are fulfilled, and that, in such case, notwithstanding the delivery of the goods to the buyer, or to a carrier or bailee for transmission to the buyer, the property in the goods docs not pass to the buyer until the conditions imposed by the seller are fulfilled. By s. 19(2), it is provided that, if by the bill of lading the goods are deliverable to the seller or his agent, the seller is *prima facie* deemed to reserve the right of disposal. It is true that all these rules, both under s. 18 and under s. 19, are *prima facie* rules, and depend on intention, but the intention in this regard by the parties is seldom or never capable of proof. It is to be ascertained, as already stated here, by having regard to the terms of the contract, the conduct of the parties and the circumstances of the case. The contract in question, though containing several complicated provisions, was in its essence a c.i.f. contract. In particular, the provision already referred to for cash against shipping documents clearly contemplated that the sellers (the appellants) were to retain the documents, including the bills of lading, until the condition of payment was fulfilled. It is true that, by the bills of lading, the goods were not in terms made deliverable to the seller or his agent, but, for all purposes of the contract, the position was the same as soon as the bills of lading (which were to the shipper's order) were indorsed in blank and transferred to the appellants. When that happened, the appellants had title in, and control over, the goods. They could deal with the goods as they liked, even though to deal with them contrary to the notice of appropriation would *prima facie* be a breach of the contract. No property passed to the respondent until the conditions stipulated in the bills of lading for the transfer of the property were fulfilled.

The contract in question here is of a type familiar in commerce, and is described as a c.i.f. contract. The initials indicate that the price is to include cost, insurance and freight. It is a type of contract which is more widely and more frequently in use than any other contract used for purposes of sea-borne commerce. An enormous number

---

4 Now Sale of Goods Act 1979.

of transactions, in value amounting to untold sums, are carried out every year under c.i.f. contracts. The essential characteristics of this contract have often been described. The seller has to ship or acquire after that shipment the contract goods, as to which, if unascertained, he is generally required to give a notice of appropriation. On or after shipment, he has to obtain proper bills of lading and proper policies of insurance. He fulfils his contract by transferring the bills of lading and the policies to the buyer. As a general rule, he does so only against payment of the price, less the freight, which the buyer has to pay. In the invoice which accompanies the tender of the documents on the "prompt"—that is, the date fixed for payment—the freight is deducted, for this reason. In this course of business, the general property in the goods remains in the seller until he transfers the bills of lading. These rules, which are simple enough to state in general terms, are of the utmost importance in commercial transactions. I have dwelt upon them perhaps unnecessarily, because the judgment of the Court of Appeal might seem to throw doubt on one of their most essential aspects. The property which the seller retains while he or his agent, or the banker to whom he has pledged the documents, retains the bills of lading is the general property, and not a special property by way of security. In general, however, the importance of the retention of the property is not only to secure payment from the buyer but for purposes of finance. The general course of international commerce involves the practice of raising money on the documents so as to bridge the period between shipment and the time of obtaining payment against documents. These credit facilities, which are of the first importance, would be completely unsettled if the incidence of the property were made a matter of doubt. By mercantile law, the bills of lading are the symbols of the goods. The general property in the goods must be in the seller if he is to be able to pledge them. The whole system of commercial credits depends on the seller's ability to give a charge on the goods and the policies of insurance. A mere unpaid seller's lien would, for obvious reasons, be inadequate and unsatisfactory. I need not observe that particular contracts may contain special terms, or otherwise indicate a special intention, taking the contract outside these rules. Such a case, to take one example, was *The Parchim*,[5] as explained by Lord SUMNER in *The Kronprinsessan Margareta*.[6] These special cases, however, may be ignored when I am stating the general practice.

---

5 [1918] A.C. 157, P.C.
6 [1921] 1 A.C., at p. 516.

Law & Bonar Ltd. *v.* British American Tobacco Co. Ltd.

(1916), 115 L.T. 612

In the case of a c.i.f. contract no notice need be given to the buyer to enable him to take out an additional insurance policy.[7]

In May, 1914, the sellers sold a quantity of hessian to the buyers c.i.f. Smyrna, and the goods were to arrive there in September. The goods were shipped at Calcutta on 20th July, and the sellers insured them under a policy which excluded war risks. War broke out on 4th August, and the vessel carrying the goods was sunk by enemy action on 13th August. The buyers refused to take up the shipping documents, and did not pay the price, contending that under s. 32(3) of the Sale of Goods Act 1893,[8] the sellers should have given them notice of shipment so that a policy against war risks could have been effected by the buyers.

Held, by the King's Bench Division, that this contention failed for s. 32(3) did not apply to c.i.f. contracts in normal circumstances (e.g., in peacetime when the contract was concluded).

ROWLATT, J. (at page 612)

In my opinion s. 32(3) of the Sale of Goods Act 1893[9] clearly does not apply to this case. It does not apply to a c.i.f. contract in time of peace when war is not contemplated, because such a contract provides for all the insurance which is customary. The contract in this case is a c.i.f. contract and was made at a time when no one anticipated that within three months a state of war would be in existence. Subsequently, it is true, strained relations between Great Britain and Germany came into being, followed by an outbreak of hostilities, and there were risks which were in addition to those insured against in times of peace. But I do not think that a new obligation thereby arose for the seller, for s. 32(3) applies to a contract as at the time that contract is made—that is to say, in this case, in May, 1914. The question whether s. 32(3) would apply to a c.i.f. contract made when insurances other than those to be provided by the seller—*e.g.*, war risks—are usual does not arise, and I leave it quite open. There is no real evidence here that it was usual to insure against war risks at any material time.

---

[7] But a notice to the buyer to enable him to insure is necessary in the case of an f.o.b. contract. See *Wimble v. Rosenberg* (1913), 109 L.T. 294, C.A., p. 159, *post*.
[8] Now Sale of Goods Act 1979.
[9] Now Sale of Goods Act 1979.

James Finlay & Co. Ltd. *v.* N.V. Kwik Hoo Tong, Handel Maatschappij[10]

[1928] All E.R. Rep. 110

In the case of a c.i.f. contract the seller must tender to the buyer a bill of lading showing the true date of shipment.

The sellers agreed to sell to the buyers a quantity of sugar c.i.f. Bombay, and one-third of it was to be shipped from Java in September, 1920. The bill of lading which was tendered stated that the goods had been shipped on 30th September, but in fact they had not been loaded until 1st October.

Held, by the Court of Appeal, that under a c.i.f. contract accurate documents must be tendered. Since the bill of lading was inaccurate as to the date of shipment, the sellers were guilty of a breach of contract.

SCRUTTON, L.J. (at page 112)

The sellers sold sugar to an English firm carrying on business in India, James Finlay & Co. The contract was for shipment of a quantity of sugar in three months, one-third of it to be in September, 1920. The question only arises as to the September shipment, and it is well settled since *Bowes* v. *Shand*[11] that these conditions as to the time of shipment are vital conditions with regard to the sale of goods. It is useless, if you have contracted to sell a September shipment, to tender goods shipped in October and to say that that difference in time is only a very little one. The term as to the time of shipment is of the essence of the contract. On 30th September the sellers had sugar which would have satisfied this contract ready for shipment at a port in Java, and the ship in which they were going to ship it arrived on that date at the port and lay there, but none of the sugar was shipped on board the ship during the month of September. Consequently, the sellers broke their contract of sale with Messrs Finlay. But more happened than that, because, this being a c.i.f. contract, the sellers had not only to ship the goods under a contract that they should be carried to the port of destination named in the contract, but they had also to furnish the buyer with certain documents. In the first place, they had to furnish him with a contract of carriage relating to the goods specified in the contract, so that, if these goods were lost during the voyage by matters for which the shipowner was responsible, the buyer would be able to recover his loss from the shipowner. They had also to furnish to the buyer a policy of insurance covering goods which were goods complying with the contract, so that, if the goods were lost during the voyage by matters coming within the policy, the buyer could recover their value from the underwriters. It is as much a part of the contract that the seller should ship the goods as that he should provide the buyer

---

[10] Another aspect of this case is considered under "Mitigation of Damages", see p. 106, *ante.*
[11] (1877), 2 App. Cas. 455.

with the documents. It is not necessary to discuss whether it is accurate to say that a c.i.f. contract is a sale of documents or a sale of goods. In view of the fact that the goods may be lost before the documents are tendered and before the property has passed, there is a good deal to be said for the view that at any rate a very large proportion of the contract is a sale of documents. But at any rate it is an essential part of the contract that accurate documents relating to goods complying with the contract should be furnished to the buyer.

Re an Arbitration between Keighley, Maxted & Co. and Bryan, Durant & Co. (No. 2)

(1894), 70 L.T. 155

In the case of a c.i.f. contract the bill of lading tendered by the seller must, as regards the quantity of goods shipped, correspond exactly with the amount specified in the contract of sale.

The sellers shipped 3,800 tons of wheat at Bombay, and stated that they had appropriated 3,000 tons to the contract made with the buyers. There were two bills of lading representing 1,750 tons each and two for 250 tons each, and the sellers offered to deliver to the buyers either all the bills of lading or two for 1,750 tons each. The buyers refused to accept the offer or pay any part of the price.

Held, by the Court of Appeal, that the buyers were justified in doing so, for they were entitled to a bill of lading representing the amount specified in the contract.

LORD HALSBURY (at page 157)

As to the question which arises for our decision here, whether there was a good tender by the sellers, when the facts are properly understood and made plain, it is not at all difficult to see what our decision must be. The contract is for the sale and delivery of wheat, the amount of which is to be ascertained thus: there is in the contract what is called a "maximum" and "minimum" clause, which provides that the sellers may ship less than the minimum quantity, in which case the price of the quantity short shipped of the medium quantity is to be settled at the value of the day of the appropriation; or that the sellers may ship more than the maximum quantity in which case the excess over the medium amount will remain for their account. The only question really is, whether there were shipping documents corresponding to the amount bought which the purchasers could have to deal with as they pleased. It has been argued that the seller could give a bill of lading for as much wheat as he liked under this contract. That, however, can only be so if contradictory words are added to the contract. It seems to me, therefore, that the purchasers had a right to have a bill of lading for the amount which they bought, 3,000 tons. Such a bill of lading was not offered to them, and the tender by the sellers was therefore bad, and the purchasers are not liable.

LOPES, L.J. (at page 157)

I am of the same opinion. It is conceded that, if the contract had been for 3,000 tons, and there had been no maximum and minimum clause, the purchasers would have been entitled to a bill of lading for that amount, and that no other bill of lading would have been a good tender. It seems to me that the true construction of this contract was determined upon shipment of the wheat, and that the contract there became one for 3,000 tons. A bill of lading was tendered to the purchasers for 3,800 tons, and consequently the shipping documents tendered by the sellers were not in conformity with the contract. The purchasers were entitled to have a bill of lading which would, if they so desired, transfer the whole thing bought to anyone else, and were not bound to take a bill of lading for a larger amount which would make them trustees of a part of the cargo which they had not contracted to buy or to be trustees of. The tender by the sellers was therefore bad and the purchasers were not bound to accept it.

DAVEY, L.J. (at page 157)

I agree. The case is perfectly clear when the facts are once understood. It is conceded that purchasers in an ordinary case are entitled to a bill of lading for the amount which they have purchased. The question is, whether the clause which has been indorsed upon this contract amounts to a special contract that that right of the purchasers shall be altered. It has been argued that this special clause will have no effect unless it is so construed. I think that is not so, and that the clause has another effect. I am not disposed in this case to alter the rule of law and of common sense that a purchaser of 3,000 tons of wheat is entitled to a bill of lading for 3,000 tons, unless there is a very express contract otherwise. This clause in this contract says nothing at all about a bill of lading, and to support the argument of the [sellers] it would be necessary to read in words to the effect that the sellers should be at liberty to give the purchasers a bill of lading for more than the amount purchased. I cannot think that it was intended to insert such an important stipulation into this contract by such a clause as this framed in such words.

Hansson *v.* Hamel & Horley Ltd.

[1922] All E.R. Rep. 237

Under a c.i.f. contract the bill of lading tendered by the seller must protect the buyer from the port of shipment to the port of destination.

The sellers sold to the buyers a quantity of cod guano to be shipped from Norway c.i.f. Kobe or Yokohama. It was shipped on board the *Kiev* from Braatvag (in Norway) to Hamburg under a bill of lading dated 22nd April, 1920, and thence transhipped in the *Atlas Maru* for delivery in Japan. At Hamburg the agent of the *Atlas Maru* issued a through bill of lading dated 5th May, 1920, stating that the goods had been "shipped from Braatvag according to bill of lading on 22nd April, 1920. Shipped in apparent good order and condition by [the seller] on board the . . . *Kiev*, lying in or off the port of Braatvag and bound to Hamburg for transhipment into the . . . *Atlas Maru*". The buyers refused to accept the bill of lading when tendered to them.

Held, by the House of Lords, that they were entitled to do so. The through bill of lading only contained the contract with the owners of the *Atlas Maru* and in no way bound the owners of the *Kiev*, for the statement in it was only a recital of the facts and not words of contract. Under a c.i.f. contract the bill of lading tendered must protect the buyer from shipment to destination. In any event, the bill of lading should be procured on shipment, and this bill was issued 13 days after shipment in another port in another country.

LORD SUMNER (at page 240)

This bill of lading, accordingly, was itself dated after the contract time of shipment, viz., March-April, but it is stated in the margin, and truly so, that, according to a bill of lading (that is the local one), shipment at Braatvag was within the contract time. It stated further that the goods, when shipped in the *Kiev*, were in apparent good order and condition, but it was silent as to their condition at Hamburg. There was no express statement that any goods had been shipped in the *Atlas Maru* at all, or, if so, in what order and condition they were when shipped, and it was reasonably plain that the *Kiev* did not belong to the Japanese owners of the *Atlas Maru*. The undertaking to deliver in Japan would, in the absence of special authority to those signing the bill of lading, apply only to such cargo as might, in fact, have been shipped at Hamburg on board the *Atlas Maru*, and no one would assume without actual evidence of it that a person like Mr Lind, signing on behalf of the captain of the *Atlas Maru* had any authority to bind her owners for the carriage by the *Kiev* or the owners of the *Kiev* for anything at all. The question is whether this ocean bill of lading was a good tender under the contract of sale and whether the respondents were bound to take it up and pay for the consignment.

A c.f. and i. seller, as has often been pointed out, has to cover the buyer by procuring and tendering documents which will be available for his protection from shipment to destination and I think that this ocean bill of lading afforded the buyer no protection in regard to the interval of 13 days which elapsed between the dates of the two bills of lading and presumably between the departure from Braatvag and the arrival at Hamburg. The initial words, on which the matter depends, may be put as a mere recital of a fact, or as words of contract, and in the latter case the contract may be that the owners of the *Atlas Maru* will (i) be answerable for the safe carriage of the goods from Braatvag to Hamburg, though they have not actually carried them, subject always to the perils excepted in their own bill of lading, though these do not correspond with the exceptions in the *Kiev* bill of lading, or (ii) will make good any loss or damage to the goods during the transit from Braatvag to Hamburg, if the owners of the *Kiev* fail to do so, or (iii) will indemnify the respondents against loss or damage affecting the goods during the voyage. Unless the words are words of contract to the effect first above-mentioned, they are useless to the respondents, and even so the question arises on the face of the document what authority, if any, the captain of the *Atlas Maru* or his agent, Mr Lind, who signs for him, has to bind his owners by words of promise in respect of a voyage, which is already over before he has anything to do with the goods on behalf of the Osaka company. *Prima facie* he has none, and there is nothing shown to rebut the presumption. No doubt a question may arise on any bill of lading whether the captain has, in fact, signed for more goods than were put on board, and, if so, whether he has any special authority to do so, but the doubt raised here, if no dissimilar in kind, is different in its actual form and much greater in degree. Of course, no contract by way of indemnity or by way of guarantee or of answering for the default of another will satisfy those requirements of a c.f. and i. sale which involve a contract of affreightment, since different defences are available on them and different incidents attach to them to those applicable to a bill of lading. Still less can a mere recital of facts avail.

With all deference to the very weighty opinion of BAILHACHE, J., to the contrary, in my judgment, these words are mere words of recital, but even if they were what the appellant contends that they are, I think it is clear that they do not make the ocean bill of lading a good tender in this case. The bill of lading by the *Kiev* was originally a contract with the appellant himself, and never was, nor in any normal course of business ever would be, tendered to the respondents. As there were not, I suppose, to be two contracts for carriage as far as Hamburg, this is strong to show that the appellant never intended the ocean bill of lading to be a contract of carriage from Braatvag to Hamburg. When documents are to be taken up, the buyer is entitled to documents which substantially confer protective rights throughout. He is not buying a litigation, as A. T. LAWRENCE, J., says in the *General Trading Co. Case*.[12] These documents have to be handled by banks, they have to be taken up or rejected promptly

---

[12] (1911), 16 Com. Cas. 95, at p. 101.

and without any opportunity for prolonged inquiry, they have to be such as can be retendered to sub-purchasers, and it is essential that they should so conform to the accustomed shipping documents as to be reasonably and readily fit to pass current in commerce. I am quite sure that, in the circumstances of this case, this ocean bill of lading does not satisfy these conditions. It bears notice of its insufficiency and ambiguity on its face: for, though called a through bill of lading, it is not really so. It is the contract of the subsequent carrier only, without any complementary promises to bind the prior carriers in the through transit. The appellant's contract with Mr Lind was not transferable by endorsement and delivery, nor was it tendered; the *Kiev* bill of lading he kept to himself, and endorsed to Mr Lind under his own contract with him. I do not suggest that tender of either document would have carried matters any further, but, as things stood, the buyer was plainly left with a considerable lacuna in the documentary cover to which the contract entitled him.

The point is also put in a slightly different way, which equally relates especially to bills of lading. SCRUTTON, J., points out in *Landauer & Co.* v. *Craven and Speeding Bros.*,[13] that in a sale of goods c.f. and i., the contract of affreightment must be procured "on shipment". Of course, this is practicable and common even when a through bill of lading is necessary, containing provision for transhipment at an intermediate port from a local to an ocean steamer not in the same ownership. I do not understand this proposition as meaning that the bill of lading would be bad, unless it was signed contemporaneously with the actual placing of the goods on board. "On shipment" is an expression of some latitude. Bills of lading are constantly signed after the loading is complete and, in some cases, after the ship has sailed. I do not think that they thereby necessarily cease to be procured "on shipment", nor do I suppose that the learned Judge so intended his words. It may also be that the expression would be satisfied, even though some local carriage on inland waters or by canal or in an estuary by barge or otherwise, preceded the shipment on the ocean steamer, provided that the steamer's bill of lading covered that prior carriage by effectual words of contract. "On shipment" is referable both to time and place. In principle, however, and subject to what I have said, I accept this opinion of so great an authority, and I am quite sure that a bill of lading only issued 13 days after the original shipment, at another port in another country many hundreds of miles away, is not duly procured "on shipment". Indeed, the ocean bill of lading was not procured as part of this c.f. and i. shipment at all, and "on shipment" does not at any rate mean on re-shipment or on transhipment. It is not enough that at the time of the initial shipment the c.f. and i. seller procured a contract by correspondence with Mr Lind for the forwarding of the goods by an ocean steamer, for that was not procuring a bill of

---

13 [1912] 2 K.B. 94.

lading. If the *Kiev* had been lost with the cod guano on the coast of Norway, no contract of affreightment to Japan would have been procured or forthcoming at all. The matter was well tested thus in the Court of Appeal. In the absence of express stipulation, shipping documents under a contract of sale on c.f. and i. terms must be tendered by the buyer as soon as possible after shipment (*Biddell Bros.* v. *E. Clemens Horst*[14]). If, then, the port of transhipment was late on in the through voyage, a buyer might be entitled to tender the documents long before any through bill of lading to Japan had been signed or procured at all, and when there was no bill of lading in existence except that to the intermediate port. This ocean bill of lading was, therefore, on this ground also, in my opinion, a bad tender.

M. Golodetz & Co. Inc. *v.* Czarnikow-Rionda Co. Inc.

[1980] 1 All E.R. 501

A "clean" bill of lading is one in which there is nothing to qualify the admission by the shipowner that the goods were in apparent good order and condition, and which is a document which would ordinarily and properly have been accepted in the trade as being an appropriate document.

G. & Co. sold to the buyers 12,000/13,000 tonnes of sugar c. & f. Bandasharpur, Iran, under a contract requiring clean bills of lading as one of the documents to be tendered by the sellers. The cargo was loaded at Kandla, India. A fire broke out and 200.8 tonnes of the sugar were damaged by fire and water and were discharged. They could not be made suitable for reloading. On the face of the bill of lading there was a typewritten notation stating: "Cargo covered by this bill of lading has been discharged at Kandla . . . damaged by fire and/or water used to extinguish fire . . .". When the bill of lading was tendered to the buyers, they rejected it on the ground that it was not a "clean" bill. The sellers claimed the price of the goods.

Held, by the Court of Appeal, that there would be judgment for the sellers. The bill of lading was a "clean" one for (i) there was nothing to qualify the admission that the goods were in apparent good order and condition at the time of shipment; and (ii) there was no evidence that it was not a document which would ordinarily and properly have been accepted in the trade as being an appropriate document.

MEGAW, L.J. (at page 505)

There were in the course of the arbitration various other complaints about that bill of lading. One by one they have dropped away. But the complaint which was the original complaint, when the bills of lading were first tendered by the sellers to the buyers and when the 200 tonnes bill of lading was rejected, still remains. That complaint relates

---

[14] [1911] 1 K.B. 934, C.A.: reversed on another point by the House of Lords, *sub nom. Clemens (E.) Horst & Co.* v. *Biddell Bros.*, [1912] A.C. 18.

to the fact that, on the face of the bill of lading, presumably before the signature was put on the bill, there was put on it a typewritten notation, which was in these terms: "Cargo covered by this bill of lading has been discharged Kandla view damaged by fire and/or water used to extinguish fire for which general average declared". That notation accurately stated the facts. It was contended on behalf of the buyers, in rejecting that bill of lading, that it was not a "clean" bill of lading. I do not find it necessary to refer to the precise terms of the various ways in which it was expressed in the correspondence which passed between the parties at the time of the rejection.

The issue in the first arbitration was, and the first issue before us is, whether the buyers were entitled to reject that bill of lading. The award made by the arbitrators reads: "(c) The said Bills of Lading were not clean 'On Board' Bills of Lading within the meaning of the said contract by reason of the notation referred to in paragraph A.8 hereof". (That is, the notation above set out).

The relevant question of law which was stated for the decision of the Court in that award is: "On the facts found and on the true construction of the contract (1) Whether the sellers are entitled to the price of the 2,008 bags of sugar alternatively to damages for the buyers' failure to accept the same or to take up and pay for the shipping documents in respect thereof". A further question was stated, which does not now call for an answer.

The learned Judge[15] held that the correct answer to the question was in the affirmative. This is because, in the learned Judge's view, the bill of lading was a clean bill of lading and the buyers should have accepted it and paid the price.

I think that, without disrespect to the very interesting and careful arguments which have been put before us by counsel on that issue, I can deal with them quite shortly.

The learned Judge was asked, on behalf of the buyers, to uphold the arbitrators' view of the matter on a large number of grounds. The first ground was that the bill of lading was not "clean" and that, therefore, it did not comply with the provisions of the contract for a clean "On Board" bill of lading; and that indeed was what the arbitrators appear to have held in their award. The learned Judge, having gone into the authorities, arrived at the conclusion that a clean bill of lading is one in which there is nothing to qualify the admission that the goods were in apparent good order and condition at the time of shipment.

Counsel for the buyers accepted in this Court that that meaning of "clean", in respect of "clean bill of lading", was indeed, as he put it, the correct meaning of the word "clean". There is also authority to that effect. But, said counsel, though that is

---

15 DONALDSON, J.

the correct meaning of "clean", it has another, wider, meaning in which it can be used: namely, that a bill of lading is not "clean" if it contains a clause the effect of which is to make the bill of lading unacceptable or unmerchantable, so that it would not be accepted in the ordinary way in the trade as being a proper document. He says that, on the true construction of the award with which we are concerned, the arbitrators ought to be taken to have been using the words "not clean" in that wider sense. They ought not to be taken to have been using the words in the narrower sense.

I have no doubt but that the learned Judge was right in saying that, on the correct approach in law, this bill of lading, with the typewritten notation on it, is a "clean" bill of lading in the proper sense of that word; and therefore, if indeed the arbitrators' finding that it was not a "clean" bill of lading is a finding which has got to be treated as using the word "clean" in its proper legal sense, the arbitrators had erred in law. That is the view the learned Judge took.

However, counsel for the buyers, as I have said, submits that, on the construction of the award as a whole and by reference to various documents which passed between the parties, and, I think he also submits, as a matter of ordinary good sense, the arbitrators ought, by way of necessary inference, to be taken as saying that the bill of lading was not "clean" in the sense that it was not a document which would ordinarily and properly have been accepted in the trade as being an appropriate document. That there is such a requirement in relation to bills of lading is, I think, sufficiently clear. The authority in that regard which is usually quoted, and which was quoted by the learned Judge in this case, is a passage from the speech of Lord SUMNER in *Hansson* v. *Hamel & Horley Ltd.*[16] The passage cited by the learned Judge contains these words:

> "These documents have to be handled by banks, they have to be taken up or rejected promptly and without any opportunity for prolonged inquiry, they have to be such as can be retendered to sub-purchasers, and it is essential that they should so conform to the accustomed shipping documents as to be reasonably and readily fit to pass current in commerce".

DONALDSON, J., unreservedly accepted that proposition. He said that if the arbitrators had found that a bill of lading in this form was not acceptable in the trade, his decision "would, of course, have been different". In that event he would have upheld their decision on this issue. But the learned Judge found himself unable to take the view that that was what the arbitrators were to be treated as having said, either by the words that they used or any inference that could properly be drawn in respect of them from the award as a whole or any relevant matters referred to therein.

---

[16] [1922] 2 A.C. 36, at p. 46.

For myself, I find that view supported by the fact that, in the second award dealing with what has been called the "insurance" issue, the self-same arbitrators, in dealing with the question whether a policy of insurance taken out by the buyers was in accordance with the contract, made an express finding, first, that the policy was defective in certain stated respects, and then went on to say: "We further find and/or hold that the policy was not one which was usual or merchantable in the trade".

The arbitrators, therefore, when they were minded to find that a document was not one which was usual or merchantable in the trade, were prepared to express that view specifically. That lends strength, in my view, to the conclusion reached by the learned Judge. I would agree with him, in any event, that here it cannot be assumed or accepted, even on a balance of probability (if that were the appropriate test), that the arbitrators were intending to say, "We, having considered this matter, find here that this document is one which was unusual and which was not merchantable in the trade". In my judgment, accepting the conclusion of the learned Judge, the arbitrators here must be taken, incorrectly as a matter of law, to have held that the bill of lading in question was not "clean" by reason of the notation referred to. If the arbitrators have not found that this bill of lading, with its notation, is not reasonably and readily fit to pass current in commerce, there is no reason for the Court so to hold.

Diamond Alkali Export Corporation *v.* Bourgeois

[1921] All E.R. Rep. 283

In the case of a c.i.f. contract the seller must tender to the buyer an insurance policy. A certificate of insurance is insufficient.

A contract for the sale of a quantity of soda ash stated that the goods were to be delivered c.i.f. Gothenburg. The seller tendered the shipping documents to the buyer, but these did not include a *policy* of insurance but only a certificate of insurance.

Held, by the King's Bench Division, that this was not a good tender under the contract. In the absence of an agreement to the contrary, it was the duty of the seller to supply a *policy*.

McCARDIE, J. (at page 290)

Is this certificate a proper policy of insurance within the c.i.f. contract here made? I have read, I believe, all the cases on the rights and obligations of buyer and seller under c.i.f. contract from *Ireland* v. *Livingston*[17] and *Hickox* v. *Adams*,[18] to *Johnson* v. *Taylor Bros. & Co. Ltd.*[19] Many decisions are cited in *Benjamin on Sale* (6th Edn.),

---

[17] (1872), L.R. 5 H.L. 395.
[18] (1876), 34 L.T. 404, C.A.
[19] [1920] A.C. 144, H.L.

p. 850,[20] and so on. In all the cases a "policy of insurance" is mentioned as an essential document. The law is settled and established. I may point out that in *Burstall & Co.* v. *Grimsdale & Sons*[21] it was expressly provided by the contract that a certificate of insurance might be an alternative for an actual policy. I ventured in *Manbre Saccharine Co.* v. *Corn Products Co.*[22] to discuss the relevant authorities, including the lucid judgment of ATKIN, J., in *C. Groom Ltd.* v. *Barber*,[23] a judgment which I have again most carefully read. It seems plain that a mere written statement by the sellers that they hold the buyers covered by insurance in respect of a specified policy of insurance, is not a policy of insurance within a c.i.f. contract: see the *Manbre Case*.[24] It seems plain also that a broker's cover note or an ordinary certificate of insurance are not adequate agreements within such a contract: see BAILHACHE, J., in *Wilson, Holgate & Co. Ltd.* v. *Belgian Grain and Produce Co. Ltd.*[25] Does the present document fulfil the sellers' contractual duty? In the *Wilson Holgate Case* BAILHACHE, J., said:[26]

> "It must be borne in mind that in dealing with certificates of insurance I am not referring to American certificates of insurance which stand on a different footing and are equivalent to policies, being accepted in this country as policies".

It will be observed that BAILHACHE, J., used the word "accepted" and not the words "bound to accept". The sellers here rely on that passage and also on the notes to *Scrutton and Mackinnon on Charterparties* (10th Edn.), p. 185, where it is said:

> "A certificate of insurance issued by an insurance company under a floating policy upon which document the company can be sued would suffice in any case".

The buyer strongly challenges that view, and his counsel require me to express an independent opinion on the point.

I do so with the greatest diffidence and reluctance in view of the weight carried by even the *dicta* of such experienced and distinguished Judges as SCRUTTON, L.J., and BAILHACHE, J. I feel bound to express my view, not upon a question of business convenience, but upon the strict law of the matter. I assume that this document (which is not stamped) was given under a floating policy issued by the insurance company to D. A. Horan. Now the certificate is not a policy. It does not purport to be a policy. This is conceded by counsel in his able argument for the sellers. It is a certificate that a policy was issued to D. A. Horan, and it incorporates the terms of that policy. Those terms I do not know, nor is there anything before me to indicate that the buyers knew them. The certificate does not show whether that policy was in

---

[20] See now Benjamin, *Sale of Goods* (1st Edn. 1974), par. 1525.
[21] (1906), 11 Com. Cas. 280.
[22] [1918-19] All E.R. Rep. 980. This case is considered on another point, see p. 148, *post*.
[23] [1914-15] All E.R. Rep. 194. This case is treated on another point, see p. 147, *post*.
[24] *Supra*.
[25] [1920] 2 K.B. 1.
[26] *Ibid.*, at p. 7.

a recognised or usual form or not. The certificate, therefore, does not contain all the terms of the insurance. Those terms have to be sought for in two documents—namely, the original policy and the certificate. But even if this document is not a policy, yet the sellers say it is "equivalent to a policy". In connection with that phrase it is well to quote from another part of the judgment of BAILHACHE, J., in the *Wilson Holgate Case*. He says:[27]

> "He, the buyer, cannot be compelled to take a document which is something like that which he has agreed to take. He is entitled to have a document of the very kind which he has agreed to take or at least one which does not differ from it in any material respect".

This leads me to ask whether the document before me differs in any material respect from a policy of insurance. The latter is a well-known document with clearly defined features. It comes within definite, established, and statutory legal rights. A certificate, however, is an ambiguous thing; it is unclassified and undefined by law. It is not even mentioned in *Arnould on Marine Insurance*. No rules have been laid down upon it. Would the buyer sue upon the certificate, or upon the original policy plus the certificate? If he sued simply on the certificate, he could put in a part only of the contract, for the other terms of the contract, namely, the conditions of the actual policy, would be contained in a document not in his control, and to the possession of which he is not entitled. In the third place, I point out that before the buyer could sue at all, he would have to show that he was the assignee of the certificate: see *Arnould, Marine Insurance* (9th Edn.) ss. 175-177. In what way can he become the assignee? It is vital to remember the provisions of the Marine Insurance Act 1906. The relevant statutory provision is s. 50(3) which says: "A marine policy may be assigned by endorsement thereon or in any other customary manner". This sub-section, however, only applies so far as I can see, to that which is an actual marine policy. Section 90, the interpretation clause, says: "In this Act unless the context or subject-matter otherwise require", policy means "a marine policy". The Act contains no reference, express or implied, to a certificate of insurance. Section 22 says:

> "Subject to the provisions of any statute a contract of marine insurance is inadmissible in evidence unless it is embodied in a marine policy in accordance with this Act".

. . . In my humble view, a document of insurance is not a good tender in England under an ordinary c.i.f. contract unless it be an actual policy, and unless it falls within the provisions of the Marine Insurance Act 1906, as to assignment and otherwise. I must, therefore, hold that the buyers were entitled to reject the documents upon the ground that . . . no proper policy of insurance [was] tendered by the sellers in conformity with the c.i.f. contract.

---

[27] [1920] 2 K.B. 1, at p. 9.

C. Groom Ltd. *v.* Barber

[1914-15] All E.R. Rep. 194

The insurance policy tendered by the seller under a c.i.f. contract must be a policy containing the terms usual in the trade.

A contract for the sale of bales of cloth c.i.f. London was signed on 8th June, 1914, shipment to be made from Calcutta. One of its terms stated "war risk for buyer's account". The goods were shipped on 5th July, 1914. The sellers took out a policy of insurance which did not cover war risks. War broke out on 4th August, and the vessel carrying the goods was sunk by an enemy cruiser on 6th August. The buyers claimed that the sellers ought to have taken out a policy covering war risks.

Held, by the King's Bench Division, that this contention failed. It was peacetime when the goods were shipped, and the sellers had taken out a policy on the terms current in the trade.

ATKIN, J. (at page 197)

I think it is an incident of a c.i.f. contract as stated by HAMILTON, J., in his judgment in *Biddell Bros.* v. *E. Clemens Horst Co.*[28] that a seller under a contract of sale has, among other things, to arrange for an insurance on the terms current in the trade which will be available for the benefit of the buyer. I am satisfied that, at the time this contract was made, the terms current in the trade were terms which would exclude war risk—in other words, that the terms of the policy would contain the f.c.s. clause. I am, therefore, of opinion that, apart from the special terms of the contract, a policy in such terms would in fact be in order. The finding of the appeal committee in that respect makes the matter quite certain. But this contract contains the words: "War risk for buyer's account". This is said to mean that the seller must, by virtue of the contract, take out a policy covering the war risk, but that he may charge the buyer with the expense of it. The contention amounts to this: that at all times, in times of peace, a war risk policy ought to be taken out at the expense of the buyer. I am perfectly satisfied myself that no seller or buyer ever contemplated such a thing being done, and that, if a buyer was charged with such a policy in ordinary times of peace, he would be the very first person to object. To my mind, those words mean that war risk is the buyer's concern; if the buyer wants to cover a war risk, he must take the necessary steps himself. The words may mean that, in the proper course of business, the buyer is entitled to ask the seller to take out a policy of insurance against war risk, at the buyer's expense, at the time when he is taking out the other policy. I do not decide that it does mean that, but it may do so. If it does, I am quite satisfied that, in this case, the buyers never did, in fact, request the seller to take out a war risk policy

---

[28] [1911] 1 K.B. 214.

on those terms, because, when they did make their request, the buyers never intended themselves to pay the cost. They merely intimated that the seller was under the obligation to take out the policy at the seller's expense. Under those circumstances, I am satisfied that, on this point, the contention of the buyers fails, that the award is perfectly right, and that the policy was in order.

Manbre Saccharine Co. Ltd. *v.* Corn Products Co. Ltd.

[1918-19] All E.R. Rep. 980

The seller is entitled to tender the shipping documents under a c.i.f. contract to the buyer even though he knows that at the time of the tender the goods have already been lost.

A quantity of corn syrup was sold c.i.f. London. On 14th March, 1917, the sellers tendered the shipping documents to the buyers, even though they knew that the vessel carrying the goods had already been sunk by a German submarine. The buyers refused to accept the documents.

Held, by the King's Bench Division, that the tender of the documents by the sellers was good, for the buyers had obtained the documents they bargained for, and if the loss was covered by insurance, they could recover on the insurance policy.

McCardie, J. (at page 983)

The first question arising can be briefly stated as follows: Can a vendor, under an ordinary c.i.f. contract, effectively tender appropriate documents to the buyer in respect of goods shipped in a vessel which at the time of tender the vendor knows to have been totally lost? . . .

I conceive that the essential feature of a c.i.f. contract as compared with an ordinary contract for the sale of goods rests in the fact that performance of the bargain is to be fulfilled by delivery of documents and not by the actual physical delivery of goods by the vendor. All that the buyer can call for is delivery of the customary documents. This represents the measure of the buyer's right and the extent of the vendor's duty. The buyer cannot refuse the documents and ask for the actual goods, nor can the vendor withhold the documents and tender the goods. The position and rights of the parties are stated with great clearness in *Scrutton and Mackinnon on Charterparties* (8th Edn.), p. 167, in the notes to art. 59.[29]

In *Arnhold Karberg & Co.* v. *Blythe, Green, Jourdain & Co.*[30] Scrutton, J., described a c.i.f. contract as being a sale of documents relating to goods and not a

---

[29] See now the notes to art. 94 in 18th Edn. (1974), pp. 184-189.
[30] [1915] 2 K.B. 379.

sale of goods. But when the Court of Appeal considered that case,[31] BANKES and WARRINGTON, L.JJ., commented on the language of SCRUTTON, J., and indicated their view that a c.i.f. contract is a contract for the sale of goods to be performed by delivery of documents. But I respectfully venture to think that the difference is one of phrase only. For in reality, as I have said, the obligation of the vendor is to deliver documents rather than goods—to transfer symbols rather than the physical property represented thereby. If the vendor fulfils his contract by shipping the appropriate goods in the appropriate manner under a proper contract of carriage, and if he also obtains the proper documents for tender to the purchaser, I am unable to see how the rights or duties of either party are affected by the loss of ship or goods, or by knowledge of such loss by the vendor prior to actual tender of the documents. If the ship be lost prior to tender, but without the knowledge of the seller, it was, I assume, always clear that he could make an effective proffer of the documents to the buyers. In my opinion, it is also clear that he can make an effective tender even though he possessed at the time of tender actual knowledge of the loss of the ship or goods. For the purchaser in case of loss will get the document he bargained for, and if the policy be that required by the contract and if the loss be covered thereby, he will secure the insurance moneys. The contingency of loss is within and not outside the contemplation of the parties to a c.i.f. contract. The views I have expressed are, I feel, in full accord with the observations of ATKIN, J., in *C. Groom Ltd* v. *Barber*[32] as to the requirements of a c.i.f. contract, and with the judgment of BAILHACHE, J., in *Re Weis & Co. Ltd. and Credit Colonial et Commercial, Antwerp.*[33] I therefore hold that the plaintiffs were not entitled to reject the tender of documents in the present case, upon the ground that the *Algonquin* had, to the knowledge of the defendants, sank prior to the tender of documents. This view will simplify the performance of c.i.f. contracts and prevent delay either through doubts as to the loss of ship or goods or through difficult questions with regard to the knowledge or suspicion of a vendor as to the actual occurrence of loss.

---

[31] [1916] 1 K.B. 495, at pp. 510, 514, C.A.
[32] [1914-15] All E.R. Rep. 194, at p. 198. This case is considered on another point, p. 147, *ante*.
[33] [1916] 1 K.B. 346.

Orient Co. Ltd. *v.* Brekke

(1913), 108 L.T. 507

All the shipping documents must be tendered by the seller under a c.i.f. contract even though the goods have arrived safely.

Twenty cases of French walnuts c.i.f. Hull were sold to the buyers. The sellers shipped the goods at Bordeaux, but did not tender to the buyers a policy of insurance in respect of them. The goods arrived safely, but the buyers maintained that they were entitled to reject them since they had not been given the policy of insurance.

Held, by the Divisional Court of the King's Bench Division, that this contention was correct, for there had been no "delivery" in accordance with the contract.

LUSH, J. (at page 508)

The contract was a c.i.f. contract for the sale of 20 cases of French walnuts c.i.f. to Hull on the terms I have mentioned—namely, payment 30 days after delivery. The plaintiffs accordingly had to prove that the goods were, in accordance with that contract, delivered at the port of shipment. That the goods were put on board and that the bill of lading was tendered is not in dispute, but in point of fact the plaintiffs not only did not tender the policy of insurance as one of the shipping documents, but they did not even effect an insurance in respect of these goods either at the time of shipment or, so far as I can see, at any time whilst the goods were afloat. The goods were delayed and arrived at Hull a month or two after the time when they would in ordinary course have arrived. Thereupon a correspondence passed between the plaintiffs and the defendants, the plaintiffs, on the one hand, insisting that the time for payment had arrived, and the defendants, on the other hand, insisting that they were not bound to pay first for one reason and then for another. One reason they gave was that they were entitled to examine the goods before they could be called upon to pay for them. But among the reasons against payment which they took at that time is not to be found the one which they now suggest—viz., that no insurance had been effected upon the goods, and that no policy had been tendered. When the action was commenced, the defendants raised the point which has been argued before us—namely, that the plaintiffs could not succeed in the action because they were not in a position to prove, and had not proved, that the goods had ever been delivered. . . . Mr Roche contended that the obligation of vendors under a c.i.f. contract such as the present is to effect complete delivery of the goods, and that that delivery is not complete unless among the shipping documents a policy of insurance is tendered to the buyer, and he contends that in any case, whether the policy is actually tendered or not, it is certainly essential, in order to constitute a delivery, that the vendors must have effected an appropriate policy of insurance for the transit of the goods. He points out that the price which the buyers have to pay under the contract is one which includes, amongst other things, the necessary premiums which the vendor has to pay for the insurance.

That was Mr Roche's contention, and he submitted that, inasmuch as there was no delivery in the present case, the plaintiffs necessarily failed in their action. Mr Powell, on the other hand, contends that the view put forward by Mr Roche is erroneous. It may well be, he says, that the vendors are under an obligation to tender a policy of insurance in a case where the goods are lost, and obviously they are. It may also be, he says, their proper course to insure, but, if the buyers do not ask for the policy and the goods arrive safely, then the fact that they never have been insured becomes an irrelevant fact, and, says Mr Powell, in that event, which was the event which happened in the present case, the vendors are entitled to sue for the price, although they never have effected the policy of insurance which it was their duty to effect under the contract. He says, as I understand it, that the property in the goods has passed, and that all that has happened is that there is an obligation to insure on the part of the vendors which has not been fulfilled, but the non-fulfilment of which does not affect the transfer of the property or the tender of the goods.

Various cases have been cited to us, and, after considering them, I have come to the conclusion that Mr Roche's contention is well founded, and that the plaintiffs have not discharged the obligation cast upon them of proving a complete delivery of the goods, the proof of which was essential to their success in the action. . . .

If it is an essential condition of delivery that the goods shall be insured in favour of the buyer so that he shall be in a position to dispose of the goods with all the shipping documents which are necessary to give him a title and secure him against loss, then, apart from the question whether the document must be tendered to him, it is quite clear that that condition has not been fulfilled, and it is clear that when the plaintiffs brought their action, they were not in a position to prove enough to show that they had delivered the goods at all. With regard to the point as to the tender of the policy, I think again that in the absence of waiver it is an essential condition of delivery under a contract like this that among the shipping documents which must be tendered to the buyer the policy of insurance is an essential unit. It is one of the documents which must be transferred to the buyer in order to effect a complete delivery to him of goods under a c.i.f. contract. In this case, the goods never having been insured and the policy never having been tendered, I think that the goods were never delivered.

Chao v. British Traders & Shippers Ltd. (N.V. Handelsmaatschappij J. Smits Import-Export, Third Party)[34]

[1954] 1 All E.R. 779

In the case of a c.i.f. contract the buyer has two rights to reject: (1) *the documents if they are not in order; and* (2) *the goods if they do not conform to the contract of sale.*

The sellers agreed to sell to the buyers a quantity of bleaching chemical under a c.i.f. contract. The goods were to be shipped not later than 31st October, 1951. The goods arrived at the quay on 31st October, but were not loaded until 3rd November. The bills of lading were endorsed, "Received for shipment and since shipped 31st October". But they were tendered to the buyers' bank after the words "Received for shipment and since" had been erased, and the date of shipment therefore appeared to be 31st October. The bills of lading were accepted by the bank on the buyers' behalf, but when the goods arrived, the buyers discovered that the true date of shipment was 3rd November, so they maintained that they were entitled to reject them.

Held, by the Queen's Bench Division, that they were entitled to do so, for in a c.i.f. contract the buyers had two rights to reject: (1) to reject the documents; and (2) to reject the goods.

DEVLIN, J. (at page 790)

In the present case there is a right to reject documents, and a right to reject goods, and the two things are quite distinct. A c.i.f. contract puts a number of obligations on the seller, and for the purpose of this case one may say that they are obligations some of which are in relation to the goods and some of which are in relation to the documents. So far as the goods are concerned, the seller must put on board at the port of shipment goods that are in conformity with the contract description. He must also send forward documents, and those documents must also comply with the contract. If he commits breaches, they may, in one sense, overlap, in that they flow from the same act. If there is a late shipment, as there was in this case, the date of the shipment being part of the description of the goods, the seller has not put on board goods which conform to the contract description, and, therefore, he has broken that obligation. He may or may not break the obligation to send forward a correct bill of lading. I should think it follows that, in such a case, a seller knows that he cannot send forward a bill of lading which conforms with the contract and, at the same time, describes accurately the date of shipment, and, therefore, in that sense, it is true to say that the same act necessarily causes the two breaches of two independent obligations. There may, however, be cases where the two breaches are not necessarily reflected both in the documents and in the goods. However that may be, there are distinct obligations, and the right to reject the documents arises when the documents are tendered, and

---

[34] Another aspect of this case is considered under "Acceptance", see p. 84, *ante*.

the right to reject, or the moment for rejecting, the goods arises when they are landed and when, after examination, they are found not to be in conformity with the contract. There are many cases where the documents are accepted, but the goods are subsequently rejected. It may be that, if the actual date of shipment is not in conformity with the contract, the buyer, by accepting the documents, loses not only the right to reject the documents but also his right to reject the goods, but that would be because he had waived in advance the date of shipment. . . .

It follows, therefore, as a matter of principle, that the action of the plaintiffs on the second breach cannot affect their right to damages on the first breach. The two breaches are distinct, not merely in law, but also as a matter of business and of ordinary common sense. There being a right to reject the documents separately from a right to reject the goods, it is obvious that, as a matter of business, very different considerations will govern the buyer's mind as he applies himself to one or other of those questions. When he has to make up his mind whether he accepts the documents or not, he has not parted with any money. If he parts with his money and then has to consider whether or not to reject the goods, wholly different considerations will operate. In the interval he may have had dealings with the goods. He may have pledged them to his bank, he may have agreed to resell the specific goods, and the position may have been entirely altered.

Let me leave aside the position of a bank and take the simple case of a buyer who has bought documents. Suppose that he has not dealt with the property in any way but has accepted the documents believing them to be accurate, that the goods arrive, and that the market has fallen by, let us say, 5%. If he rejects the goods and wants to put himself into the same position, he is faced with the choice of having to go out into the market to buy a new lot of goods at 95% of the purchase price. If the seller to him was someone about whom he knew little, the buyer might well feel that he would not part with the goods by rejecting them and pay out another 95% (which he might pay to the seller himself if the seller was selling the goods in the market, the property having returned to him) and be faced merely with an unsecured claim for the recovery back from the seller of the price which he had originally paid. Very different considerations would naturally govern his mind at that stage, when he was considering whether or not to reject the goods, from those which would govern his mind when he was considering whether to reject the documents. If I might call the breach of the term to deliver correct documents breach (a) and the failure to ship goods in conformity with the contract, i.e., on the contract date, breach (b), it seems to me that the right to damages for breach vests when (a) the breach is committed, that the measure is then determined as being the proper measure to put the buyer in as good a position as he would have been in if the breach had not been committed; and that, when a separate breach, breach (b), is committed, the buyer has a separate and independent right to elect on that breach how he is going to deal with it, whether he treats it as a condition or as a warranty, and that he cannot be fettered in the exercise of that right by his election altering the measure of damages which he could have recovered from the earlier breach. That measure of damages must remain the same, however the buyer elects to deal with breach (b).

Sharpe & Co. Ltd. *v.* Nosawa & Co.

(1918), 118 L.T. 91

Where the seller does not deliver the goods under a c.i.f. contract, damages are calculated according to the market price ruling at the time when the shipping documents (and not the goods themselves) should have been delivered.

The sellers sold two parcels of Japanese peas c.i.f. London, one parcel to be shipped in May and the other in June, 1914. The whole of the first parcel was shipped, and part of the second was shipped at the proper time. A dispute arose and the sellers refused to ship the rest of the second parcel. The shipping documents representing the goods would have reached the buyers on 20th July, so they claimed damages for non-delivery.

Held, by the King's Bench Division, that the damages should be calculated according to the market price on 20th July, for this was the time when the documents should have been delivered.

ATKIN, J. (at page 92)

The only question here is whether the damages are to be measured by the market price in July, when the documents would have arrived in the ordinary course, on a June shipment of the goods, or the price in August when the goods would have arrived, on the assumption that the voyage took about two months. The correct answer to that question depends upon the true meaning of a contract of this kind. I think that it is reasonably plain that such a contract is performed by the vendor taking reasonable steps to deliver as soon as possible after shipment the shipping documents, including the bill of lading and policy of insurance, to the buyer, and by the buyer paying the price against the documents, unless there is some special stipulation as to payment in the contract. The performance of the contract on the seller's part is by delivery of the documents which represent the goods; in other words, by delivery of the bill of lading. . . .

I think the date of performance of a c.i.f. contract is the date at which the documents would, in the ordinary course, come forward if the vendor performed his duty to make every reasonable effort to send forward the shipping documents as early as possible. In this case, on the evidence, such a period would be about 20 or 21 days after the goods had in fact been shipped. I am quite clear, not merely from the course of business in this case, but from ordinary commercial usage in business of this nature, that in a case of this kind it would be reasonable for the vendor to send forward the shipping documents by mail by the Trans-Siberian Railway as soon as they had been shipped, by which route they would arrive in this country in a substantially shorter time than they would if sent by ship. Therefore it appears to me that the date of performance of the contract would be somewhere about 20th or 21st July. The contract was not performed, as the documents did not come forward at that time. . . .

Then as to the time or times when the goods ought to have been delivered, within the meaning of s. 51 of the Sale of Goods Act 1893.[35] It seems to me that the words of that section mean the time or times when they ought to be delivered according to the mode of delivery contemplated by the contract. If the contract provides for delivery of the goods by delivery of the shipping documents, or by handing over to the buyer the key to the warehouse, the date for that event is the time "when they ought to have been delivered". In this case the date on which the documents ought to have arrived— namely, 20th or 21st July—is the important date in considering when the plaintiffs ought to have bought on the market; and the plaintiffs ought to be allowed a reasonable time in which to consider their position. I do not think, however, that the time can be indefinitely extended on the assumption that the plaintiffs could waive the terms as to the June shipment. The question must be considered as between vendor and vendee on a contract which must be performed strictly as to time. In these circumstances it only remains for me to determine at what price the plaintiffs ought to have bought on the footing that the contract ought to have been performed strictly. Accordingly, I fix the time for ascertaining the market price as somewhere about the last week in July.

E. Clemens Horst Co. *v.* Biddell Brothers

(1911), 105 L.T. 563

Under a c.i.f. contract the buyer must pay the price when the shipping documents are tendered and cannot delay payment until the goods themselves are delivered.

A contract was made for the sale of hops to be shipped from San Francisco to London c.i.f. net cash. The shipping documents were tendered to the buyers, but they refused to pay until the goods themselves were actually delivered.

Held, by the House of Lords, that the sellers were entitled to payment on tender of the shipping documents.

EARL LOREBURN (at page 564)

This contract is what is known as a cost, insurance, and freight, or c.i.f. contract, and under it the buyer was to pay cash. But when? The contract does not say. The

---

[35] Now Sale of Goods Act 1979.

[sellers] say on the physical delivery and acceptance of the goods when they have come to England. Section 28 of the Sale of Goods Act 1893[36] says in effect that, unless otherwise agreed, payment must be made on delivery—that is, on giving possession of the goods. It does not say what is meant by delivery. Accordingly, we have to supply from the general law the answer to that question. The question is, when is there delivery of goods on board ship? That may be quite different from delivery of goods on shore. The answer is that delivery of the bill of lading when goods are at sea may be treated as delivery of the goods themselves. That is so old and so well established that it is unnecessary to refer to authorities on the subject.

In my judgment, it is wrong to say, upon this contract, that the vendor must defer tendering the bill of lading until the ship has arrived in this country, and still more wrong to say that he must wait until the goods are landed and examination made by the buyer.

B. F.O.B. CONTRACTS

Maine Spinning Co. *v*. Sutcliffe & Co.

[1916-17] All E.R. Rep. 537

In the case of an f.o.b. contract the seller is entitled to insist on making delivery on board the ship concerned, even though the buyer may wish to take delivery beforehand.

The sellers sold to the buyers a quantity of wool "delivery Liverpool" for export to America. Although the buyers wished to obtain delivery of the goods before they were loaded on board a vessel bound for America, the sellers insisted on making delivery on board.

Held, by the King's Bench Division, that the words of the contract meant "f.o.b. Liverpool", and that the sellers were entitled to insist on making delivery on board. The condition in an f.o.b. contract as to the place of delivery was intended for the benefit of both parties, and not merely for that of the buyer. Consequently it could not be waived by one party without the other's consent.

BAILHACHE, J. (at page 538)

Counsel for the plaintiffs calls attention to the fact that the contract provides for "delivery Liverpool", and he says that his clients, the plaintiffs, were always ready and willing to take delivery in Liverpool, and, inasmuch as they were ready and willing to take delivery in Liverpool, whether they could get the goods to the United States or not was a matter for them and did not concern the defendants who were bound to hand over the goods in Liverpool. Delivery in Liverpool is to some extent ambiguous.

---

[36] Now Sale of Goods Act 1979.

When one considers that the wool was being bought for export to the plaintiffs, it is easy to come to the conclusion that "delivery Liverpool" did not mean "delivery on rail Liverpool", but meant delivery in the way in which goods are delivered in Liverpool when they are delivered for export at Liverpool, that is to say, "delivery f.o.b. Liverpool", and if there is any ambiguity in "delivery Liverpool", I think I am fully entitled to look at the cables and letters which passed between the parties at the time the arrangement was made. Without those cables and letters I should have come to the conclusion that the true construction of the words "delivery Liverpool" meant "delivery f.o.b. Liverpool". If I look at the cables and letters leading up to and immediately after this contract, they state in the most express terms that the price was 27½d. a pound, and that the contract was f.o.b. Liverpool. Counsel for the plaintiffs, although he contests that, says, even if that be so, it is open to one of the parties to the contract—the plaintiffs in this case—to waive "f.o.b. Liverpool" and to take delivery of these goods short of Liverpool, or at Liverpool off rail instead of on board ship. He might have taken delivery at Bradford, the place where the goods were being prepared and combed for fulfilment of this contract, but in my opinion that is a mistaken view of the law. It is quite true, of course, that where a condition in a contract is wholly for the benefit of, and entirely for the benefit of, one of the parties to the contract, such a condition may be waived by the person for whose benefit, entirely and solely, it was inserted in the contract; but where one of the terms of the contract is the mode of delivery, it is not a condition which the other party may waive, but it is a part of the contract which has to be fulfilled by the seller making delivery at that particular place and the buyer receiving delivery there, and it is not a condition which is entirely for the benefit of either party to the contract, and neither party can waive it without the consent of the other. Of course, if they both agreed to waive it, there is an end of the matter, but either party is entitled to insist upon making or receiving delivery in strict accordance with the terms of the contract.

The best statement I know of the law in this respect is contained in a very short sentence in a judgment of Lord WATSON in his speech in the House of Lords in *Sailing Ship Blairmore Co. Ltd.* v. *Macredie.*[37] That case was a different case from this. The sailing ship *Blairmore* had gone to the bottom of the sea, and she was insured against a total loss. It would have cost a great deal more than she was worth to bring her up to the surface and repair her, but if she had been brought to the surface, she was not so far damaged but that the repairs would have come to considerably less than she was worth. If, therefore, she could have been got up to the surface without expense to the owner, she could have been repaired at a sum which would not have left her a constructive total loss, and in that case the underwriters would not be liable.

---

37 [1898] A.C. 593, at p. 607.

The underwriters therefore subscribed between themselves a sufficient sum of money to raise the ship, and, having got her to the surface, said to the owners: "There is the ship. Go and repair her. We have got her to the surface, and she can be repaired at an expense very much less than her value when repaired. She is no longer a constructive total loss, and we are no longer liable to pay on our policy". It was held that the underwriters were not entitled to defeat their contract by spending a considerable sum of money in raising the *Blairmore* from the bottom of the sea, and what Lord WATSON says is this:

> "The rule of law applicable to contracts is that neither of the parties can by his own act or default defeat the obligations which he has undertaken to fulfil".

That is the rule of law which I must apply in this case. I have instanced *Sailing Ship Blairmore Co. Ltd.* v. *Macredie*,[38] which is a case not at all analogous to this; but counsel for the defendants has referred me to *Wackerbarth* v. *Masson*.[39] The headnote is this:

> "Where, in a contract for the sale of sugar, there is the following term, 'free on board a foreign ship', the seller is not bound to deliver it into the hands of the purchaser, or to transfer it into his name in the books of the warehouse where it lies, but only to put it on board a foreign ship, which it is the duty of the purchaser to name".

That is a decision of Lord ELLENBOROUGH as long ago as 1812. I was not aware of that decision; but I was quite prepared without it, applying the rule laid down by Lord WATSON, to say that in this case the plaintiffs were not entitled to demand delivery of this wool anywhere but on board ship at Liverpool.

Colley *v*. Overseas Exporters (1919) Ltd.

[1921] All E.R. Rep. 596

In the case of an f.o.b. contract, in the absence of a special agreement, the property and risk in the goods do not pass to the buyer until the goods are actually placed on board the ship concerned.

A quantity of unascertained leather goods was sold to the buyers f.o.b. Liverpool. No effective ship was named by the buyers, and the goods were left at the docks. The sellers thereupon sued for the price.

Held, by the King's Bench Division, that the action failed. Since the goods had not been shipped, property in them had not passed, and therefore the sellers were not entitled to sue for the price under s. 49(1) of the Sale of Goods Act 1893.[39a]

---

[38] *Supra*.
[39] (1812), 3 Camp. 270.
[39a] Now Sale of Goods Act 1979.

McCARDIE, J. (at page 598)

The buyers committed no deliberate breach of contract. They suffered a series of misfortunes, they failed, however, to name an effective ship. The seller, on his part, did all he could to carry out his obligations. In these circumstances the seller seeks to recover the price of the goods in question. The circumstances, however, under which a claim to the price may be made (as distinguished from a claim for damages for breach of contract) are indicated in s. 49 of the Sale of Goods Act.[40] . . . Here sub-s. (2) of s. 49 does not apply. . . . The parties before me here made no special arrangement as to the payment of the price. Nor can it be said that sub-s. (1) of s. 49 applies, for the property in the goods has not in fact and in law passed to the buyer. Several rules for the passing of property in sale of goods contracts are indicated in ss. 16, 17, 18 of the Act, and also in s. 32. The Act does not deal specifically with f.o.b. or c.i.f. contracts. Judicially settled rules exist, however, with respect to them. I need only deal with f.o.b. contracts. It seems clear that, in the absence of special agreement, the property and risk in goods does not, in the case of an f.o.b. contract, pass from the seller to the buyer till the goods are actually put on board. . . . In my opinion . . . no action will lie for the price of goods until the property has passed save only in the special cases provided for by s. 49(2). That seems plain both on the Act and on common law principle. I have searched in vain for authority to the contrary.

Wimble *v.* Rosenberg

(1913), 109 L.T. 294

Section 32(3) of the Sale of Goods Act 1979 applies to f.o.b. contracts.[41]

On 27th June, 1912, the sellers sold 200 bags of rice to the buyers f.o.b. Antwerp. On 9th August the buyers instructed them to ship the goods on a vessel bound for Odessa. On 24th August, the rice was shipped, and the vessel was lost on 26th August. On 29th August the buyers learnt for the first time that the goods had been shipped. The goods had not been insured so the buyers claimed that the sellers were in breach of s. 32(3) of the Sale of Goods Act 1893[42] in that the sellers ought to have given the buyers notice so as to enable them to insure. The sellers contended that s. 32(3) did not apply to f.o.b. contracts.

Held, by a majority of the Court of Appeal,[43] that s. 32(3) applied.

Held further, by VAUGHAN WILLIAMS, L.J., that the contract alone did not afford sufficient information to enable the buyers to insure. BUCKLEY, L.J., however, was of the contrary opinion.

---

[40] Now Sale of Goods Act 1979.
[41] But s. 32(3) does not apply to c.i.f. contracts. See *Law & Bonar Ltd.* v. *British American Tobacco Co. Ltd.* (1916), 115 L.T. 612; p. 134, *ante.*
[42] Now Sale of Goods Act 1979.
[43] VAUGHAN WILLIAMS and BUCKLEY, L.JJ.; HAMILTON, L.J. dissenting.

VAUGHAN WILLIAMS, L.J. (at page 296)

An argument before us was on the basis that sub-s. (3) of s. 32 had, and could have, no application to a contract of sale f.o.b. It was argued also that the buyers did not require a notice because they might have insured these goods by a "general cover contract", or by a "ship or ships' " contract. . . .

At the conclusion of [counsel's] argument on behalf of the plaintiffs, [junior counsel following him] put forward a new point that notice enabling the buyers to insure already had been given, for that the contract of purchase itself was notice. . . .

I think it is agreed that sub-s. 3, and indeed the whole of s. 32, includes agreements, if any, outside the contract, and includes also the proof of "the circumstances in which it is usual to insure", and, I think, includes cases where it has been usual *inter partes* to insure, although the agreement of sale itself contains no reference to insurance. . . .

This case, to my mind, turns on construction. No facts are in dispute. I am of opinion that sub-s. (3) of s. 32 of the Sale of Goods Act covers an f.o.b. contract. . . .

The natural meaning of the words of sub-s. (3) does not exclude an f.o.b. contract. The real ground for the suggested exclusion is that the sub-section, construed according to its natural meaning, is hard to reconcile with some of the previous law laid down in the cases relating to the carriage of goods under an f.o.b. contract, and that it is highly improbable that the Legislature intended to alter or modify law which is the result of a series of decisions laid down by great commercial lawyers. . . .

I construe the word "send" both in sub-s. (1) of s. 32 and in sub-s. (3) in the sense of "forward" or "dispatch", and in my opinion the word "send" covers every obligation of the seller in reference to effecting or securing the arrival of the goods, the subject of sale at the destination intended.

It is not true in fact to say that the purchased goods are being sent to the ship on which they are placed for the purpose of delivery at the port of destination. The purchased goods are not the less being sent to the buyer at the port of destination because delivery f.o.b. is *prima facie* delivery to the buyer, or because the property has passed to the buyer.

Sub-s. (3) in my opinion casts the duty on the seller forwarding the goods to the buyer by a route involving sea transit, under circumstances which it is usual to insure, to give such notice as may enable the buyer (to whom, be it observed, the property in the purchased goods has passed) to insure them during the sea transit. The penalty for not performing this duty is that the goods, though the goods of the buyer, shall be at the risk of the seller during such sea transit. Moreover, the same result is arrived at if the words "when the goods are sent by the seller to the buyer", at the beginning of sub-s. (3), are construed as describing the whole transaction.

I have already said that I cannot agree with the argument of [junior counsel], that the contract of sale itself was notice within the meaning of sub-s. (3), and I have arrived at this conclusion, not only on the ground that the contract did not afford sufficient information to enable the buyer to insure the purchased goods during their sea transit, but also on the ground that knowledge of the buyer, actual, inferred or assumed, which would enable the buyer to insure does not dispense with the statutory obligation of the seller, when the route involves sea transit, under circumstances in which it is usual to insure, to give such notice to the buyer as may enable him to insure the goods during their sea transit. The obligation, unless dispensed with by the agreement, and in this case there was no dispensing agreement, on the seller is to give such notice, with such details to the buyer as may be necessary to effect insurance of the goods during sea transit. It is to my mind impossible to construe those words as meaning that the obligation to insure does not arise in case the buyer happens to have sufficient information from some other source than the statutory notice to enable him to insure the goods.

I have only to add that whichever of the suggested constructions relieving the seller from obligation to give the statutory notice in the case of an f.o.b. contract is adopted, the practical utility and application of sub-s. (3) of s. 32 is reduced to nothing.

BUCKLEY, L.J. (at page 297)

The contention is that sub-s. (3) is a qualification of sub-s. (1), and may be read as if it were prefaced by the words "provided always that". To this I agree. Then it is said sub-s. (1) applies only where the seller is authorised or required to send the goods to the buyer, and that this is not the case where the contract of sale is f.o.b., inasmuch as the delivery is complete so soon as the goods are handed over the ship's rail; that the sending by the seller to the buyer is then complete.

In my opinion this is erroneous. The sending of the goods is not within the language of the section equivalent to the delivery of the goods to the buyer. The first sub-section uses the word "send" and the word "transmission" and the word "delivery". The word "send" is so used as to bear the same meaning as that for which the word "transmission" is next employed, and both the one and the other are contrasted with "delivery", the word last used. In sub-s. (1) the word "send" means, I think, "despatch" or "transmit" in a physical sense, and not "deliver" so as to pass the property at law. The same meaning is, I think, to be attributed to the word "sent" in sub-s. (3). After the property has passed by placing the goods on shipboard under an f.o.b. contract the goods may, I think, within the meaning of the sub-s. (3) be "sent"—that is to say, transmitted or despatched by the seller to the buyer. Goods are capable of being sent by the vendor, in whom the property is not, to the buyer, in whom it is.

Next I wish to deal with the words "unless otherwise agreed". The operative words which follow that expression are "the seller must give such notice", etc. The agreement must therefore be an agreement agreeing "otherwise" in respect of the giving such notice as is mentioned. An f.o.b. contract is one under which the seller is to put the goods on board at his own expense on account of the buyer, but it is a contract in which neither expressly nor by implication is there involved any agreement as to notice to be given by the former to the latter. Whether notice ought to be given or not depends not upon anything expressed in or implied from the contract as an f.o.b. contract, but might arise *aliunde*, say, from the course of business between the parties. Neither from the use of the word "sent" nor from the words "unless otherwise agreed" therefore can I see that there is anything to render sub-s. (3) inapplicable to an f.o.b. contract of sale. On the contrary, it seems to me that the effect of sub-s. (1) is to add to every contract *prima facie* as an incident that which is involved in an f.o.b. contract—namely, that delivery to a carrier is delivery to the buyer.

The effect of the section seems to me to be as follows: Where in pursuance of a contract of sale goods are to be sent, it shall be an incident of every contract, as it already is of an f.o.b. contract, that delivery to a carrier is delivery to the buyer, with the result that the goods at sea will be at risk of the buyer. But nevertheless (unless otherwise agreed) if the seller fails to comply with sub-s. (3), the risk shall be that not of the buyer but of the seller. From these provisions I can find no exception of an f.o.b. contract, but, on the contrary, I find a reduction of every contract for this purpose to the position of an f.o.b. contract.

So far, therefore, it seems to me that the appellants are right, and that it is necessary to see whether in the present case sub-s. (3) has been complied with. Sub-s. (3) requires the seller to give such notice to the buyer as will enable the latter to insure. These words will be satisfied if either (a) the buyer is already in possession of knowledge of all the facts which it is necessary to know in order that he may insure the goods, in which case nothing is wanting to enable him to insure them; or (b) if such notice (if any) as has been given him, completes his knowledge of the facts so as to enable him to insure.

The contract of 27th June, 1912, was a contract for sale of 200 double bags of rice f.o.b. Antwerp to be shipped as required by the buyers within three months. From this document the buyer knew the particulars of the goods and the port of loading, but not the port of discharge. It was for him to name the port to which he asked the goods to be shipped. The shipping instructions of August named the port—namely, Odessa; and also contained further matter in the nature of a request to the seller with which they were not bound, but, out of courtesy in business, no doubt, would comply. This request, in fact, left it to the sellers to select the ship, and asked them to pay the freight on the buyers' account. In naming the port to which the goods were to be shipped the buyer was but completing a term of the contract of 27th June which was left to his determination. To that extent the shipping instructions formed part of, and put the sellers in a position to complete, the contract. Further, the shipping instructions in leaving it, as impliedly they did, to the seller to select the ship, were a further completion by the action of the buyers of the terms of the contract. All was now complete; port of discharge and ship—namely, as regards the latter, any ship which the seller selected sailing to Odessa. The further request that the seller should pay the freight formed no part of the contract, and was a matter with which the seller was not bound to comply. The conjoint effect of the documents of June and August was this, that in August the buyer had a complete knowledge of the particulars of the goods, the port of shipment, and the port of discharge, and he had waived any right to know the name of the ship by leaving it to the seller to select one.

In this state of facts it was contended that the buyer could have protected himself by a general covering policy. For this purpose a knowledge of all the facts which I have been detailing would be unnecessary. In my judgment this would not constitute a good answer to the buyers' contention. To say that he could cover himself by a general policy is equivalent to saying that in every case without any knowledge of the particulars he is already in possession of all the information which enables him to insure. The result is that the sub-section is reduced to silence. This argument I think proves too much. But in the facts which I have stated it seems to me that no notice to "enable" the buyer was wanted, for he already had ability; he had all materials necessary to enable him to insure. Those words of the section, therefore, which require the seller to give notice do not apply, for no notice was wanted to enable him to insure. But if this is not so, and the seller was under an obligation to give him such notice, etc., then I think he had done so. The contract itself of 27th June, 1912, was a sufficient notice. It gave the buyer knowledge of all the necessary particulars other than knowledge which rested with himself or was determined by himself—namely, first, the port of discharge; and, secondly, the name of the ship. The former lay within his own knowledge, and was supplied by him in August. The latter was not necessary to enable him to insure, and in fact he waived knowledge of it by leaving it to the seller to select the ship. For these reasons I am of opinion that, although sub-s. (3) is applicable to this case, notwithstanding that the contract was an f.o.b. contract, yet that the seller has not failed to do anything which by sub-s. (3) he was bound to do.

C. EX SHIP CONTRACTS

Comptoir d'Achat et de Vente du Boerenbond Belge S.A. *v.* Luis de Ridder Limitada

[1949] 1 All E.R. 269

In the case of an "ex ship" contract the property and risk in the goods do not pass to the buyer until they are delivered at the port of destination.

A quantity of rye was sold under a contract expressed to be on c.i.f. terms, and the goods were to be delivered c.i.f. Antwerp. The contract stated that payment was to be made against presentation of a delivery order. The buyers paid the purchase price, but the delivery order they were given was addressed to the cargo agents of the sellers, and stated that the bearer was given a share in a certificate of insurance covering a bulk cargo of rye, and an undertaking by the sellers' agents to honour it according to the bill of lading. If the goods had arrived at Antwerp, the property in them would not have passed to the buyers until they were discharged from the ship, and at no time did the buyers have a delivery order entitling them to demand delivery from the ship. The vessel never arrived at Antwerp, so the buyers contended that the contract was really a contract for sale ex ship and not on c.i.f. terms, and claimed the recovery of the whole of the price they had paid.

Held, by the House of Lords, that the action succeeded. The contract on its true construction was not a c.i.f. one, even though expressed to be so. The consideration for the purchase price had wholly failed.

LORD PORTER (at page 274)

My Lords, the obligations imposed on a seller under a c.i.f. contract are well known, and in the ordinary case include the tender of a bill of lading covering the goods contracted to be sold and no others, coupled with an insurance policy in the normal form and accompanied by an invoice which shows the price and, as in this case, usually contains a deduction of the freight which the buyer pays before delivery at the port of discharge. Against tender of these documents the purchaser must pay the price. In such a case the property may pass either on shipment or on tender, the risk generally passes on shipment or as from shipment, but possession does not pass until the documents which represent the goods are handed over in exchange for the price. In the result, the buyer, after receipt of the documents, can claim against the ship for breach of the contract of carriage and against the underwriters for any loss covered by the policy. The strict form of c.i.f. contract may, however, be modified. A provision that a delivery order may be substituted for a bill of lading or a certificate of insurance for a policy would not, I think, make the contract be concluded on something other than c.i.f. terms, but, in deciding whether it comes within that category or not, all the permutations and combinations of provision and circumstance must be taken into consideration. Not every contract which is expressed to be a c.i.f. contract is such. Sometimes, as in *The Parchim*,[44] terms are introduced into contracts so described which conflict with c.i.f. provisions. In the present case, therefore, it is not as if a usual form of delivery order had been given and accepted or an insurance certificate covering the parcel was in the hands of Messrs Van Bree as agents for the buyers, nor can a solution be found in the mere designation of the contract as c.i.f. This is not a case in which the over-riding provision is the term c.i.f., under which antagonistic terms can be neglected on the ground that they are repugnant to the transaction, as was done by ROWLATT, J., in *Law & Bonar Ltd.* v. *British American Tobacco Co. Ltd.*[45] The true effect of all its terms must be taken into account, though, of course, the description c.i.f. must not be neglected. . . .

My Lords, the object and the result of a c.i.f. contract is to enable sellers and buyers to deal with cargoes or parcels afloat and to transfer them freely from hand to hand by giving constructive possession of the goods which are being dealt with. Undoubtedly, the practice of shipping and insuring produce in bulk is to make the process more difficult, but a ship's delivery order and a certificate of insurance transferred to or held for a buyer still leave it possible for some, though less satisfactory, dealing with the goods while at sea to take place. The practice adopted between buyers and sellers in the present case renders such dealing wellnigh impossible. The buyer gets neither property nor possession until the goods are delivered to him at Antwerp, and the certificate of insurance, if it enures to his benefit at all, except on the journey from ship to warehouse, has never been held for or delivered to him. Indeed, it is difficult to see how a parcel is at the buyer's risk when he has neither property nor possession, except in such cases as *Inglis* v. *Stock*[46] and *Sterns Ltd.* v. *Vickers Ltd.*,[47] where the purchaser had an interest in an undivided part of a bulk parcel on board a ship, or elsewhere, obtained by attornment of the bailee to him. The vital question in the present case, as I see it, is whether the buyers paid for the documents as representing the goods or for the delivery of the goods themselves. The time and place of payment are elements to be considered, but are by no means conclusive of the question. Such considerations may, on the one hand, indicate a payment in advance, or, on the other, they may show a payment postponed until the arrival of the ship, though the property in the goods or the risk has passed to the buyer while the goods are still at sea, as in *Castle* v. *Playford*.[48] But the whole circumstances have to be looked at and where, as, in my opinion, is the case here, no further security beyond that contained in the original contract passed to the buyer as a result of payment, where the property and possession both remained in the seller until delivery in Antwerp, where the seller was

---

44 [1918] A.C. 157, P.C.
45 (1916), 115 L.T. 612. This case is treated in another connection, p. 134, *ante*.
46 (1885), 10 App. Cas. 263, H.L.
47 [1923] 1 K.B. 78.
48 (1872), L.R. 7 Ex. 98, Ex. Ch.

to pay for deficiency in bill of lading weight, guaranteed condition on arrival, and made himself responsible for all averages, the true view, I think, is that it is not a c.i.f. contract, even in a modified form, but a contract to deliver at Antwerp. Nor do I think it matters that payment is said to be not only on presentation but "in exchange for" documents. There are many ways of carrying out the contract to which that expression would apply, but, in truth, whether the payment is described as made on presentation of or in exchange for a document, the document was not a fulfilment, or even a partial fulfilment, of the contract. It was but a step on the way. What the buyer wanted was delivery of the goods in Antwerp. What the seller wanted was payment of the price before that date and the delivery of the documents furnished the date for payment, but had no effect on the property or possession of the goods or the buyer's rights against the vendor. If this be the true view, there was plainly a frustration of the adventure—indeed, the sellers admit so much in their pleadings—and no part performance, and the consideration had wholly failed.

D. EXPORT LICENCES

Peter Cassidy Seed Co. Ltd. *v.* Osuustukkukauppa I.L.

[1957] 1 All E.R. 484

Whether the party concerned is under an obligation to use reasonable diligence to obtain an export licence or is under an absolute duty to obtain one is a matter of construction, and depends on the circumstances of each case.

The sellers, a Finnish company, sold to English buyers some ants' eggs f.o.b. Helsinki. A clause in the contract of sale stated "Delivery: prompt, as soon as export licence granted". The sellers applied for a licence, but by Finnish law licences were only granted if the Ant Egg Exporters' Association approved the application. The Association, however, never approved an application by a person who was not one of its members. The sellers were not members, and did not know of this practice. The licence was refused, so the eggs could not be exported. The buyers claimed damages for non-delivery.

Held, by the Queen's Bench Division, that the action succeeded, because, as a matter of construction, the clause in the contract imposed an absolute liability on the sellers to obtain an export licence, and not merely to use all reasonable diligence to obtain one.

DEVLIN, J. (at page 487)

The parties in this case, on 16th September, 1953, entered into a contract for the purchase and sale of a certain quantity of ants' eggs. The sellers were a Finnish concern, and the buyers carried on business in England; delivery was to be made f.o.b. Helsinki. The contract contained this term: "Delivery: prompt, as soon as export licence granted". The position under Finnish law was that it was unlawful to export ants' eggs unless a licence for their export had been granted by the State Board of

Licences. The State Board of Licences could not lawfully grant a licence for the export of ants' eggs unless the Ant Egg Exporters' Association approved, and it was the practice of the Ant Egg Exporters' Association not to concur in any application to export ants' eggs unless the exporter was a member of the Association. The sellers were not members of the Association, and, consequently, when they applied for a licence to fulfil their obligations under the contract, it was rejected, the reason being: "The applicant is not a member of the Ant Egg Exporters' Association". The sellers were, therefore, unable, in accordance with the law of Finland, to fulfil their contract.

The question, in those circumstances, is whether or not the sellers are liable to pay damages. If the contract said nothing at all about the obtaining of a licence, it is clear that some provision concerning that matter would have to be implied into it. The contract could not be fulfilled legally under the law of Finland unless one or other, either the buyers or the sellers, obtained a licence, and it would, therefore, be necessary to imply a term as to whose duty it was to apply for a licence. In this case it is accepted (and I think obviously rightly) that it was the sellers' duty to apply for a licence. It is then necessary to imply a term as to what the nature of that obligation was. The person whose duty it is to apply for a licence may either warrant that he will get it, that is an absolute warranty, or he may warrant that he will use all due diligence in getting it. When nothing is said in the contract, it is usually—probably almost invariably—the latter class of warranty which is implied, but each case must be decided according to its own circumstances and the question of implication must be settled in the ordinary way in which implied terms are settled. Thus, in *Re Anglo-Russian Merchant Traders & John Batt & Co. (London) Ltd.*,[49] one of the very early cases where the nature of the obligation had to be considered, Viscount READING, C.J., dealing with this point,[50] held that in the case before him there was an obligation only to use due diligence. He said:[51]

> "A party to a contract may warrant that he will obtain a licence, but no such term can be implied in this case".

On the other hand, an absolute obligation was held to apply in *Partabmull Rameshwar v. K. C. Sethia (1944) Ltd.*[52] a decision of the House of Lords. I refer particularly to what was said by Lord PORTER.[53] The circumstances in the case were unusual; I need not detail them here, and the only purpose for which I wish to refer

---

[49] [1917] 2 K.B. 679.
[50] *Ibid.*, at p. 686.
[51] *Ibid.*
[52] [1951] 2 Lloyd's Rep. 89, H.L.
[53] *Ibid.*, at p. 95.

to the case is plain enough, namely, that there are always these two alternatives which have to be considered. As DENNING, L.J., said in *Brauer & Co. (Great Britain) Ltd.* v. *James Clark (Brush Materials) Ltd.*[54]

"The question for decision depends on the true construction of the words: 'This contract is subject to any Brazilian export licence'. Those words serve a most useful purpose. The parties to the contract knew that the goods could not lawfully be exported from Brazil without an export licence. If this clause had not been inserted, the buyers might have contended that the sellers undertook absolutely to obtain a licence and ship the goods, and that it was no excuse for the sellers to say that they could not get a licence . . .".

Lastly, in *A. V. Pound & Co. Ltd.* v. *M. W. Hardy & Co. Inc.*[55] in the House of Lords, while it was, again, not necessary for the House to consider the nature of the obligation, Lord SOMERVELL OF HARROW said:[56]

"It is also unnecessary to decide other points which were referred to in argument. Had the sellers undertaken an absolute obligation to get a licence for any destination? Was their obligation only to take reasonable steps? Apart from the general objection to dealing with points which it is unnecessary to decide, there is, I think, a special difficulty arising from the absence of certain findings".

That shows once again that the nature of the obligation has to be decided in relation to the circumstances of each particular case.

In the present case there is no "subject to licence" clause in the contract. If there had been such a clause, I think that, on the authorities, it would have concluded the matter. In the absence of a "subject to licence" clause, and further, if there were no other relevant clause in the contract, it would be necessary for me to determine, in relation to all the circumstances of the case, what would be the appropriate terms to be implied regarding the duty to obtain a licence. There is, however, a clause in the contract which, on its true construction, gives considerable assistance to the contention of counsel for the buyers that an absolute obligation on the part of the sellers to obtain a licence was intended in this case. The clause, which reads: "Delivery: prompt, as soon as export licence granted", seems to show clearly that the assumption which was underlying the contract, and which was in the minds of both parties, was that an export licence certainly would be granted. The only question was at what precise moment of time this would take place, because delivery could not be made until it was granted. If that be right, if that be the underlying assumption, there would be no hardship in holding that the sellers, being the parties responsible, were undertaking absolutely to do that which both parties had assumed would, in fact, be done, or could be done,

---

54 [1952] 2 All E.R. 497, at p. 501.
55 [1956] 1 All E.R. 639, H.L.
56 *Ibid.*, at p. 651.

sooner or later. I think that, on the true construction of that clause, the sellers are saying, in effect: "We can get a licence, but we cannot say for certain just when we will get it, and therefore the time for delivery must depend on the getting of it".

Having regard to what I think is the right construction of that clause and to the circumstances in this case, I think that the proper conclusion is that the sellers were warranting absolutely that they would get a licence.

H. O. Brandt & Co. *v.* H. N. Morris & Co. Ltd.[57]

[1916-17] All E.R. Rep. 925

In the case of an f.o.b. contract it will depend upon the circumstances whether the duty of obtaining an export licence falls on the seller or on the buyer.

In September, 1914, the sellers who carried on business in Manchester, sold to the buyers, who were chemical manufacturers in Manchester, 60 tons of pure aniline oil f.o.b. Manchester. After the contract had been made the export of aniline oil was prohibited, and licences were only granted in special cases.

Held, by the Court of Appeal, that the obligation to obtain the licence was on the buyers.

SCRUTTON, L.J. (at page 929)

There is one question of general importance which I desire to deal with first. The contract is: "We have this day bought from you sixty tons pure aniline oil, f.o.b. Manchester". At the time that contract was made there was no prohibition on the export of aniline oil. That is some distinction from the case which has already been decided in this Court (*Re Anglo-Russian Merchant Traders Ltd. & John Batt & Co. (London) Ltd.*[58]), in which a contract was made at the time when there was an existing prohibition, and a question arose whose duty it was to provide the licences, exportation not being possible without a licence. In that case, which was a c.i.f. contract, BAILHACHE, J., had held that a man who contracted to sell at a time when there was a prohibition of export except by licence undertook to get the licence or pay damages. This Court held that, as there was a finding of fact that the seller had done all in his power to get a licence, at any rate his obligation was not higher than that, and he was not liable. In the present case I think it becomes necessary to go further, and to decide whether in this f.o.b. contract the obligation to get a licence in case there should, after the making of the contract, be a prohibition against export except with a licence, lies upon the seller or the buyer. In my view it lies upon the buyer. The buyer must provide an effective ship—that is to say, a ship that can legally, and as it is bound to

---

57 It is important to read this decision in the light of the later case of *A. V. Pound & Co.* v. *M. W. Hardy & Co. Inc.*, [1956] 1 All E.R. 639, H.L., p. 170, *post.*
58 [1917] 2 K.B. 679, C.A.

by contract, carry the goods. When the buyer has done that, the seller may ship the goods he has contracted to ship. If that is so, the licence to export is a buyer's matter. It is the sending of a ship out of the country after the goods are put on board, and it is not made a seller's matter by a statutory prohibition of the goods being put on the quay if their export is prohibited. Putting on the quay is only subsidiary to the exporting, which is the real matter of the licence. In my view, therefore, on the general question in a contract of this description, it is for the buyer to get the licence.

VISCOUNT READING (at page 927)

I am, however, not able to agree with the learned Judge's view that the duty was upon the defendants to apply for a licence. They had contracted to sell and put on board the vessel—not the vessel selected by them, but the vessel selected by the buyers. It was the duty of the buyers to find the ship and to give all the information which was necessary in order to get the licence. It is very noteworthy that, apart from the present case, or it may be the special circumstances such as the war and the export of oil of this character, when there is a prohibition and a licence has to be obtained, the material facts are in the possession of the buyer, not in the possession of the seller. All that the seller knows is that he has sold the goods to his buyer. What his buyer is going to do with them is immaterial to him. If he has undertaken to put them f.o.b., that has no reference to any particular vessel, and it may even be not a vessel going to any particular destination.

A. V. Pound & Co. *v.* M. W. Hardy & Co. Inc.

[1956] 1 All E.R. 639

In the case of an f.a.s. contract it will depend upon the circumstances whether the duty of obtaining an export licence falls on the seller or on the buyer.

The sellers, an English company, agreed to sell to the buyers, an American company, some Portuguese turpentine f.a.s. Lisbon, and the buyers chartered a vessel so that the goods could be loaded on her for delivery at Rostock (a German port). By Portuguese law turpentine could not be exported except under licence, and this was never granted except to Portuguese suppliers, though the sellers did not know of this. The sellers bought the turpentine from Portuguese suppliers, who applied for a licence to export it to Rostock, but this was refused. No mention of a licence being necessary was made in the contract of sale made between the sellers and the buyers. The sellers asked the buyers to name another port instead of Rostock, but the buyers refused to do so. The sellers claimed damages for breach of contract, and one of the issues was whether the duty of obtaining a licence fell on the sellers or on the buyers.

Held, by the House of Lords, that there was no general rule for f.a.s. contracts that the buyer had to obtain a licence, but each case depended on the contract and the surrounding circumstances, and in the present case the duty was on the sellers.

VISCOUNT KILMUIR, L.C. (at page 643)

The sellers' main contention, in accordance with the judgment of McNAIR, J., on which they relied, was that the principles applicable were those laid down by the Court of Appeal in *H. O. Brandt & Co.* v. *H. N. Morris & Co. Ltd.*[59] In that case, the goods had been sold f.o.b. Manchester by English merchants to English merchants seeking to export from England. Subsequent to the contract, an order rendering a licence necessary was made in the United Kingdom under United Kingdom statutory powers. In these circumstances, the Court held that it was for the buyers to supply any necessary licence which is required to enable the goods to be placed on the ship. In my opinion, it is necessary to remember, in comparing *Brandt* v. *Morris* with any other case in this field, (i) that the parties had not contracted with reference to an existing licensing system; (ii) that a United Kingdom licensing system overtook their contract; (iii) that either party could have applied to the British authorities; (iv) that the buyers alone knew the facts which it was necessary to state when a licence was applied for. The sellers, however, argued that the effect of this decision, and especially of the judgment of SCRUTTON, L.J., was that, in the case of any f.o.b. contract it was the duty of the buyers to provide a ship alongside which the goods could legally be placed, and, therefore, their duty to procure any licence required.

In my opinion, the decision in *Brandt* v. *Morris* is authority only for the proposition that, where a British buyer has bought goods for export from Britain, and a British prohibition on export except with a licence supervenes, then there is a duty on such a buyer to apply for a licence, because not only is he entitled to apply to the relevant British authority but he alone knows the full facts regarding the destination of the goods. It is not without importance to note that SCRUTTON, L.J., introduces the part of his judgment which deals with this point by saying:[60]

"This is a contract to sell 60 tons of aniline oil f.o.b. Manchester. At the date of the contract there was no prohibition against the export of aniline oil. In *Re Anglo-Russian Merchant Traders & John Batt & Co. (London) Ltd.*[61] the contract was a c. and f. contract, and at the date thereof there was an existing prohibition against export except under a licence. A question arose as to whose duty it was to obtain a licence. BAILHACHE, J., held that the person who had contracted to sell undertook to obtain the licence or to pay damages. This Court held that, as there was a finding of fact that the seller had done all in his power to get a licence, at any rate his obligation was not higher than that, and that therefore he was not liable. In this case it becomes necessary to go further and to decide whether in this f.o.b. contract the obligation to obtain a licence, in case there should after the making of the contract be a prohibition against export, lies upon the sellers or the buyers. In my opinion it lies upon the buyers".

---

[59] [1917] 2 K.B. 784, C.A.; p. 169, *ante.*
[60] *Ibid.*, at p. 798.
[61] [1917] 2 K.B. 679, C.A.

In my view, significance must be attached to the words "in this f.o.b. contract". Further, it must be observed that the Lord Justice draws attention not only to the fact that one was a c. and f. contract while the other was f.o.b., but also to the fact that in one case the prohibition was existing and that in the other it supervened. It is in the second case that the words following become applicable, namely:

> "The buyers must provide an effective ship, that is to say, a ship which can legally carry the goods".

Also, in the case of a supervenient prohibition, once it has become the duty of the buyers to obtain the licence and so legalise the ship, it is immaterial that there is a duty on the sellers to perform the act subsidiary to export, namely, to bring the goods through Customs on to the quay. Moreover, it is, in my view, essential for us, 39 years later, to read that judgment as SCRUTTON, L.J., was delivering it, in contradistinction to his decision in *Re Anglo-Russian Merchant Traders & John Batt & Co. (London) Ltd.*[62] I draw attention to the words in which the Lord Justice there posed the problem:[63]

> "The sellers could only export aluminium under a licence. They contracted to export it. There are two alternatives suggested. Have they contracted to get a licence or pay damages though it may be illegal to export? Or have they contracted to use reasonable diligence to get a licence, and, having been unable to obtain one, are they relieved from any liability because a contract which is illegal cannot be enforced?".

SCRUTTON, L.J., reaches the conclusion that the second of these alternatives is the term that must be implied in the contract.

Against that background, I cannot extract from *Brandt* v. *Morris*[64] a general rule that, on every f.o.b. or f.a.s. contract, the buyer must supply a ship into which, or alongside which, the goods can legally be placed where there exists a prohibition on export except with a licence. My view is supported by an examination of *McMaster & Co.* v. *Cox, McEuen & Co.*[65] on which the sellers also relied. In that case, a firm of jute manufacturers in Dundee accepted order-notes for jute goods dated 1st and 2nd November, 1917, from a firm of merchants also in Dundee. The notes stipulated for delivery f.o.b. Dundee. There supervened the Jute (Export) Order, of 23rd November, 1917, which prohibited the manufacture and delivery of jute goods without a permit. Thereupon the sellers wrote to the buyers asking for a guarantee that the goods on order were not to be exported, or, if they were for export, for a government permit authorising their manufacture and delivery. The buyers intimated that the goods in question were for export. Thereupon they applied for, and were refused, a permit for

---

[62] *Supra.*
[63] *Ibid.,* at p. 688.
[64] *Supra.*
[65] 1921 S.C. (H.L.) 24.

the manufacture of the goods, whereupon they cancelled the contract. In an action for damages by the sellers against the buyers for breach of contract, your Lordships' House held that the buyers were liable in damages. In his opinion Lord BIRKENHEAD, L.C., said:[66]

> "I find that [the agreement] is one in which a vendor has undertaken to supply a certain article to a purchaser. He is not concerned to ask, and he does not ask, in what market the purchaser proposes to dispose of that which he buys, and I have already pointed out that every attempt to show that the vendor was affected with any knowledge that the purchaser intended to dispose of these goods in a foreign market has failed".

VISCOUNT FINLAY said:[67]

> "Something was said about the words 'f.o.b.' They, of course, would be equally applicable to any transit by sea whether coastwise or to foreign ports; but it appears to me quite impossible to find in the documents or in the surrounding circumstances any sufficient foundation for making it a term of the contract that liberty of export should exist at the time it was to be performed".

Lord DUNEDIN took as the basis of his concurrence that the right of the buyers to dispose of the goods was a right due to the fact that, after delivery, they became owners of the goods. Lord ATKINSON agreed with him. Counsel for the sellers, however, placed great reliance on the reasoning of Lord SHAW OF DUNFERMLINE,[68] and especially on the terms in which he rejected the view of the majority of the Second Division, that the buyer

> "seems to have had a certain recourse at law under which he could, while holding the seller bound under the concluded contract, yet assert his own, the buyer's, freedom therefrom".

In my opinion, the applicability of that reasoning to a simple contract of sale which was overtaken by such a departmental order does not make it applicable to the facts of this case. The opinions in your Lordships' House do not, in my view, support a general rule for f.o.b. contracts. The outcome must depend on the contract, and the surrounding circumstances in each case.

The sellers can only succeed in this action if they can establish that there was a breach of contract by the buyers. In my opinion, they have failed to do so. The essential facts seem to me to be (i) that the sellers knew that the buyers wished to export to Eastern Germany, and (ii) that only the suppliers (whose identity the sellers deliberately withheld from the buyers) could apply for the necessary licence. In these circumstances, it was for the sellers to do their best to obtain a licence for Eastern Germany through the suppliers and, if they found that they could not, further performance of the contract was excused.

---

[66] *Ibid.*, at p. 26.
[67] *Ibid.*, at p. 27.
[68] *Ibid.*, at pp. 29, 30.

PART VI

BANKERS' COMMERCIAL CREDITS[1]

Ian Stach Ltd. *v.* Baker Bosly Ltd.

[1958] 1 All E.R. 542

The credit must be made available to the seller by at least the earliest date stated in the contract of sale for the shipment of the goods.

The buyers of a quantity of steel to be delivered f.o.b. a Benelux port, delivery to be made in August/September, 1956, agreed to open an irrevocable confirmed credit in favour of the sellers. But by 14th August, in spite of repeated requests to do so, the buyers had still not opened the credit.

Held, by the Queen's Bench Division, the credit should have been opened by 1st August, 1956, i.e., the earliest shipping date under the contract, so the sellers were entitled to claim damages from the buyers for their failure to do so.

DIPLOCK, J. (at page 546)

There is clear authority binding on me that in c.i.f. contracts the confirmed credit must be opened at least by the beginning of the shipment period. That was decided by the Court of Appeal in *Pavia & Co. S.P.A.* v. *Thurmann-Nielsen*,[2] where SOMERVELL, L.J., said:[3]

"When a seller is given a right to ship over a period and there is machinery for payment, that machinery must be available over the whole of that period".

DENNING, L.J., put the matter succinctly in the following words:[4]

"The question in the present case is this. In a contract which provides for payment by confirmed credit, when must the buyer open the credit? In the absence of express stipulation, the credit must be made available to the seller at the beginning of the shipment period. The reason is because the seller is entitled, before he ships the goods, to be assured that, on shipment, he will get paid. The seller is not bound to tell the buyer the precise date when he is going to ship, and whenever he does ship the goods, he must be able to draw on

---

[1] The cases included in this Part set out the general law relating to Bankers' Commercial Credits. They must, however, be read in the light of the "Uniform Customs and Practice for Documentary Credits" (1974 Revision) which "apply to all documentary credits and are binding upon all parties thereto unless otherwise expressly agreed": "General Provisions and Definitions" par. (a).
[2] [1952] 1 All E.R. 492, C.A.
[3] *Ibid.*, at p. 494.
[4] *Ibid.*, at p. 495.

the credit. He may ship on the very first day of the shipment period. If the buyer is to fulfil his obligations, he must, therefore, make the credit available to the seller at the very first date when the goods may be lawfully shipped in compliance with the contract".

. . . It is said, therefore, that there is a distinction to be drawn between a c.i.f. contract and a classic f.o.b. contract . . . namely that in the classic f.o.b. contract, where the buyer can dictate the date of shipment, the seller is not obliged to commence any of the operations directed to performing his obligations under the contract until he has had shipping instructions or calling forward instructions from the buyer. It was contended by counsel for the [buyers] that, applying the *ratio decidendi* in the c.i.f. contract cases (such as *Pavia & Co. S.P.A.* v. *Thurmann-Nielsen*),[5] the time at which the confirmed credit had to be opened was a reasonable time before the shipping instructions took effect. The rival contention by counsel for the [sellers] was that the credit had to be opened a reasonable time before the earliest shipping date; but in his reply he was prepared to put it as, at the latest, by the earliest shipping date. Counsel for the [buyers], on the other hand, said that it must be a reasonable time before the actual shipping date.

As I have said, there is no authority which guides me in this matter. It seems to me, however, that the contention of counsel for the [sellers] is the sensible one, and, since it is the sensible one, and since there is no authority to the contrary, the one which I am inclined to hold, and do hold, is good law. I am fortified in this view by the fact that it is apparent from the correspondence and from the conduct of the parties in this case (and, so far as one can see, from that of the parties to the other contracts) that it was their view that that was the requirement of the contract. In a trade of this kind, where (as is known to all parties participating) there may well be a string of contracts, all of which are financed by, and can only be financed by, the credit which is opened by the ultimate user, and which goes down the string, getting less and less until it comes to the ultimate supplier, it seems to me that the business sense of the arrangement requires that by the time the shipping period starts each of the sellers should receive the assurance from the banker that, if the seller performs his part of the contract, he will receive payment. That seems to me to have the advantage that there would, at least, be a definite date at which the parties know that they have to fulfil the obligation of opening a credit.

The alternative view put forward by counsel for the [buyers], namely, that the date for opening the credit has to be a reasonable time before the actual shipping date, seems to me to lead to an uncertainty on the part of buyer and seller which I should be reluctant to import into any commercial contract. I asked counsel for the [buyers],

---

5 *Supra.*

whether when the Court had to consider what was a reasonable time (which must depend on the circumstances), it depended on the circumstances known to the parties at the time of the contract, or the circumstances as ascertained later on before the shipping instructions were given, or, as a third alternative, the circumstances as they actually were, whether known to the parties or not. It seems to me that that sort of uncertainty is open to the same criticism which SOMERVELL, L.J., directed to the argument put forward to him in *Pavia & Co. S.P.A.* v. *Thurmann-Nielsen.*[6] It was argued in that case that the buyers need not open the credit until the sellers were ready to deliver and had got bills of lading. SOMERVELL, L.J., said:[7]

> "My view is that the suggestion which counsel for the buyers put forward—that the buyers under this form of contract were under no obligation until a date, which they could not possibly know and which there was no machinery for their finding out, namely, when the sellers actually had the goods at the port ready to be put in the ship— is unworkable".

In the present case, too, the contention of counsel for the [buyers] was that the buyer's obligation did not arise until a date which the buyer could not possibly know because it was a date which must depend on circumstances, and on circumstances which would not normally be known to the buyer: he did not know, and would not normally know, how long a chain there was between him, and the actual manufacturer or stockist; he would not know how long it would take to bring the goods from the place where they were and transport them to the port: he would not know in a case of this kind, and the [buyers] in this case did not know, whether or not the goods had to be rolled to order or whether they were in stock or whether they were partly rolled. It seems to me that in a case of this kind, and in the case of an ordinary f.o.b. contract financed by a banker's confirmed credit, the *prima facie* rule is that the credit must be opened at the latest (and that is as far as I need go for the purposes of this case) by the earliest shipping date. In that way one gets certainty into what is a very common commercial contract, and in any other way one can only get a position in which neither buyer nor seller knows what his rights are until all the facts have been ascertained—and it may become necessary for two or three Courts to direct their minds to the question whether in all the circumstances that was a reasonable time.

I, therefore, hold that it was the duty of the [buyers] under this contract to open their letter of credit or to get a banker's pre-advice of it by 1st August, 1956, at the latest.

---

[6] *Supra.*
[7] *Ibid.*, at p. 494.

J. H. Rayner & Co. Ltd. and Oilseeds Trading Co. Ltd. *v.* Hambros Bank

[1942] 2 All E.R. 694

The seller must tender to the bank the exact documents stated in the credit. If he does not do so, the bank must not pay the purchase price in respect of the goods.

The buyers of some groundnuts instructed their bank to pay the sellers by means of a banker's commercial credit, instructing payment to be made against bills of lading covering 1,400 tons of "Coromandel groundnuts". The sellers presented bills of lading stating that the goods were "machine shelled groundnut kernels". The bank refused to pay.

Held, by the Court of Appeal, that it was entitled to do so, in view of the discrepancy of the documents, even though the terms "Coromandel groundnuts", and "machine shelled groundnut kernels" by a custom of the trade were the same. In any event the bank was under no duty to know the custom of the trade.

GODDARD, L.J. (at page 703)

I protest against the view that a bank is to be deemed to have a knowledge of the trade of its various customers. But quite apart from that, even if the bank did know this custom or trade practice, by which Coromandel groundnuts were described as "machine-shelled groundnut kernels", I do not think that would be conclusive of the case. There are three people concerned where a banker's credit is in question: there is the person who requests the bank to establish the credit, there is the bank who establishes it, and there is the beneficiary who has the opportunity of drawing on the credit. The person who requests the bank to establish the credit can impose what terms he likes. If he says to the bank: "I want a bill of lading in a particular form", he is entitled to do so. If the bank accepts the mandate which he gives to them, they must accept it on the terms which their customer imposes. The bank can impose, as between themselves and the beneficiary, extra terms if they like. . . . The bank can say to the beneficiary: "These are the terms upon which we will pay", and, if they have only been authorised by their customer to pay on certain terms, they must see that those terms are included in the notification which they give to the beneficiary, and they must not pay on any other terms. If they do pay on any other terms, they run the risk of their customer refusing to reimburse them. It does not matter whether the terms imposed by the person who requires them to open the credit are reasonable, or seem to be reasonable, or unreasonable. Of course, they may be terms, which, as between themselves and the beneficiary, they would not be entitled to impose. The bank is not concerned with that. The bank, if it accepts the mandate to open the credit, must do exactly what its customer requires it to do, and if the customer says: "I require a bill of lading for Coromandel groundnuts", the bank is not justified, in my judgment, in paying against a bill of lading for anything except Coromandel groundnuts, and it is no answer to say: "You know perfectly well machine-shelled groundnut kernels are the same as Coromandel groundnuts". For all the bank knows, its customer may have a particular reason for wanting "Coromandel groundnuts" in the bill of lading. At any rate, that is the instruction which the customer has given to the bank, and if the bank wants to be reimbursed by the customer, it must show that it has performed its mandate. If I ask a person to pay money for me—the bank, of course, is remunerated for its letter of credit—or if I employ somebody at remuneration to pay money for me on getting a receipt in a particular form, and he pays the money and does not get the receipt in a particular form, he has not carried out the duty which I imposed upon him, and it would be no answer to say: "But I got a receipt which, in fact, gives you all reasonable protection". My answer to that is: "You are not concerned with the protection which you have given me. You are concerned to carry out the orders which I gave you, and you have not done it". In my opinion, in this case, whether Hambros knew or not that there was this trade description is nothing to the point. They were told to establish a credit and to pay against a bill of lading describing particular goods, and the beneficiary under that credit presented to them a bill of lading which was not what they had promised to pay against. Therefore, it seems to me whether it is reasonable or unreasonable for [the buyers] to say that they want a bill of lading for Coromandel groundnuts or whether or not Hambros had knowledge of some of the trade practices which are referred to is not the question. The question is: What was the promise that they made to the beneficiary under the credit, and has the beneficiary availed himself of that promise? In my opinion, he had not, and, therefore, I think Hambros were justified in refusing to pay.

MacKinnon, L.J. (at page 701)

It is quite impossible to suggest the banker is to be affected with knowledge of the customs and customary terms of every one of the thousands of trades in regard to the dealings in which he may issue letters of credit. As I suggested as a homely illustration which is suggested by the books in front of me, if a banker was ordered to issue a letter of credit with respect to the shipment of so many copies of the 1942 *Annual Practice* and he was handed a bill of lading for so many copies of the 1942 *White Book*, it would be entirely beside the mark to call a lawyer, if that were necessary, to say that all lawyers know that the 1942 *White Book* means the 1942 *Annual Practice*. It would be quite impossible for business to be carried on and for bankers to be in any way protected in such matters, if it was said that they must be affected by a knowledge of all the particular details of the way in which particular traders carry on their business.

Moralice (London) Ltd. *v.* E. D. & F. Man

[1954] 2 Lloyd's Rep. 526

The de minimis *rule does not apply in the case of bankers' commercial credits.*[8]

The sellers sold 5,000 bags of sugar each containing 100 kilos to the buyer c.i.f. Tripoli. Payment was to be made against documents in accordance with an irrevocable credit established by the buyer with a London bank in favour of the sellers. The documents tendered by the sellers were for 4,997 bags only. The bank refused to allow the sellers to draw against the credit except upon an indemnity being given in respect of the discrepancy.

Held, by the Queen's Bench Division, that the bank was justified in so doing because the *de minimis* rule did not apply to bankers' commercial credits.

McNair, J. (at page 532)

. . . The question I have to consider is whether the plaintiffs did in fact incur any liability to the bank. The determination of that issue, as it seems to me, depends upon whether or not I take the view that these documents, showing the deficiency of the 300 kilos, were documents which the bank would have been obliged to take up. Clearly the bank would not be obliged to take up those documents, seeing that they were documents which differed from the documents required by the credit, unless it is true to say that the maxim *de minimis non curat lex*, or, as it is sometimes called, the rule of insignificance, applies (a) on the facts of this case, and (b) as between confirming banker and the beneficiary of the credit—namely, the seller.

On the first question (a), I think that as between a buyer and a seller, if the contract was not complicated by the intervention of a letter of credit, and seeing that the seller was not calling upon the buyer to pay for 500 tons, but only for 500 tons less 300 kilos, it would be a case in which the maxim or rule I have already referred to would apply. . . .

But on the second question, (b), I have been referred to no authority, and I have found none, in which this rule has ever been applied as between a buyer and his bank, or between a confirming bank and the beneficiary seller, and there are indeed quite definite indications that the rule should not be so applied.

---

[8] Article 34(b) of the "Uniform Customs and Practice for Documentary Credits" (1974 Revison) states that: ". . . Unless a credit stipulates that the quantity of the goods specified must not be exceeded or reduced, a tolerance of 3 % more or 3 % less will be permissible, always provided that the total amount of the drawings does not exceed the amount of the credit. This tolerance does not apply when the credit specifies quantity in terms of packing units or containers or individual items".

British Imex Industries Ltd. *v.* Midland Bank Ltd.

[1958] 1 All E.R. 264

Where the credit states that payment will be made against bills of lading, this means "clean" bills of lading.[9]

The sellers sold the buyers a quantity of steel bars. The Midland Bank Ltd. issued an irrevocable credit to the sellers under which it promised to pay them up to £23,000 on presentation of the shipping documents including bills of lading representing the goods. On the back of the bills of lading was a clause stating that the shipowners were not responsible for correct delivery unless every bar were marked with oil paint. The description of the goods was given in the bills of lading presented to the bank, but there was no acknowledgment by the shipowners that the condition concerning the marking of the goods had been complied with. The bank therefore refused to pay, claiming that the bills of lading were not a good tender under the credit, because they were not "clean".

Held, by the Queen's Bench Division, that the bank was wrong in refusing to pay. The bills of lading were "clean", and this was all that was necessary, even though they did not contain an acknowledgment that the clause had been complied with.

SALMON, J. (at page 267)

The point raised in this case is both novel and important, namely: Is it necessary for bills of lading in this form to contain an acknowledgment that the printed terms as to marking and securing have been complied with, or is the bill of lading acceptable so long as it contains no indorsement or clausing to the effect that this printed clause has not been complied with?

The plaintiffs have called before me a witness, Mr Donald, of the widest experience in the exporting and importing business, including the exporting and importing of iron and steel. I understand that he has 30 years' experience; that he is on the council of the London Chamber of Commerce; that he is deputy chairman of its exporting and importing section, and on the trade terms committee. He tells me that a clause in similar terms to clause B is not unusual in bills of lading. A great many bills of lading contain no such clause, but a great many bills of lading do contain such a clause. This witness had never heard of a bill of lading containing the clause in question being objected to on the ground that it did not contain a statement that there had been compliance with such a clause. He told me that in his experience such bills of lading were invariably accepted as good without such a statement. Indeed, there has been produced to me such a bill of lading accepted by the defendants themselves without

---

[9] Article 18 of the "Uniform Customs and Practice for Documentary Credits" (1974 Revision) states that: "(a) A clean shipping document is one which bears no superimposed clause or notation which expressly declares a defective condition of the goods and/or the packaging. (b) Banks will refuse shipping documents bearing such clauses or notations unless the credit expressly states clauses or notations which may be accepted".

any such acknowledgment as they now argue is indispensable; it may be that in that particular case, special circumstances were applicable. Mr Donald's evidence was wholly uncontradicted, and not very seriously challenged. I unhesitatingly accept it.

It follows that if the defendants are right in their present contention, it will be necessary for those concerned with the exporting and importing of iron and steel to revolutionise their present practice when using bills of lading which contain a clause similar to additional clause B. There may also be a good many disappointed sellers of iron and steel who have already parted with their goods on the faith of confirmed irrevocable credits relying on the practice of banks to accept bills of lading in this form, that is to say, without any express statement that the terms relating to marking and securing of the goods have been complied with.

The letter of credit stipulated that payment would be made against bills of lading without qualification. The plaintiffs suggest that this does not necessarily mean clean bills of lading. In my judgment, when a credit calls for bills of lading, in normal circumstances it means clean bills of lading. I think that in normal circumstances the ordinary business man who undertakes to pay against the presentation of bills of lading means clean bills of lading; and he would probably consider that that was so obvious to any other business man that it was hardly necessary to state it. That seems to have been the view taken by BAILHACHE, J., in *National Bank of Egypt* v. *Hannevig's Bank Ltd.*[10] I entirely agree with it. No doubt, as was pointed out by the Court of Appeal in that case,[11] there may be circumstances when, for instance, business has been disorganised by war, in which a credit against bills of lading is not necessarily a credit against clean bills of lading. That is a point which it is unnecessary to decide in this case, for in this case there are no special circumstances, and I read "bills of lading" in the letter of credit as meaning clean bills of lading. A "clean bill of lading" has never been exhaustively defined, and I certainly do not propose to attempt that task now. I incline to the view, however, that a clean bill of lading is one that does not contain any reservation as to the apparent good order or condition of the goods or the packing. In my judgment, the bills of lading in this case are plainly clean bills of lading. They contain no reservation by way of indorsement, clausing or otherwise, to suggest that the goods or the packing are or may be defective in any respect.

The defendants contend that inasmuch as the bills of lading do not contain on their face an express acknowledgment that the goods have been marked in accordance with the provisions of additional clause B, then either they are not clean bills of lading—I have dealt with that point—or they are so seriously defective that the defendants are

---

[10] (1919), 1 Ll.L. Rep. 69.
[11] *Ibid.*, at p. 70.

entitled to refuse payment. It is to be observed that the letter of credit did not call for bills of lading to be indorsed with any acknowledgment that the provisions of the additional clause B had been complied with. I do not consider that the defendants have any right to insist on such an acknowledgment before payment. According to their case it was their duty for the remuneration of £18 to read through the multifarious clauses in minute print on the back of these bills of lading, and having observed additional clause B, to consider its legal effect and then to call for an acknowledgment that there had been compliance with it. I respectfully share the doubts that SCRUTTON, L.J., expressed in *National Bank of Egypt* v. *Hannevig's Bank Ltd.*[12] whether any such duty is cast on a bank. I doubt whether they are under any greater duty to their correspondents than to satisfy themselves that the correct documents are presented to them, and that the bills of lading bear no indorsement or clausing by the shipowners or shippers which could reasonably mean that there was, or might be, some defect in the goods, or their packing.

Urquhart Lindsay & Co. Ltd. *v.* Eastern Bank Ltd.

[1921] All E.R. Rep. 340

Where the credit is an irrevocable one and the seller tenders the correct documents, the bank must pay him the purchase price of the goods, even though the buyer instructs the bank not to pay.[13]

The Eastern Bank Ltd. issued an irrevocable credit to the sellers of some machinery. It promised to pay the sellers up to £70,000 on tender of the shipping documents including invoices relating to the goods. Two instalments of the machinery were sent, and the bank paid under the credit. But before the next shipment was made, the buyers discovered that the sellers were including in the invoices an additional sum representing a rise in the cost of wages and materials. So they instructed the bank not to pay when the invoices were tendered by the sellers, even though the sellers were entitled to charge the additional sum under the contract of sale. The bank refused to pay, and the sellers claimed damages on the ground that the credit was an irrevocable one, and therefore the bank was bound to pay.

Held, by the King's Bench Division, that the action succeeded. The bank was bound to pay if the correct documents were tendered to it, and was in no way concerned with the terms of the contract of sale.

---

[12] The passage referred to is not reported in (1919), 1 Ll.L. Rep. 69, but will be found in a report of *National Bank of Egypt* v. *Hannevig's Bank Ltd.* in *Legal Decisions Affecting Bankers*, Vol. III, 213, at p. 214.
[13] Article 3 of the "Uniform Customs and Practice for Documentary Credits" (1974 Revision) states that: "(a) An irrevocable credit is a definite undertaking of the issuing bank, provided that the terms and conditions are complied with: (i) to pay . . . ; (ii) to accept drafts . . . ; (iii) to purchase/negotiate . . . drafts drawn by the beneficiary . . . (b). Such undertakings can neither be amended nor cancelled without the agreement of all parties thereto. Partial acceptance of amendments is not effective without the agreement of all parties thereto".

ROWLATT, J. (at page 342)

In this case, the essential facts are few and simple. The plaintiffs in this country arranged with the Benjamin Jute Mills of Calcutta to manufacture and ship to them over a series of months a quantity of machinery at prices mentioned in a *pro forma* invoice; subject, however, to a stipulation not infrequently insisted on by manufacturers at the date when the arrangement was made that, should the cost of labour or wages advance, there would be a corresponding advance in the prices to be paid by the buyers. The goods were to be paid for by means of a confirmed, irrevocable credit to be opened by the buyers in favour of the plaintiffs with a bank in this country, who were to pay the plaintiffs for each shipment as it took place. In pursuance of this arrangement, the defendants, at the instance of the buyers, issued to the plaintiffs a document the terms of which I need not rehearse in detail, it being sufficient to state that the defendants undertook up to a certain amount within a certain limit of time to pay the plaintiffs against bills drawn on the buyers accompanied by corresponding invoices and shipping documents, the amount of the invoices. This credit was by its terms to be irrevocable and the invoices were to be for machinery. There can be no doubt that, on the plaintiffs acting on the undertaking contained in this letter of credit, consideration moved from the plaintiffs, which bound the defendants to the irrevocable character of the arrangement between the defendants and the plaintiffs; nor was it contended before me that this had not become the position when the circumstances giving rise to this action took place.

Having received the letter of credit, the plaintiffs proceeded to manufacture the machinery and actually shipped two shipments of it, receiving payment from the defendants under the letter of credit against bills accompanied by invoices and other documents called for by that instrument. Before the third shipment was made, the buyers, finding that the plaintiffs were including in their invoices an addition to the prices originally quoted, in respect of an alleged rise in the cost of wages or materials, instructed the defendants only to pay so much of the next invoices as represented the original prices. These instructions (very unfortunately, as I think, from many points of view) the defendants obeyed. The plaintiffs, however, refused to part with the documents representing their goods unless they received the full amount of the invoices, and, on the defendants maintaining their position, cancelled the contract as to further shipments, as on a repudiation by the buyers; and have brought this action against the defendants claiming as damages the loss on material thrown on their hands, and loss of profits; in other words, the same damages as they would claim against the buyers on their repudiation of the contract. After the action had been commenced, the defendants paid to the plaintiffs the amount of the invoices, the original refusal of which had caused the dispute.

In my view, the defendants committed a breach of their contract with the plaintiffs when they refused to pay the amount of the invoices as presented. Counsel for the defendants contended that the letter of credit must be taken to incorporate the contract between the plaintiffs and their buyers; and that, according to the true meaning of that contract, the amount of any increase claimed in respect of an alleged advance in manufacturing costs was not to be included in any invoice to be presented under the letter of credit, but was to be the subject of subsequent independent adjustment. The answer to this is that the defendants undertook to pay the amount of the invoices for machinery without qualification, the basis of this form of banking facility being that the buyer is taken for the purposes of all questions between himself and his banker, or between his banker and the seller, to be content to accept the invoices of the seller as correct. It seems to me that, so far from the letter of credit being qualified by the contract of sale, the latter must accommodate itself to the letter of credit. The buyer having authorised his banker to undertake to pay the amount of the invoice as presented, it follows that any adjustment must be made by way of refund by the seller, and not by way of retention by the buyer.

Malas *v*. British Imex Industries Ltd.

[1958] 1 All E.R. 262

If the seller tenders the correct documents under the credit, the Court will not grant an injunction restraining him from drawing on the credit merely because a dispute has arisen between the parties as to whether the goods are in accordance with the contract.

The sellers of a quantity of reinforced steel arranged to ship the goods in two instalments. The buyers agreed to pay for each instalment by a separate irrevocable credit. The sellers were paid under the first credit, but the buyers discovered that the goods delivered in the first instalment were not up to the quality specified in the terms of the contract. So the buyers applied for an injunction to restrain the sellers from drawing on the second credit.

Held, by the Court of Appeal, that the injunction would not be granted. It would be wrong for the Court to interfere with the established practice that if the correct documents were tendered, the seller was always entitled to payment under an irrevocable credit, even though there was a dispute between the parties as to the quality of the goods.

JENKINS, L.J. (at page 263)

In this case the [buyers] are a Jordanian firm who agreed to buy from the [sellers], a British company, a quantity of reinforced steel rods. These steel rods were to be delivered in two instalments and payment was to be effected by the opening in favour of the [sellers] of two confirmed letters of credit with the Midland Bank Ltd., in London, one in respect of each instalment. The letters of credit were duly opened. The first has been realised by the [sellers], and they are on the point of realising the second. This application is concerned with the second letter of credit.

It appears that, when the first consignment of steel rods arrived, according to the [buyers], they were by no means up to contract quality and many criticisms were made on that score. That is a matter in issue between the parties. In the meantime the [buyers] wish to secure themselves in respect of any damage to which they may be found to be entitled when this dispute is ultimately tried out, by preventing the [sellers] from dealing with this outstanding letter of credit. Counsel for the [buyers], in effect, treats this as no more than part of the price, a sum earmarked to pay for the goods bought under the contract, which the [buyers] have become entitled to repudiate; and he says that, accordingly, the [sellers] ought to be restrained from dealing with the amount of this letter of credit. He points out that he is seeking an order against the [sellers], not against the bank.

We were referred to several authorities, and it seems to be plain that the opening of a confirmed letter of credit constitutes a bargain between the banker and the vendor of the goods, which imposes on the banker an absolute obligation to pay, irrespective of any dispute which there may be between the parties on the question whether the goods are up to contract or not. An elaborate commercial system has been built up on the footing that bankers' confirmed credits are of that character, and, in my judgment, it would be wrong for this Court in the present case to interfere with that established practice. It has also to be remembered that a vendor of goods selling against a confirmed letter of credit is selling under the assurance that nothing will prevent him from receiving the price. That is no mean advantage when goods manufactured in one country are being sold in another. Furthermore, vendors are often reselling goods bought from third parties. When they are doing that, and when they are being paid by a confirmed letter of credit, their practice—and I think it was followed by the defendants in this case—is to finance the payments necessary to be made to their suppliers against the letter of credit. That system of financing these operations, as I see it, would break down completely if a dispute between the vendor and the purchaser were to have the effect of "freezing", if I may use the expression, the sum in respect of which the letter of credit was opened.

I agree with counsel for the [buyers] that this is not a case where it can be said that the Court has no jurisdiction to interfere. The Court's jurisdiction to grant injunctions is wide, but, in my judgment, this is not a case in which, in the exercise of the Court's discretion, it ought to grant an injunction. Accordingly, I think that this application should be refused.

Discount Records Ltd. *v*. Barclays Bank Ltd.

[1975] 1 All E.R. 1071

An injunction to prevent a seller drawing under a bankers' commercial credit may be granted where actual fraud is shown. A plea alleging fraud is insufficient.

The sellers sold to the buyers a quantity of cassettes. Payment for the goods was to be made by an irrevocable bankers' commercial credit. The credit was opened by the buyers, but they discovered that some of the cartons containing the cassettes were filled with rubbish or packing, so they applied for an injunction to stop the sellers drawing under the credit on the ground that the sellers were guilty of fraud.

Held, by the Chancery Division, that an injunction would not be granted for fraud on the part of the sellers had not been established.

MEGARRY, J. (at page 1074)

Counsel for the plaintiffs puts his claim for an injunction on two grounds. First of all, he says that this is a case where Promodisc has been guilty of fraud, and that fraud is one of the instances in which the Court will intervene even in the case of bankers' irrevocable confirmed credits. He told me that there was no English authority directly on the point or anywhere near it, but he did put before me *Sztejn* v. *J. Henry Schroder Banking Corpn*,[14] a case which is summarised in *Gutteridge and Megrah, The Law of Bankers' Commercial Credits*.[15] There, it was alleged that the seller had shipped rubbish and then passed his draft for collection. SHIENTAG, J.,[16] referred to the well-established rule that a letter of credit is independent of the primary contract of sale between the buyer and the seller, so that unless the letter of credit otherwise provides, the bank is neither obliged nor allowed to enter into controversies between buyer and seller regarding the quality of the merchandise shipped. However, the learned Judge (and I use the phrase as no empty compliment) distinguished mere breaches of warranty of quality from cases where the seller has intentionally failed to ship any of the goods ordered by the buyer. In relation to the latter case, the Judge uttered a sentence[17] (quoted in the book)[18] on which counsel for the plaintiffs placed great reliance:

"In such a situation, where the seller's fraud has been called to the bank's attention before the drafts and documents have been presented for payment, the principle of the independence of the bank's obligation under the letter of credit should not be extended to protect the unscrupulous seller".

[14] (1941), 31 N.Y.S. 2d 631.
[15] 4th Edn. 1968, pp. 133, 134. See now 5th Edn. 1976, pp. 136, 137.
[16] (1941), 31 N.Y.S. 2d, at p. 633.
[17] *Ibid.*, at p. 634.
[18] *Op. cit.*

During the argument on this point before me, the familiar English phrase "Fraud unravels all" was also discussed. However, it is important to notice that in the *Sztejn* case[19] the proceedings consisted of a motion to dismiss the formal complaint on the ground that it disclosed no cause of action. That being so, the Court had to assume that the facts stated in the complaint were true. The complaint alleged fraud, and so the Court was dealing with a case of established fraud. In the present case there is, of course, no established fraud, but merely an allegation of fraud. The defendants, who were not concerned with that matter, have understandably adduced no evidence on the issue of fraud. Indeed, it seems unlikely that any action to which Promodisc was not a party would contain the evidence required to resolve this issue. Accordingly, the matter has to be dealt with on the footing that this is a case in which fraud is alleged but has not been established. I should also add that on the facts required to be assumed in the *Sztejn* case[20] the collecting bank there was not a holder in due course, who would not be defeated by the fraud, but was merely an agent for the fraudulent seller.

Counsel for the plaintiffs' second ground was that there was a lack of correspondence between the documents and the goods, and that whatever might be said about the allegation that the plaintiffs had in some way waived the lack of conformity, there remained the fact that the goods were shipped 13 days after the latest day for shipment stated in the documents establishing the credit. However, in claiming the relief before me, counsel for the plaintiffs accepted that the first head of the notice of motion might not be entirely appropriate. He relied primarily on the second head, but preferred to leave the precise formulation of that claim until he had heard counsel for the defendants.

For his part, counsel for the defendants did not seek to deal with the points on fraud or a lack of correspondence between the goods and the documents. His case was that the claim for an injunction was misconceived. He said that what would happen was this. Somewhere there is a bill of exchange which has already been accepted by the Discount Bank. That bill may well have been negotiated; it may indeed have passed into the hands of a holder in due course. That bill will be presented for payment, and the Discount Bank is bound to pay it on 20th July. The Discount Bank will then debit Barclays Bank S.A. Barclays Bank S.A. will then debit the second defendants and the second defendants will then debit the first defendants. The injunction against the two defendants, if granted, would not achieve counsel for the plaintiffs' avowed purpose, which was to prevent Promodisc from being paid.

---

[19] *Supra.*
[20] *Supra.*

Promodisc, indeed, may already have been paid by discounting the bill. All that the injunction would do would be to prevent the banks concerned from honouring their obligations. As regards the two defendants (as distinct from whatever claim there might be against Promodisc), the plaintiffs' only real claim, counsel for the defendants said, was against the first defendants, and the first defendants alone, and there was, and could be, no suggestion that the first defendants were not good for the money.

Faced with that, and with an invitation from the Bench to reconsider the terms of the injunction, counsel for the plaintiffs, after a certain amount of hesitation, accepted that a revised form of injunction against the first defendants alone would sufficiently protect him. He amended his notice of motion so as to claim an injunction restraining the first defendants from paying out the £4,000 deposited on or about 7th June, 1974, in the joint names of the plaintiffs and the first defendants, to any party at all, any sums pursuant to the irrevocable credit requested by the plaintiffs to be opened in favour of Promodisc, and so on. He accepted that he had a money claim against the bank for breach of contract, but asserted that it was better to have a proprietary claim against the £4,000 as well. When invited to explain why this was better, he said that he could not explain it exactly, but that he felt in his bones that it was better; and he said that, in particular, he was not satisfied that the same matters must be determined however his case was put.

I would not dismiss counsel for the plaintiffs' contentions merely because he failed to particularise them. The sense of litigation of an experienced silk is not something to be cast lightly overboard. Nevertheless, I do not think that this is a case for an injunction at all. It cannot harm the plaintiffs in any way if Promodisc is paid, so long as the money does not come out of the plaintiffs' funds; and the revised form of injunction is, I think, the most that the plaintiffs should ever have sought. Even in that form I cannot see any real justification for it. If the first defendants have acted in breach of contract, the plaintiffs will have their claim against them. As I have said, there is no question of them not being good for the money. I see no need to keep the £4,000 in any state of security, nor have adequate grounds been put before me for doing anything except leaving the plaintiffs to their claim in contract. I would be slow to interfere with bankers' irrevocable credits, and not least in the sphere of international banking, unless a sufficiently grave cause is shown; for interventions by the Court that are too ready or too frequent might gravely impair the reliance which, quite properly, is placed on such credits. The *Sztejn* case[21] is plainly distinguishable in relation both to established fraud and to the absence there of any possible holder in due course. I do not say that the doctrine of that case is wrong or that it is incapable

---

[21] *Supra.*

of extension to cases in which fraud is alleged but has not been established, provided a sufficient case is made out. That may or may not be the case. What I do say is that the present case falls far short of establishing any ground on which it would be right for the Court to intervene by granting the interlocutory injunction claimed, even in its revised form. The motion accordingly fails and will be dismissed.

PART VII

PERFORMANCE GUARANTEES

Edward Owen Engineering Ltd. v. Barclays Bank International Ltd.

[1978] 1 All E.R. 976

It is only in exceptional circumstances that the Courts will interfere with the operation of a performance guarantee.

E. Ltd. entered into a contract to supply a quantity of greenhouses to buyers in Libya. The price of over £500,000 was to be paid in Libyan dinars by instalments. The buyers were to open an irrevocable letter of credit in favour of the sellers through Barclays Bank International Ltd. The sellers arranged for Barclays to give a performance guarantee for £50,203 to Umma Bank of Libya, which in turn was to issue a performance guarantee to the buyers. The credit was not made available, so the sellers said that they could not go on with the contract. The buyers sought payment under the guarantee from Umma Bank which sought payment from Barclays. The sellers applied for an injunction to restrain Barclays from paying the £50,203 either to Umma Bank or to the buyers.

Held, by the Court of Appeal, that an injunction would not be granted. Banks were not concerned with relations between buyers and sellers. Unless Barclays had knowledge of fraud, they must honour their guarantee. It was only in exceptional circumstances that the Courts would interfere with irrevocable obligations assumed by banks.

LORD DENNING, M.R. (at page 983)

All this leads to the conclusion that the performance guarantee stands on a similar footing to a letter of credit. A bank which gives a performance guarantee must honour that guarantee according to its terms. It is not concerned in the least with the relations between the supplier and the customer; nor with the question whether the supplier has performed his contracted obligation or not; nor with the question whether the supplier is in default or not. The bank must pay according to its guarantee, on demand if so stipulated, without proof or conditions. The only exception is when there is a clear fraud of which the bank has notice.

Such has been the course of decision in all the cases there have been this year in our Courts here in England. First of all, there was *R. D. Harbottle (Mercantile) Ltd. v. National Westminster Bank Ltd.*[1] before KERR, J. The learned Judge considered the position in principle. I would like to adopt a passage from his judgment:

---

[1] [1977] **2** All E.R. 862, at p. 870.

"It is only in exceptional cases that the Courts will interfere with the machinery of irrevocable obligations assumed by banks. They are the life-blood of international commerce. Such obligations are regarded as collateral to the underlying rights and obligations between the merchants at either end of the banking chain. Except possibly in clear cases of fraud of which the banks have notice, the Courts will leave the merchants to settle their disputes under the contracts by litigation or arbitration as available to them or stipulated in the contracts. The Courts are not concerned with their difficulties to enforce such claims; these are risks which the merchants take. In this case the plaintiffs took the risk of the unconditional wording of the guarantees. The machinery and commitments of banks are on a different level. They must be allowed to be honoured, free from interference by the Courts. Otherwise, trust in international commerce could be irreparably damaged".

Since that time there has been before DONALDSON, J., and afterwards in this Court the case of *Howe Richardson Scale Co. Ltd.* v. *Polimex-Cekop.*[2] In that case ROSKILL, L.J., spoke to the same effect. He said:

"Whether the obligation arises under a letter of credit or under a guarantee, the obligation of the bank is to perform that which it is required to perform by that particular contract, and that obligation does not in the ordinary way depend on the correct resolution of a dispute as to the sufficiency of performance by the seller to the buyer or by the buyer to the seller as the case may be under the sale and purchase contract; the bank here is simply concerned to see whether the event has happened on which its obligation to pay has arisen".

So there it is. Barclays Bank International has given its guarantee, I might almost say its promise to pay, to Umma Bank on demand without proof or conditions. They gave that promise, the demand was made. The bank must honour it. This Court cannot interfere with the obligations of the bank.

---

2 [1977] Court of Appeal Transcript 270.

INDEX